THE GATES OF THE SEA

THE GATES OF THE SEA

MIGRATION AND RESCUE AT THE EDGES OF EUROPE

LUNA VIVES

Fernwood Publishing
Halifax and Winnipeg

Copyright © 2025 Luna Vives

All rights reserved. No part of this book may be reproduced or transmitted in any form by any means without permission in writing from the publisher, except by a reviewer, who may quote brief passages in a review.

Development Editor: Fiona Jeffries
Copyediting: Amber Riaz
Cover Design: John van der Woude
Text Design: Lauren Jeanneau
Printed and bound in the UK

Published by Fernwood Publishing
2970 Oxford Street, Halifax, Nova Scotia, B3L 2W4
Halifax and Winnipeg
www.fernwoodpublishing.ca

Fernwood Publishing Company Limited gratefully acknowledges the financial support of the Government of Canada through the Canada Book Fund and the Canada Council for the Arts. We acknowledge the Province of Manitoba for support through the Manitoba Publishers Marketing Assistance Program and the Book Publishing Tax Credit. We acknowledge the Nova Scotia Department of Communities, Culture and Heritage for support through the Publishers Assistance Fund.

This book has been published with the help of a grant from the Federation for the Humanities and Social Sciences, through the Awards to Scholarly Publications Program, using funds provided by the Social Sciences and Humanities Research Council of Canada.

Library and Archives Canada Cataloguing in Publication
Title: The gates of the sea : migration and rescue at the edges of Europe / Luna Vives.
Names: Vives, Luna, author.
Description: Includes bibliographical references and index.
Identifiers: Canadiana 2025020830X | ISBN 9781773637662 (softcover)
Subjects: LCSH: Search and rescue operations—Spain. | LCSH: Rescue work—Spain. | LCSH: Immigrants—Government policy—Spain. | LCSH: Border security—Spain. | LCSH: Spain—Emigration and immigration.
Classification: LCC TL553.8 .V58 2025 | DDC 363.34/810946—dc23

*To Inara and Aurora,
who are brave and know the way forward.
And to Alex, always.*

> We are very lucky in Spain, because the protection of human life is kept separate from the protection of the border. The problem begins when we mix maritime search and rescue and border control. This has not happened in Spain. Here, we have the protection of human life, regardless of whether or not [the people in distress] are undocumented. Let's bring them to a safe place and let the judicial system decide, but mixing the two is dangerous.
>
> —Ismael Furió, General Secretary GGT Mar y Puertos (2023)

Contents

Acronyms, Organizations, and Conventions viii

Voices of Note x

Acknowledgements xii

Preface xvi

1   Sea Migration and the Politics of a Manufactured Crisis 1
    Death at Sea 2
    Human Migration as a Hydraulic System 7
    The Creation of the Sea Border, One Rescue Operation at a Time 11
    Looking Back to Look Ahead: Structure of This Book 16

2   Defining Safety, Jurisdiction, and Responsibility at Sea
    throughout the Twentieth Century 20
    The Sinking of the Titanic 23
    Regulating Safety at Sea 24
    The Sinking of the Titanic and the Safety of Life at Sea Convention 26
    Bounding the World's Oceans 32
    Maritime Sovereignty and Jurisdiction According to the United Nation's
    Convention on the Law of the Sea 36
    Protecting Human Life at Sea: The Search and Rescue Convention 41
    The Politics of Organized Abandonment at Sea 47

3   A Brief History of the Spanish Maritime Search and Rescue System 50
    Paving the Way: Rescue in the 1960s and 1970s 52
    The 1990s: A Coordinated Rescue System Is Born 56
    Environmental Disasters Shaped the Early Spanish Search and Rescue System 59
    The Creation of a Two-Tier Rescue System 68
    SASEMAR Today 72
    The End of an Era: Rescue Becomes Entangled with Migration Control 80

4	The Spectacle of Militarization and Abandonment in the Western Mediterranean	83
	Ceuta	85
	Border Crossings and Co-operation in the Western Mediterranean	89
	A Turning Point in the Militarization of Maritime Rescue in the Western Mediterranean	99
	Doing Away with Universal Rescue: The Birth of a Two-Tier System	103
	Developing Morocco's Rescue Capacity	105
	Migration, Rescue, and Geopolitics in the Western Mediterranean	109
	Rescue and Migration in the Western Mediterranean: A View from Tarajal Beach	112
5	The Canary Islands: A Stealthy Takeover of Maritime Search and Rescue by the Military	115
	The Many Deadly Routes of the Atlantic Zone	118
	The Atlantic Zone of Responsibility: Two Decades of Arrivals and Externalization	121
	SASEMAR during the First "*Cayuco* Crisis"	130
	The Return of the Cayucos	133
	An Exhausted Rescue Fleet	137
	Geopolitics and Rescue Responsibilities in the Atlantic	141
6	The Rescuers' Union: Resistance from Within	147
	The Arrival of the Anarchists	150
	Anarcho-Syndicalism in Spain: A Brief History of the CGT	154
	CGT SASEMAR: A Workers' Organization and an Actor of Change	157
	The Union's Newsletter	160
	"The Two Huawei Dudes"	163
	Labour Struggles: The Government as an Employer	166
	Looking into the Future	173
7	Death, Resistance, Hope	174
	Death	176
	Resistance	180
	Hope	181
Endnotes		184
References		185
Index		196

Acronyms, Organizations, and Conventions

AIS: Automated Identification System.

Alarm Phone: Hotline for people crossing the maritime border on their way to the Europe.

Caminando Fronteras (also known as Walking Borders): non-governmental human rights organization.

CATE (Centro de Atención Temporal de Extranjeros): Temporary holding centre for foreigners.

CGT (Confederación General del Trabajo): Spanish anarchist labour union.

CGT Mar y Puertos: Section of the CGT that represents seafarers and dockworkers.

CGT SASEMAR: Section of the CGT Mar y Puertos that represents SASEMAR rescue crews in the maritime units (boats).

CNT (Confederación Nacional del Trabajo): Spanish confederation of anarchist labour unions.

CCOO (Confederación Sindical de Comisiones Obreras): Spanish labour union historically aligned with the communist left.

CCOE (Centro de Coordinación de Operaciones de Emergencia): Emergency Operation Coordination Centre.

Defensor del Pueblo: High Commissioner of the Parliament responsible for defending citizens' fundamental rights and civil liberties.

ECHR: European Court of Human Rights.

EEZ: Exclusive Economic Zone.

EUROSUR: European Border Surveillance System.

Frontex/EBCG: European Border and Coast Guard.

GEAS (Grupo Especial de Actividades Subacuáticas): elite underwater unit of the Guardia Civil.

GMDSS: Global Maritime Distress Safety System.

IMO: International Maritime Organization.

MRCC: Maritime Rescue Coordination Centre.

MUO (Mando Único Operativo): Military Single Operative command for rescue operations involving migrant boats in the Western Mediterranean.

NRCC: National Rescue Coordination Centre.

REMOLMAR/REMASA (Remolques Marítimos Sociedad Anónima or Maritime Towing Inc.): Spanish private tugboat company crucial to the early development of SASEMAR.

RNLI: Royal National Lifeboat Institution.

SAR Convention: Search and Rescue Convention, 1979/1985.

SASEMAR (Sociedad Española de Salvamento Marítimo, commonly known as Salvamento Marítimo): Spanish maritime search and rescue agency.

SEMAR (Servicio Marítimo de la Guardia Civil): Guardia Civil Maritime Service.

SESN (Sociedad Española de Salvamento de Náufragos): Spanish Society for the Rescue of Shipwreck Victims.

SIVE (Sistema Integrado de Vigilancia Exterior): Spanish Integrated System for the Surveillance of the External Border.

SNSM (Société Nationale de Sauvetage en Mer): French National Maritime Rescue Society.

SOLAS Convention: Safety of Life at Sea Convention, 1974/1980.

TRAGSA (Empresa de Transformación Agraria): Agrarian Transformation Inc., Spanish publicly owned company dedicated to rural development and nature protection.

UGT (Unión General de Trabajadores): Spanish labour union historically aligned with the Spanish socialist party.

UNCLOS: United Nations Convention on the Law of the Sea, 1982/1994.

Voices of Note

ALHASSANE BANGOURA: Baby born in a migrant boat on his way to the Canary Islands. He was probably stillborn and is buried at Teguise cemetery in Lanzarote.

ARAN SOL JUANOLA: Volunteer for the *Prestige* disaster cleanup efforts in 2003.

DÁCIL TRUJILLO HERNÁNDEZ: Municipal social worker and volunteer. She lives in El Hierro with her family.

ENRIC TARRIDA: Retired rescue captain and anarchist union leader with the CGT. Enric started working in maritime search and rescue in 1989 (before SASEMAR was established) and is responsible for creating the section of the CGT representing rescue workers. He currently lives in Valencia with his wife and children.

HELENA MALENO: Founder and coordinator of the NGO Caminando Fronteras. She lives in Tangiers with her family.

ISMAEL FURIÓ GENOVÉS: Guardamar captain and secretary of both sections of the CGT devoted to seafarers and dockworkers (CGT Mar y Puertos) and rescue crews (CGT SASEMAR) between 2019 and 2024. He lives in Valencia with his family.

HARIDIAN MARICHAL NIEBLA: Journalist and activist. She lives in El Hierro with her family and her dog Sol.

JOSEP BORRELL FONTELLES: Spanish politician and main architect of Spain's first maritime search and rescue service. Borrell was involved in Spanish politics (being a member of Felipe González's cabinet between 1982 and 1998 and candidate for leadership of the Socialist Party in 1998) and transitioned to European politics in 2002. He was the EU's High Representative of the Union for Foreign Affairs and Security Policy between 2019 and 2024.

JUAN CARLOS ARBEX: Writer and documentarian specialized in maritime issues, he was SASEMAR's first Director of Communications in 1992-1993. He lives in Gijón with his family.

JULIE CAMPAGNE: Co-founder and member of Lanzarote's Network of Solidarity with Migrant People, created in 2020. She lives near Timanfaya National Park (Lanzarote) with her children.

LAETITIA MARTHE: Co-founder and member of Lanzarote's Citizens' Network of Solidarity with Migrant People, created in 2020. She lives in Tías (Lanzarote) with her children and collaborates with other organizations in Spain and abroad.

MANUEL CAPA: Second officer employed with SASEMAR since 2012 and union spokesperson with the CGT SASEMAR. When not aboard one of the agency's Guardamares, he lives in Almería with his children.

ORIOL ESTRADA: rescue crew employed with SASEMAR since 1993 and spokesperson with the CGT SASEMAR. He lives in Almería and works in one of the agency's Salvamares.

PATUCA (PATRICIA) FERNÁNDEZ: Spanish lawyer specialized in childhood, social exclusion and migrations and leader of the pro bono legal team that has been pushing for a legal decision on the Tarajal massacre since February 2014.

Acknowledgements

AS USUAL, IT IS IMPOSSIBLE TO THANK EVERYONE who made this book what it is, and all the mistakes are mine.

A number of institutions have generously supported my research on migration, borders, and the sea over the last two decades. I would like to acknowledge the support of the Fonds de Recherche du Québec – Société et Culture's Programme de soutien à la recherche pour la relève professorale (grant 2019-NP-253366), Social Sciences and Humanities Research Council of Canada's Insight Development Program (grant 430-2020-00700) and Insight Program (grant 435-2023-0819, Principal Investigator Danièle Bélanger), and the Spanish Ministry of Education and Science. I am indebted to the people in the many institutions where I have been over the years: the Universidad Complutense de Madrid, the University of British Columbia, McGill University, and the Université de Montréal. In this trip across countries, continents, languages, and intellectual traditions I have had the best teachers. María Lois, Heriberto Cairo, Dan Hiebert, David Ley, and Vandna Sinha have changed not just how I think about space and power, but about the responsibility that comes with being a social scientist nowadays.

Other colleagues have also made this journey possible. Laurie Beaudonnet and Kathryn Furlong have been steadfast supports through gale and fair weather: thank you. I am thankful to the wonderful colleagues and friends in migration and border studies who have supported my work, people like Danièle Bélanger, Christina Clark-Kazak, Karine Côté-Boucher, François Crépeau, Francisco Durán, Adèle Garnier, Shauna Labman, Jamie Liew, Patricia Martin, Laura Madokoro, Mireille Paquet, Stephanie Silverman, Özgün Topak, Lyubov Zhyznomirska — what a joy and privilege to walk this path alongside you. Co-conspirators Arnaud Banos, Kira Williams, Camille Martel, and Lizzie Hessek have generously allowed me to incorporate materials from our common projects and publications in the chapters on the Atlantic and Western Mediterranean. Historian Enrique Tudela Vázquez read and commented on an early draft of the chapter on the rescuers' union, for which I am grateful. A group of labour historians I met in Amsterdam as I was beginning to write this book have provided insightful feedback and inspiration, both directly and through their work: Peter Cole, Brendan von Briesen, and Nandita Sharma (who may not be a historian by title, but has profoundly influenced how I view history). They have made me see the radical potential of the past to change the future, and the strength of collectivity. Writer Taras Grescoe helped me trust I could tell this story before I even put pen to paper.

This book is also better thanks to the contributions of research assistants whom I have had the pleasure of working with throughout the years: Jeanne Beauchemin, Jessie Bigras-Lauzon, Marianne Turcotte-Plamondon, Shaima Jorio, Vivien Geoffray, and Ismael de la Villa Hervás. Lizzie Hessek, a promising migration scholar and fabulous person, has made all the maps and graphs included in this book and edited the text for clarity and language. The word "research assistant" does not do justice to her crucial role in bringing this project to life.

Thanks also to the many colleagues who influenced the content of this book through their thoughtful comments on texts and presentations I gave at the biannual Borderwalls Conference organized by Élisabet Vallet in Montréal in 2022; at a workshop organized by Idil Atak and Anna Triandafyllidou at Toronto Metropolitan University in March 2023; at the Maritime Solidarity Conference at the University of Amsterdam's International Institute of Social History in the fall of 2023; at an internal meeting of Alarm Phone in late 2023; and at a conference on Borders in the Iberian Peninsula I co-organized with long-term colleague María Lois in early 2024. I also workshopped some of the ideas presented in this book at a talk I gave at the University of Osnabrück, Germany, in the spring of 2024 at the invitation of Maurice Stierl, member of the Institute for Migration Research and Intercultural Studies. This book has benefited from all these exchanges.

A massive thank you to the incredible team at Fernwood Publishing, especially Fiona Jeffries, whose support and guidance have been invaluable at every step. You are a treasure. I also want to express my gratitude to the three anonymous reviewers whose insights and feedback made this book better. Our profession depends on this kind of unpaid labour, which often goes unrecognized. Thank you.

My deepest thanks to the activists and labour leaders whose work has inspired mine. I was thinking of other things when I met Manuel Capa in

Almería in the summer of 2019. He made me realize how unique the Spanish search and rescue system is and fed me more than once so that we could keep talking: thank you. At SASEMAR, I can only thank the union leaders publicly: besides Capa, they are Ismael Furió Genovés, Enric Tarrida, Oriol Estrada, and Juan Miguel Font from CGT SASEMAR, and Cristian Castaño from CCOO. Thanks to them, I was able to interview other rescue workers who asked to remain anonymous out of fear that talking to me would cost them dearly. To the captains, the machinists, the sailors, the cooks, the winch operators, the pilots, and the helicopter rescuers who talked to me: I hope you will see yourselves in this book. To the activists: Natalia García Caballos (and her parents), Julie Campagne, Laetitia Marthe, Loueila Sid Ahmed Ndiaye (referred to in some of the publications used in this book as Loueila Mint El Mamy), Saliou Diouf, Diego Boza, Maurice Stierl, Haridian Marichal Niebla, Dácil Trujillo Hernández, Naé, and all the people who devote their time and energy to push against oppression and violence: you make this world a better place. Your dedication has been the guiding thread and the compass of this book.

Journalists do not often make it into the acknowledgements section of books written by academics, but this book would not exist without a few dedicated journalists whose work has been an inspiration. One evening in late 2023, I was incredibly fortunate to share a dinner with a dream team of reporters in Gran Canaria: María Martín and Guillermo Vega from *El País*, José María Rodríguez (EFE), and Txema Santana (who is a journalist and so much more). Through their work over the last decade, they have consistently and rigorously tracked the state of migration in Spain. Another journalist, Pepe Naranjo, was not at the table that night, but his reporting has had a definite impact on own work ever since I first landed in Dakar over fifteen years ago to study sea migration to Spain. Thank you for your critical, incisive perspectives on these crucial issues. Your articles are referenced throughout this book.

Not everything in life is work, though. I wrote this book during my sabbatical in Spain in the 2023–24 academic year. Natalia helped me settle in and find my feet — thank you for the walks, the conversations, the friendship, and the encouragement. Noe and Sergio welcomed us as part of their chosen family. I am so very grateful for all the hiking and the climbing and the sleeping under the stars and the canyoning and the spelunking and the cans of soda at the end of our adventures: you made this year unforgettable. Kelly offered the best pen advice, as usual, along with a steady supply of matcha and support whenever my motivation faltered. And finally, after two decades abroad, I had the chance to be close to my family again — my dad, his wife Yolanda, my two beautiful sisters, my cousins, aunts and uncles — thank you for welcoming me back as though no time had passed. I am so lucky to have you in my life.

Last but certainly not the least, above everyone and everything, thanks to my kids for always asking all the hard questions with a steady gaze. You make me proud.

Preface

PORT OF ALMERÍA, JULY 2019. I came to meet rescue crews employed by the Spanish search and rescue agency, SASEMAR. Instead, I ended up talking to union representatives. Due to a recent gag order from the government, only they were allowed to talk to me without explicit authorization from the agency. On the dock, I met union leaders Manuel Capa and Ismael Furió, who lamented that most people do not understand what they do. "People think we are some kind of NGO," said Capa, "but I am just a public worker doing my job. I rescue people. I am not a hero. I am not a martyr. I am just a worker." Ismael Furió, then secretary general for the section of the main union representing sea rescue crews, nodded from across the table and added: "and as rescue workers we don't rescue migrants: we rescue shipwreck victims."

By then, I had spent a decade and a half studying migration policy in Spain, with a special focus on sea migration. And yet, listening to the union reps, I realized I did not understand SASEMAR very well either. If they were not an NGO, but they were independent from the military, then what were they? What was their relationship to other government agencies, state security forces, and NGOs elsewhere along the European Union's (EU) maritime border who were struggling to do their work in an increasingly hostile political climate? How exactly did search and rescue work in Spain, and how was it similar to, or different from, how it was done in other places? How had rescue crews' work changed as the number of boats carrying migrants across the sea grew, and how had the politicization of these arrivals impacted their everyday? What explains the intriguing fact that the majority of these government workers elected an anarcho-syndicalist union openly opposed to border control to represent their interests? How has this shaped the agency's response to sea migration since its creation more than three decades ago?

My goal in this book is to answer these questions. I focus on the Spanish approach to maritime rescue at sea: what it is supposed to do, what it actually does, and who is responsible for it. I am also interested in how this approach has evolved over the last thirty years, as shielding the border against certain groups of people has become an increasingly contentious political issue.

Undocumented border crossers are often simply labelled as "illegal migrants." But the categories that states have created to serve their own needs and priorities (categories like economic migrant, asylum seeker, refugee, or the most striking of them all, "illegal alien") do not always reflect the lived experiences of people on the move who frequently shift between categories over time or occupy several at once. To understand what really happens when people cross the border, we need to rid ourselves of this "categorical fetishism" (Crawley and Skleparis 2018). Moreover, these categories are dehumanizing. For this reason, and following the lead of other scholars and activists, I have used alternative terms such as "people on the move" whenever possible.

Spain has a long-standing history of human mobility, shaped over millennia by commerce, invasions, and its proximity to Africa (only fourteen kilometres away at the Strait of Gibraltar). More recently, the country was the origin of a significant exodus: for much of the second half of the twentieth century, political exiles and poor workers left, looking for safety and prosperity beyond the country's borders, mainly in Western Europe and Latin America. This dynamic shifted dramatically in the early 1990s, coinciding with Spain's entry into the European Communities (replaced by the European Union in 1993), as the country transitioned from a place of emigration to a destination for immigration. Spain's growing economy, political stability, and status as a member state were attractive factors for people on the move on the other side of the Mediterranean.

Sea migration has played a pivotal role in Spain's migration patterns all along. Initially, boats arrived from the Maghreb to the southern and eastern coasts of the Iberian Peninsula; after the turn of the twenty-first century, these flows expanded to include the Canary Islands. Meanwhile, citizens from former colonies in Latin America arrived by plane in much larger numbers, but these arrivals did not stir as much political and social anxiety. In stark contrast, irregular arrivals — particularly by boat — have been at the centre of public concern and heated political debates. Alongside other southern European nations like Greece and Italy, Spain has often been described as the "soft underbelly" of the EU's border regime. Against this backdrop, policymakers have increasingly turned their attention to the rescue infrastructure already in place along Spain's maritime border, repurposing these resources for the enforcement and control of the southern border.

In 2024, nearly 47,000 people arrived in the Canary Islands by boat — 17 percent more than the year before, marking the highest number on record. The emergence of sea migration as a political issue has evolved in parallel to the evolution of SASEMAR. But SASEMAR is very poorly positioned to play the role of the border guard. The agency, a government-run civil body with no law enforcement mandate and unarmed personnel, is increasingly becoming an outlier in the European context.

Across areas of migration in the continent, a two-tier rescue system has emerged: one system for migrant people, and another one (typically more aligned with member states' international obligations) for tourists and locals. Rescue assets (boats, planes, and personnel already at sea) have been reclaimed to act as border guards. In many places this "mission creep" has been rather successful. This has been especially the case in contexts where rescue responsibilities were in the hands of state security forces — in Italy, Greece, or Malta, for example. So far, this is less the case in Spain, but this may change soon. In the following pages, I continuously return to the most crucial question in maritime search and rescue work: why is it that some lives are considered worth saving, while others are not? The answer speaks the quiet part out loud, not just about maritime rescue, but about the construction of self and other in contemporary Europe.

This question is also an existential issue for SASEMAR. As populist discourses throughout Europe successfully exploit sea migration for political gain, the agency's position is becoming untenable. The growing gap between EU member states' international obligations in maritime rescue that SASEMAR upholds and actual rescue practices in zones of migration is a source of endless tension and criticism. In fact, anyone with seafaring experience understands the duty of rescue. Rescuers — alongside a diverse group of actors who have taken up the moral compass politicians have discarded in their pursuit of votes — uphold Spain's international rescue obligations. Among them are activists, union leaders, and senior Navy personnel. Their voices echo Furió's and remind us that the first responsibility at sea is to save lives; the questions come later, once at port. In this sense, this book is not just about changes, but also about resistance to those changes and the power of collectivity to envision better futures and bring them to life.

1

Sea Migration and the Politics of a Manufactured Crisis

IN THE EARLY DAYS OF 2020, a boat left the Moroccan city of Tantan bound for the Canary Islands. The wind was strong as the grey rigid-hull inflatable boat left the beach. Aboard were forty-three people from various African countries, including the Ivory Coast, The Gambia, Cameroon, Senegal, and Guinea Conakry (Rosati and Martín 2020). Among them were nineteen minors and fifteen women, three of whom were pregnant. Most of the passengers could not swim, and few had lifejackets. Under normal conditions, the journey would have taken about seven hours. But the weather was bad, the engine was weak, their compass was broken, and the boat entered an area with no phone reception shortly after leaving Tantan. The journey quickly turned into a nightmare. By the end of the first day, they had run out of food and water. Some drank seawater, which made them sick. On the second day, they ran out of fuel, and some tried to paddle with their hands in the direction they thought they would find the islands. Caminando Fronteras, an NGO led by activist Helena Maleno with a mandate to defend the rights of migrant people, began receiving calls from worried relatives and alerted emergency services. Shortly after, the regional rescue coordination centre dispatched a helicopter and a plane, but they were unable to locate the tiny boat in the immense ocean. On board, people prayed for mercy, certain they would not survive.

Then, on the third night, a wail pierced the darkness: nineteen-year-old Daria[1] had gone into labour. "God have mercy on me!" she cried. The men looked away as another passenger, a heavily pregnant woman travelling with her eight-year-old daughter, stepped in to assist with the birth (Rosati and Martín 2020). That night, fifteen nautical miles (twenty-eight kilometres) from the island of Lanzarote, Alhassane Bangoura was born. The baby did not cry. It was then that one of the young men turned on his cellphone and received a message: "Welcome to Spain." He called Caminando Fronteras, and eventually emergency services were able to locate the boat and dispatch the Salvamar *Altair*, one of the fast rescue boats owned and operated by SASEMAR, the Spanish search and rescue agency. The captain of the *Altair* tried to resuscitate Alhassane Bangoura but was unsuccessful.

Hours later, they arrived at the port of Los Mármoles in Lanzarote. Daria and others were taken to the hospital (Murillo and Martín 2020), while the body of Alhassane Bangoura was taken from his mother and brought to the courthouse morgue for investigation. The young mother spent the next ten days recovering at the hospital, surrounded by some of the other women who had travelled with her, unable to accept that her baby had died. Daria was not allowed to see her son's body. A volunteer working with an organization that supports women through perinatal grief took pictures of baby Alhassane Bangoura and brought them to Daria, who slowly came to terms with the painful fact that her baby had likely been stillborn.

The funeral was held weeks later, on January 25, in the village of Teguise on Lanzarote. Daria could not attend; she had been sent to Gran Canaria, two hundred kilometres away. Heartbroken, she asked that a small stone bearing Alhassane Bangoura's name be placed on his grave. Laetitia Marthe and Julie Campagne, co-founders of Lanzarote's Network of Solidarity with Migrant People, attended the funeral. Laetitia had been volunteering as an interpreter the night the passengers of the ill-fated boat arrived on the island; at the hospital, she also helped translate for the doctors who attended to Daria and the other women, as well as for the volunteers supporting the young mother through her grief. As Laetitia was heading to her car after the funeral, she recognized a young man standing by the cemetery gates as another passenger from the boat. Overcome with emotion, the man told Laetitia that he believed Alhassane Bangoura gave up his life so the others could survive — he was convinced that the rescue operation would never have happened had Daria not gone into labour. Perhaps he was right.

DEATH AT SEA

Alhassane Bangoura is far from the only person, or the only child, to have lost their life attempting to reach the Canary Islands. In 2023 alone, 6,618 people on the move drowned on their way to Spain according to the organization Caminando Fronteras (2023). The vast majority of these deaths (6,007) occurred in the Atlantic. Most of them happened within Spain's Search and Rescue Region (SRR), also known as a Search and Rescue (SAR) zone or zone of responsibility. These deaths stand as a stark testament to the failure of punitive migration and border policies in contemporary Europe.

Migration, particularly sea migration, has become a hot-button issue in European and Spanish politics. Its political salience outweighs its statistical significance: according to data from the International Organization for Migration (IOM n.d.), 207,000 people entered the European Union by sea in 2024 — less than 0.5 percent of its population of 450 million people. And yet, sea migration is systematically misrepresented, criminalized, and instrumentalized. Indeed, the clandestine movement of poor people (because no wealthy person risks their life on a boat to reach the European Union) appears to offer endless avenues for profiting and for political manoeuvring. On one hand, business-minded people (a mix of small entrepreneurs, criminal networks, and legitimate private companies providing border control technologies) fuel a thriving migration industry. On the other hand, elected politicians across the political spectrum capitalize on increasingly populist rhetoric to gain votes while doing little to address the root causes that drive people to leave their communities and cross borders. In some cases, they contribute through their actions to the political and economic instability that fuels the unwelcomed mobility of the poor. Despite their different agendas, these actors have successfully reframed the conversation and turned sea migration into a crisis that demands a swift and drastic solution. Even worse, by portraying the people who arrive by boat as a national security threat, governments legitimize repression as the only rational and effective response to migration, as if the only possible way to stop the arrival of people on the move was to build taller walls and fill the seas with military patrols. This rhetoric elides the fact that seven decades of experimentation along the US–Mexico border has repeatedly proven this strategy to be both ineffective and costly. It also ignores the fact that the vast majority of undocumented immigrants currently living in the European Union arrived by plane with valid travel documents, and that those crossing the external land and sea borders make up only a tiny fraction of the total. The war on sea migration continues unabated.

The urgency of the task at hand, combined with the framing of migration as a series of crises, has normalized the death toll and the violence against people on the move. Both seem now a tragic yet inevitable price to pay for containing the crises caused by the mobility of the unwanted. If a crisis is an exceptional event that demands an exceptional response, then that response is expected to be swift and decisive. We are led to believe that bypassing standard procedures and safeguards is unavoidable — that, in the "war" against undocumented migration, the ends justify the means both in terms of human suffering and in terms of financial cost; governments dig deep into their pockets in times of crisis.

Geographer Alison Mountz (2020, 38) argues that defining (certain forms of) human mobility as a crisis triggers "moments of hysteria" in policy making: moments when even those solutions that violate legal and moral boundaries are seen as conceivable. This erosion of moral and legal norms is particularly evident when those on the move are individuals entitled to specific protections, such as children, asylum seekers, and others covered by international conventions and domestic law. The very notion of a "migration crisis," thus, shifts responsibility for repressive measures onto people on the move, including those in clear need of protection.

Framing human mobility as a crisis also shifts the focus from the lived experiences of those on the move to the challenges faced by governments (Dines, Montagna, and Vaccheli 2018) and imposes a specific sense of temporality. Crises are, by definition, short-lived — and so are the policies crafted in response. Yet, migration in Europe is not a crisis, or even a series of one-time crises: it is a structural fact. Framing individual migration events (for example, population movements following the Arab Spring of 2011 and the so-called Syrian refugee crisis of 2015) as one-time crises disconnected from one another exposes a fundamental illusion in contemporary border policy which is the belief that human mobility is an anomaly, a passing challenge that can be controlled through short-term measures, be they however draconian.

In this context, the securitization of sea migration has fundamentally reshaped how maritime search and rescue is done across Europe. Migration control and sea rescue are, at least in theory, two separate policy areas. While the first is an instrument that governments use to regulate who can and cannot enter their territory, the second is a means to protecting human life at sea, regardless of people's nationality or administrative status. But, as migration control becomes a source of profit for some and of political leverage for others, the line between control and rescue has blurred. Thus, the universal mandate to save lives at sea is increasingly called into question.

Maritime rescue has become tangled in Europe's approach to migration management, which rests on three key strategies: militarizing borders to seal them against illegalized human mobility, externalizing border enforcement to regions of origin and transit, and implementing repressive policies centred on detention and deportation. These strategies are deeply interwoven. The one with the most profound impact on maritime search and rescue has been the fortification of borders, but the other two have also changed the perception of whose lives can be put at risk with no political cost and whose lives are deemed worth rescuing.

Externalization entails countries of destination delegating migration and border-related responsibilities to countries defined (within the European imagination) as spaces of origin and transit for people on the move. The European Union and its member states have, for decades now, shifted these responsibilities to non-EU countries that often lack both the capacity and the political will to uphold the fundamental rights of migrant people – including their right to life. Governments who take on these responsibilities have been rewarded with substantial financial packages. The most well-known of these co-operation agreements is the 2016 EU–Türkiye deal, in which the European Union provided six billion euros in exchange for Türkiye's commitment to curb irregular migration to Greece. But countries co-operating with the European Union also have their own political motivations to play along. For example, these agreements may help them increase their political and economic leverage within their regions. This is how Morocco, Libya, Mauritania, Tunisia, Senegal, Niger, Türkiye, and others have become the European Union's border guards across different zones of migration.

At the same time, externalization allows the European Union and its member states to expand their geopolitical sphere of influence and control: the elongated European border region now extends far beyond the Union's outer territorial limits. For instance, barriers to movement begin as far south as Niger, over two thousand kilometres from the European Union's border. In effect, Europe's border is no longer a fixed line but a sprawling, multilayered zone that encompasses both land and maritime spaces. Countries of origin and transit are increasingly integrated into the European Union's enforcement apparatus, serving as extensions of its migration control strategy. Delegated responsibilities include the monitoring of areas of departure and known nodes along migration journeys; the detention of people on the move; the criminalization of activities that facilitate migration; and the coordination of maritime rescue operations in the waters separating Europe from Africa. In outsourcing these tasks, the European Union shirks direct accountability while reinforcing a system in which migration is treated primarily as a security threat rather than recognizing it as a normal yet complex phenomenon with economic, humanitarian, and legal dimensions.

Externalization aligns closely with militarization, since the responsibility for rescue operations transferred to origin and transit countries is placed in the hands of agencies that are almost invariably a part of armed forces. This process is further facilitated by generous funding from the European Union and individual member states to equip and train security forces in countries such as Senegal, Mauritania, Morocco, Tunisia, and Libya.

The third strategy, repression, goes hand in hand with the criminalization of certain forms of human mobility, particularly (in the case of the Atlantic and Western Mediterranean) that of Black people. Repression often hinges on excluding migrants from spaces of freedom. It relies, heavily and increasingly, on the detention of people on the move in centres both within and outside EU territory — centres funded, at least partially, by the European Union.

Migrant detention in the European Union is not as widespread or profitable as in the United States yet, but it is also a component of Europe's border architecture. Often, the primary goal of detention is to facilitate deportation (the expulsion of foreigners from the territory); but detention also serves as a deterrent to future arrivals. Deportation has become a popular electoral promise, but its implementation is both difficult and costly when done within legal frameworks. Specifically, those deported from the European Union need to be taken somewhere outside the European Union, but countries of origin and transit have little interest in accepting the return of their own nationals — citizens who were so dissatisfied or felt so threatened that they risked their lives to start fresh elsewhere — or deported nationals of other countries who could fuel xenophobia at home. Politicians may promise deportation, but what actually happens after they get elected is another matter.

This relatively new border regime — characterized by militarization, externalization, and repression through detention and deportation — is reinforced by a fourth strategy: the use of advanced and highly costly technology. This technology is designed to detect irregular movements of people at and near borders, create biometric databases for identification, and share profiles with countries both within and beyond the European Union. The use of advanced technology also plays a key role in securing the co-operation of countries along migration routes in Africa and the Middle East.

These three strategies, though expensive and spectacular, have proven ineffective at stopping migration. Instead, they have made migration routes more dangerous, contributing to the emergence of a growing network of spaces of violence and death that includes the Teguise cemetery where baby Alhassane Bangoura is buried. These strategies have also fostered a highly profitable smuggling business. Because self-directed migration is less and less feasible due to towering border walls and heavily monitored seas, people on the move are left with no option but to hire the services of actors engaging in criminal smuggling. This, in turn, leads to an increase of physical, emotional, financial, and sexual violence against people on the move.

Despite mounting evidence attesting to the failure of these strategies to achieve their official goal, EU member states have doubled down. Maritime rescue has become a casualty in this "war against migrants." It is remarkable that, while there is no evidence that the presence of rescue boats increases sea migration, populist European policymakers continue to push for the removal of life-saving services from areas of sea migration to deter future arrivals. There is evidence, though, that militarization and the withdrawal and shrinking of rescue services are directly responsible for the preventable deaths of people on the move. Thus, the integration of rescue services into European anti-immigration strategies exposes the European Union's foundering commitment to the protection of human rights.

HUMAN MIGRATION AS A HYDRAULIC SYSTEM

International migration is a multifaceted and fast-changing phenomenon shaped by deep structural global inequalities. Who moves, where they move from and to, and the conditions of their mobility (both material and administrative) are influenced by many factors that range from the personal to the structural. This inequality has led researchers to talk about a "global mobility divide" (Mau et al. 2015). In their study of visa policies between 1969 and 2010, Steffen Mau and colleagues found that while nationals from wealthy countries enjoy increasing freedom to move across international borders, those from poorer countries face growing administrative obstacles to do the same. This growing disparity is particularly pronounced for citizens from African countries. In other words, the main factor determining how easily people can move is their place of birth.

Precarious migrants from poorer countries navigate routes that open and close in response to wars, natural disasters, economic conditions in their home communities, geographic proximity, the presence of established networks of people from the same community, the demand for migrant labour, and the availability of transportation (legal or otherwise) to their destinations. Over the last few decades, evidence shows that while restrictive border policies may force people on the move to find new routes, exposing them to greater risks of violence and death, these policies have never stopped migration. This is why irregular migration dynamics are often likened to a hydraulic system: when one route is shut down, the pressure on other routes increases, causing new paths to emerge (Schmoll 2015).

The hydraulic system metaphor helps explain why repressive approaches consistently fail to stop undocumented border crossings. We have seen, time and again, that when a border closes, migrants turn to alternative, more dangerous routes where they are more exposed to violence from smugglers, traffickers, and even state security forces. This metaphor also highlights how quickly migration patterns adapt to changing circumstances. For example, within a month of Russia's invasion of Ukraine in February 2022, nearly four million people fled the country, while six million others were internally displaced. Similarly, within weeks of Senegalese President Malick Sall's renewed crackdown on political dissent in 2023, the southern section of the Atlantic route, which had been dormant for almost fifteen years, resumed with striking intensity. Political repression, compounded by persistent unemployment, drove five thousand people (mostly young Senegalese men) to embark on boats headed toward the Canary Islands in November 2023 alone. Official statistics show that over 37,000 people arrived at the archipelago that year, with nearly 47,000 more in 2024 (Martín and Hierro 2024); an unknown number died along the way. The regional government of the Canary Islands has struggled to respond to the arrivals (many of whom are unaccompanied minors) while also denouncing the lack of solidarity from other regions in mainland Spain. But what happens when borders along the several routes that migrants use to reach the Canary Islands become even more militarized? People on the move find another way in — just as they always have and always will.

Migration Routes

In academic and policy circles, as well as in the media, the term "migration route" is commonly used. In European migration speak, there are four main sea routes: the Atlantic route and the Western, Central, and Eastern Mediterranean routes. The framing of human mobility into routes reflects a pivotal shift in EU migration policy that took place in 2005 with the adoption of the Global Approach to Migration and Mobility (GAMM). This shift redirected the focus of attention of anti-immigration policy from the border to the many spaces that were part of migrants' journeys to Europe.

However, the term "migration route," obscures the multifaceted and fluid nature of migration itself. Take, for example, the Atlantic migration zone (shown in Figure 1 below), which is often referred to as a single route ("the Atlantic route"). In reality, it consists of multiple and overlapping routes stretching thousands of kilometres.

Just like the "crisis" narrative, framing human mobility in terms of routes oversimplifies human mobility dynamics. This perspective reduces journeys to a simple path between two fixed points, obscuring the broader structural factors that drive movement. On a map, a route appears as a straight line or an arrow, implying a direct and short-lived journey from point A to point B. In reality, migration is far more complex, shaped by detours, interruptions, and changing circumstances along the way, with journeys stretching over months or even years, often taking people on the move to multiple destinations without ever necessarily reaching their original goal.

However, from a policy perspective, this simplification is useful. It portrays migration as a temporary disruption of the natural order of things, which is one with sedentary populations, and as a problem that can be fixed by interrupting the line at any given point. This approach disregards the deep historical and contemporary forces driving migration, the interconnectedness of migratory movements, and the opportunities migration offers. It also fails to acknowledge the risks people on the move face and the legal and moral obligations states have toward migrants and refugees. Most crucially, reducing the mobility of people to lines on a map dehumanizes them and enables wealthy states to evade responsibility for finding durable and just responses to this global phenomenon, which is cartographically represented as happening mostly elsewhere.

The routes perspective, thus, paves the way for governments to justify quick and simplistic policy responses to illegalized human mobility such as building border walls or withdrawing rescue services at sea. But these strategies are bound to fail because migration is a complex sociopolitical phenomenon that resists simple answers (Rittel and Webber 1973). Human mobility connects places with long and complicated relationships shaped by colonial histories and ongoing unequal power dynamics. In particular, migration from Africa to Europe is rooted in the enduring legacy of colonial power relationships. People leave their home countries because they are unable to feed their families or achieve their life aspirations due to the continued plundering of natural resources by wealthier countries — often

FIGURE 1: Map showing the different maritime routes that cross the Atlantic zone

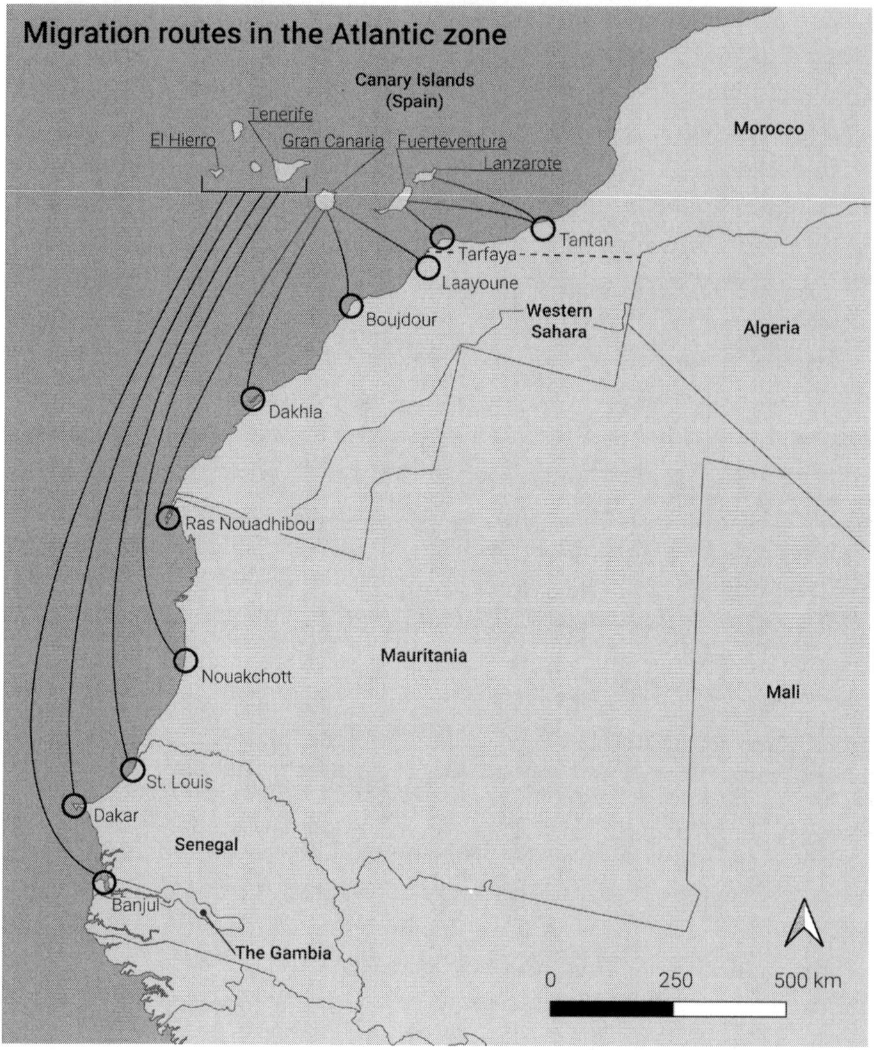

Adapted and expanded from *El País* (Rosati and Martín 2020) with data from SASEMAR and activists in Mauritania and Senegal. Created by Elizabeth Rose Hessek and reproduced with permission.

former colonial powers. For instance, would so many young Senegalese fishermen risk the dangerous journey to the Canary Islands if Spanish and Chinese industrial fishing vessels were not engaged in illegal, unreported, and unregulated fishing in the waters off Senegalese coasts (Maritimes Crimes 2023)? Probably not. But this context gets lost when governments think of human mobility as a simple line on the map.

Moreover, reducing human mobility to migration routes shifts the focus of sea rescue from human security — the core principle of search and rescue (SAR)—to national security, where the primary goal is to secure the nation from the myriads of real or imaginary threats (sea) migrants embody (Hyndman 2008). In other words, if people on the move are cast as enemies of the nation, rescuing them is no longer a priority; letting them drown becomes part of the strategy to keep them out. And so, though it is well-known that removing rescue assets from border regions does not stop migration, this strategy persists because deaths at sea are deliberately built as a deterrent into the EU's external border.

THE CREATION OF THE SEA BORDER, ONE RESCUE OPERATION AT A TIME

While border control has increasingly merged with maritime search and rescue across much of the European Union, these two policy areas remain relatively distinct in Spain. The main actor in maritime rescue is SASEMAR (commonly known as Salvamento Marítimo), a government agency. Even though SASEMAR has become a key player along the southern Spanish border, much of the company's work is unrelated to migration. For example, of the 5,356 vessels the agency assisted in 2023, only 21 percent were migrant boats. The rest were leisure boats (43 percent), merchant vessels (10 percent), fishing boats (7 percent) and others (19 percent; Ministerio de Transportes y Mobilidad Sostenible 2024).

SASEMAR's archives in Madrid are filled with case logs documenting a wide range of incidents: rescue operations triggered by boats running out of fuel at sea, fishing vessels lost in rough seas, catamarans sinking and leaving their passengers stranded, and numerous false alarms from emergency beacons (EPIRBs), some set off by mistake. Surfers, in particular, are a recurring challenge: annual surfing events in the Strait of Gibraltar (also one of the top ten routes for international maritime trade in the world) require months of planning. In short, key sectors of the economy (including tourism, maritime trade, and fishing) benefit from and depend on having a well-functioning system to safeguard human life and protect the marine environment.

Despite this broad mandate, SASEMAR increasingly finds itself responding to emergencies involving people on the move attempting to access Spanish (and, by extension, EU) territory illegally by sea and encountering difficulties along the way.

The Borders at Sea as Power Structures

Why is migration such a big issue? International migration involves people crossing borders to settle in a country other than their country of birth or regular residence. But what is a border? At its core, a border is a political object, an invention we use to organize and make sense of the world. We imbue borders with meaning through our daily actions and interactions: when we show our passport at the airport, when we accept the border guard's authority to let us in or refuse us entry, when we unconsciously reproduce markers of belonging and unbelonging in our everyday language by labelling people as citizens, migrants, expats, or aliens. While socially constructed, borders have tangible and significant consequences — attempting to argue otherwise with an officer is unlikely to benefit a critical traveller. Much more than lines on a map, borders function as power structures rooted in geography. They shape identities, determine rights, and form the foundation of the modern international order.

The maps we study in school may neatly divide the world into distinct spaces called countries, but social phenomena often defy the rigid boundaries of the nation state, which aim to unite territory, population, and political authority. For example, we are told that national territories are contiguous, but British Gibraltar is surrounded by Spain, the Canary Islands are in Africa, and Spain controls territories in northern Morocco. Sustaining the illusion of stability in a world defined by movement, circulation, and change demands considerable effort. The movement of people across international borders shatters this fragile illusion of stasis. Likewise, the sea defies the very idea of fixed and stable boundaries. Borders, as we know them, were designed with land-space in mind: a space that is solid, immovable, and predictable. How can you draw a border on the ocean, an environment defined by constant change, motion, and fluidity?

Race and Organized Abandonment at Sea

In a context where the mobility of the poor is seen as a threat to national security, Europeans — or, at least, their governments — seem to regard the lives lost at sea and the violence against migrant people as acceptable. This is only possible because those who suffer this violence are often young, racialized men from poorer countries, and apparently less deserving of humanity than Europeans. Stripping migrants of their humanity allows us to block empathy. It stops us from imagining our sisters, brothers, or, god forbid, children enduring the horrors many survivors recount: nights adrift at sea in total darkness, chemical burns, thirst, hunger, amputations from untreated infections, destitution, detention, deportation, or a forced return to a home that invested everything on the migration of their best and brightest, who then come back humiliated and emptyhanded — if they come back at all. The silent body sinking to the bottom of the sea, perhaps resurfacing on a tourist-filled beach days or weeks later, is not ours. The dehumanization of people on the move is what makes it possible for us to tolerate the many forms of violence witnessed at the border. And that dehumanization is a result of the construction of sea migrants as racial others.

No one is born a migrant. We become migrants when we cross an international border, and even then, only if the laws on the other side define us as such. For example, until 1985, Spain had no comprehensive immigration law. Poor and fresh from a forty-year-long fascist dictatorship, it was a country that people left to look for greener pastures in Europe and Latin America. Few settled there, save for the occasional British adventurer seeking sun and thrills in what they saw as an exotic, backward country. These foreigners were not called migrants. They were wealthy, white, and quirky. They ran with bulls, drank heavily, and pursued local women; they were seen not as threats, but as amusing eccentrics.[2] Even today, Britons, who number over 290,000 and rank as Spain's eighth-largest foreign group, are not viewed as immigrants. Nor are Ukrainians, even though they are widely (and fairly) accepted as refugees. Somehow, the label "immigrant" does not stick to white people.

This reveals a truth: "migrant" is not just a legal category but a political and social one, deeply tied to race. In this book, then, I have favoured terms like "people on the move" to challenge the prejudices that have become associated with the categories "migrant," "immigrant," and "refugee" (and the most shockingly dehumanizing of all, "illegal alien"). Hopefully, this subtle shift will help us regard the people whose stories I tell here in their whole humanity.

What does race have to do with the transformation of European maritime rescue systems at sea, anyway? In 2007, African American geographer Ruth Wilson Gilmore, defined racism as exposing certain groups to premature death, be it through state action or neglect (Gilmore 2007). This exposure occurs through the interlocking of distinct spaces connected by history, commerce, and migration. The "here" and "there" are geographies shaped by their interconnectedness and distinctiveness, forged through a shared history of collaboration and confrontation. This definition of racism is especially useful for understanding the borders between Europe and Africa or the Middle East — regions tied together through history and geography yet held apart through sustained effort. In many ways, the relationship between these different spaces can be summarized by the image of the colossus demigod Hercules, who (according to Greek mythology) created the Strait of Gibraltar by pushing Europe and Africa apart. Spanish and European migration policy have inherited the Herculean task of keeping the two continents and their inhabitants apart. In this sense, the border regime that keeps Africans out of Europe is far more than just a line in the sea: it is a network of laws, institutions, infrastructure, technology, and narratives about who belongs and who does not.

More recently, Gilmore (2022) used the term "organized abandonment" to define the structural, racialized violence that deems some groups unnecessary or disposable because they are no longer economically useful. The abandoned groups are subject to forms of domination that often result in exploitation and exposure to violence and death. This exploitation can take many forms. In southern Europe, it can look like a border policy so restrictive that people must rely on smugglers to cross, and one where the opportunities for criminals to make a profit are rife. It looks like the hundreds of babies born to mothers who were sexually assaulted during their journey, often by state security forces tasked with stopping migration. It looks like people being sold as slaves in Libya, repeatedly and in plain sight, in prisons at least partially funded by the European Union. It looks like migrants forced into physically gruelling, exploitative, and underpaid jobs. For example: in southern Europe, a growing percentage of those labouring in greenhouses, in homes as caregivers, and in construction are immigrants with a precarious status; in Spain, authorities estimate that more than 95 percent of sex workers are immigrant women, mostly from Latin America, Eastern Europe, and Africa.

At sea, Gilmore's concept of "organized abandonment" (2022) helps explain Europe's emerging approach to maritime search and rescue. If racism is embedded in the structures of European societies, it will manifest at their borders. The withdrawal of rescue services from migration routes is a tool of domination and control of racialized people on the move.

This abandonment is seen as acceptable not just because it happens to "others," but also because it is not direct violence: it is engineered structural neglect. By redesigning maritime rescue systems, governments can pretend that deaths at sea are inevitable — the natural consequence of the ocean's indomitable power. The waves and currents do the dirty work of keeping migrant people out by killing them.[3] But these deaths are "systemic, logical, and predictable" (Achiume 2022, 452). Blocking safe, legal pathways for migration and then leaving people to die on perilous, illegal routes is necropolitics in action. Achille Mbembe (2019), the Cameroonian historian who coined the term, defines necropolitics as the use of social and political power to determine who may live and who must die.

These ideas are not just academic. Organizations like Caminando Fronteras have claimed the concept of necropolitics to describe and explain what is happening in the Mediterranean and the Atlantic and have described Spain's approach to sea migration as a policy of "letting die."[4] Activists monitoring the Mediterranean have exposed the hypocrisy of Europe's migration policies, where governments are violating their own laws to let the sea swallow the problem of illegalized migration. In other cases, they outsource the violence, paying countries with poor human rights records (countries like Libya, Morocco, or Türkiye) to keep people on the move within their territories, where they may be incarcerated and mistreated.

The waters around Europe are more dangerous than ever, particularly for Black people. Tendayi Achiume (2022, 454), a Zambia-born, Yale-educated leading legal scholar on racial discrimination, argues that modern borders are rooted in colonialism and are inherently racist. Migration and border policies may appear racially neutral, she argues, but they are not: their ultimate goal is to protect and perpetuate the privilege of some to the detriment of the rest, "mainly along the same geopolitical and racial lines that characterized the European colonial project." Those who move freely are typically white; those who cannot are racialized: Indigenous, Arab, Black, or people from formerly colonized, impoverished nations. This is not a coincidence.

Achiume (2022) describes race as a "border infrastructure," integral to how states control movement. Who belongs within the imagined boundaries of the nation and who is excluded varies by place and is the result of a historical process of nation-building. In Spain, for example, national identity has long been constructed in opposition to Islam and the African continent (especially the Maghreb; Vives 2011). Spain's contemporary immigration policies reflect this, as they impose the harshest barriers on nationals from African countries. The country's best-funded border infrastructure exists to keep African people out. In contrast, migration from former colonies in Latin America, though statistically much higher, is seen as relatively unproblematic.

Ruth Wilson Gilmore's (2007; 2022) definition of racism and her approach to organized abandonment, Achille Mbembe's (2019) concept of necropolitics, and Tendayi Achiume's (2022) understanding of the border as a form of racial governance are important to understand how and why rescue at sea is mobilized to stop people on the move. Whether we agree entirely with these authors, incorporating race into our analysis is vital, as it reveals whose movements borders facilitate and whose they block, exposing the deep inequalities and the slow, structural violence at the heart of Europe's contemporary border regime.

LOOKING BACK TO LOOK AHEAD: STRUCTURE OF THIS BOOK

Migrants are never truly alone at sea, though at times it may seem that way. The sea is a contested place where people and organizations with different and conflicting agendas often collide. My main goal with this book is to tell the story of the birth and transformation of the Spanish maritime rescue system, with a focus on SASEMAR, the government agency created in 1993 to fulfill this mandate. I do not intend to establish a singular and absolute truth, but to share this story from the point of view of some of the people who played key roles in the survival and evolution of the system. I have not spoken to everyone who makes the maritime borders of Spain and the European Union what they are today: that would be an impossible task. Instead, I have centred the voices of individuals who have been at the forefront of maritime rescue over the past three decades. Their experiences, alongside operational data from the Spanish rescue zone, have inspired the chapters of this book.

Chapter 2 recounts the history of the evolution of maritime rescue and discusses the global events and legal frameworks that shape safety and jurisdiction at sea. Those who originally contributed to the making of safety norms at sea are long gone, and thus their voices in this chapter come to us through the archives. They include figures like the passengers of the *Titanic*, legendary labour organizer Andrew Furuseth, Captain William Caius Crutchley and the crew of the whaleship Essex, destroyed by the very whales they sought to hunt. Scholars Hugo Grotius and John Selden, often portrayed as advocating for diametrically opposed visions of sea space, also make an appearance, alongside some of the architects of the French,

British, and Spanish rescue systems from the eighteenth century onward. These individuals, whether through deliberate action or tragic circumstance, played a role in shaping the contemporary idea that governments must protect all human lives at sea.

Despite the legal and policy frameworks that have been put in place to realize this idea, their application remains uneven. Responses to two maritime tragedies in 2023 offer a stark contrast, showcasing maritime rescue at its best and its worst. Thus, while the disappearance of the *Titan* submersible and its five wealthy occupants on its way to the *Titanic* wreckage triggered a swift and massive international rescue operation (an example of the system working as intended), the sinking of the overcrowded *Adriana* and more than five hundred of its passengers (all poor people on the move) on the opposite side of the world exposes how life-saving services are often withheld when those in danger are perceived as a threat or an inconvenience. The contrast between the two events shows that the obligation for sea rescue was never as universal as the legal documents suggest.

Chapter 3 shifts the focus to Spain. It discusses the creation and decades-long construction of a national maritime rescue system where there used to be none. At the heart of this story is a small agency, SASEMAR, which, in 2024, had a total budget of 276 million euros (Ministerio de Transportes y Mobilidad Sostenible 2024). Neither an NGO nor a branch of the military, SASEMAR was created at a time when environmental disasters were the top concern for the government, and the people on the move mattered little to those in power. This chapter deals with some internal power struggles that shaped Spain's unique approach to maritime rescue, setting it apart from its European neighbours and leaving the agency ill-suited for law enforcement. These struggles were mainly between two visions for Spain's maritime search and rescue. The first was championed by former Guardia Civil chief, Luis Roldán, who sought to establish a militarized Coast Guard. The second was that of Josep Borrell Fontelles, SASEMAR's original architect (and later the European Union's top diplomat between 2019 and 2024). Drawing on archival records and media reports, the chapter brings these tensions to life through the voices of key figures, including Juan Carlos Arbex (SASEMAR's first director of communications), Enric Tarrida (retired rescuer and union leader), and anonymous SASEMAR's crew members who had orders not to talk to outsiders but wanted to do so nonetheless. Ultimately, this chapter explains why, unlike other rescue forces in Europe, SASEMAR struggles to integrate border control into its mandate.

The next two chapters address the question of how the politization of sea migration has played into the transformation of the Spanish maritime rescue service and, most particularly, of SASEMAR's evolving role. Chapter 4 focuses on the Western Mediterranean zone, an area encompassing the Strait of Gibraltar, the Alboran Sea, and the Balearic Sea. Here, big changes happened in 2018–19 when the Guardia Civil assumed control of rescue operations involving migrant boats, marking a shift toward a militarized approach. Chapter 5 turns to the Canary Islands and compares the first and second "*cayuco* crises." A similar shift toward the militarization of rescue operations emerged in the Atlantic area around the Canary Islands, though its timeline and impact follow a different trajectory. In these two chapters, we hear directly from the people who are involved in search and rescue: crews aboard SASEMAR's boats and helicopters, journalists and activists, and some people on the move.

The agency exists within a broader context where EU member states are increasingly repurposing rescue assets for border control. However, the push to integrate SASEMAR into law enforcement has faced strong internal resistance. The concluding chapter (Chapter 6) explores this resistance and the role of organized labour in both protecting the agency's mandate and challenging official discourses of belonging and mobility. Here, members of the main union representing sea rescue crews share insights about how their work has changed as the Guardia Civil's role in maritime rescue continues to expand. They argue that, as rescuers, discriminating between whom to save and whom to let die at sea based merely on nationality or race goes against not just their deontological code and the core principle of the SAR Convention, upon which the agency is built, but also against their humanity. But the union's opposition to the criminalization of migrant workers and the militarization of the sea is also deeply political: as an anarcho-syndicalist union, the CGT is committed to a struggle that is class-based and internationalist. This means that, in each person saved by a rescue boat, the union sees not an enemy but an equal — and a potential ally. This view is a far cry from the politics of fear and enmity that underpin European migration and border policy in Europe and illustrates the fundamental incompatibility of the Union's perspective within this broader context.

Where SASEMAR's work ends, others take over: rescue is just a fleeting moment in a much longer journey, but one that can mean the difference between life and death, between reaching land or being lost to the sea. For many, departure from a coast somewhere on the African continent and arrival at a Spanish port are the bookends to their migration story, but not for all. This book tells a story that happens at the border — a space of movement, rescue, and, too often, loss. It explores the sea as a not-so-new stage for the geopolitical tensions in an ever-changing world, and the consequences that high-level political manoeuvres have on the lives of people on the move leaving from places such as Morocco or Senegal and their families. This book is about the everyday work of government workers tasked with Spain's legal duty to protect human lives at sea; about citizens-turned-activists like Julie Campagne and Laetitia Marthe from Lanzarote's Network of Solidarity with Migrant People; people on the move who reach Europe, like Daria, and some who do not, like her son; and about communities burdened by the cost of violent geopolitics. It charts the evolution of Spain's national maritime rescue system, from its modest beginnings in the early 1990s to recent efforts to subordinate it to border control. This transformation remains unfinished. In that sense, this story is a like a seabird in mid-flight: we do not yet know where the bird will land.

2

Defining Safety, Jurisdiction, and Responsibility at Sea throughout the Twentieth Century

ON JUNE 18, 2023, the *Titan*, a submersible carrying five extremely wealthy people, imploded on its way to the wreck of the *RMS Titanic* off the coast of Newfoundland. The *Titan* was classified as an experimental craft, operated in international waters, and did not carry passengers from a port — three factors that explain why it was exempted from the safety regulations that usually apply to seacraft (Porter and Guenot 2023). In the weeks and months that followed the implosion, the world learned that several experts and former employees had raised serious concerns about the *Titan*, particularly regarding the unsuitability of the materials used in its construction. Neither the carbon fibre materials used for the hull nor its acrylic viewing window were designed to withstand the high pressure of the deep seas, which, at the site of the *Titanic* wreck, is equal to four hundred atmospheres, or four hundred times the pressure at sea level. The concerns went unheeded. OceanGate, the US-based private company that operated the submersible, responded with threats of legal action against anyone who dared bring the *Titan*'s design into question.

Much has been written since June 2023 on the gall of Stockton Rush, co-founder and CEO of OceanGate, who was in the *Titan* when it imploded. In interviews, Rush derided those who worried about safety by saying, "If you want to be safe, don't get out of bed, don't get in your car, don't do anything" (Anderson, Angelovski, and Kelley 2024). In his view, safety regulations hindered innovation. "There are a lot of rules that didn't make engineering sense to me," Rush told journalist David Pogue in 2022 (*CBC News* 2023, 3:38). So, he simply ignored them, and built the *Titan* by "MacGyver-ing off-the-shelf parts," according to Pogue. Then, on its first descent in 2023, the submersible lost communication with its transport, the *Polar Prince*. The US Coast Guard was alerted a few hours after the *Titan* was due to resurface.

What followed was one of the largest and costliest rescue operations in history. The initial area of the operation was closest to the Canadian coast, but it was in the United States' zone of responsibility. Both countries led the search and rescue efforts with ships and air units. Eventually, the operation brought together rescue assets from Canada, France, the United Kingdom, and the United States: boats, planes, helicopters, and underwater remotely operated vehicles (ROVs) gathered on site for a frantic search in the days after the *Titan* disappeared. Private carriers already present in the area participated in the recovery efforts as well. The efforts to save the *Titan*'s passengers were a textbook demonstration of how maritime search and rescue operations are meant to unfold according to international law.

The SAR Convention defines a modus operandi where the protection of human life is paramount; in this view, borders and boundaries are largely irrelevant. This ideal, which prevailed during the rescue efforts for the *Titan*, is not upheld in contexts where those at risk are poor people on the move, however. An event that illustrates this double standard occurred just four days before the underwater implosion of the *Titan*, when the *Adriana* sank off the Greek coast near Pylos. The sinking of the *Adriana* was one of the worst incidents involving a migrant boat to ever occur in the Mediterranean (Piper, Lee, and Parker 2023). The circumstances of this tragedy could not have been more different from that of the *Titan* and its passengers. Instead of a submersible offering a luxury tour of the *Titanic* wreck at a quarter million dollars per head, the *Adriana* was a "junk boat," a rusty and terribly overcrowded fishing boat carrying poor migrants and asylum seekers mostly from Syria, Pakistan, and Egypt. Collectively, the *Titan*'s four passengers, not including Rush, had paid $1 million for their trip; the *Adriana*'s estimated 750 passengers had paid $3.5 million to be taken to Italy (Stevis-Gridneff and Shoumali 2023).

The *Adriana* left from the Libyan city of Tobruk on June 10. Three days later, it was in extreme distress. The first to raise the alarm (a few minutes before 10:00 a.m. on June 13) was Nawal Soufi, a Moroccan Italian human rights activist. Like many other activists at the time, Soufi used her Twitter account to bring attention to the boat in distress and to call for emergency services. Soufi had received information that there were 750 live passengers on board, in addition to 6 who had already died. An hour after the initial distress call, Italian authorities alerted the Greek Coast Guard and Frontex. Greek officers would later state that they approached the *Adriana* but the captain and some of the passengers refused their assistance, so they stayed nearby. Other merchant vessels in the area gave food and water to the migrants, who started making distress calls using their own phones. The activist network Alarm Phone, who received some of those calls, contacted Greece, the United Nations, and Frontex. The latter, having no authorization from Greece, stood by. At least two mayday relay signals were heard by nearby boats that night in the area where the *Adriana* was already drifting. These usually trigger an immediate search and rescue operation, but only one Greek Coast Guard vessel stayed nearby as the tragedy slowly unfolded.

Hours passed with other vessels reporting that the *Adriana* was rocking dangerously. There were strong winds that night. At 1:44 a.m., the engine of the *Adriana* broke down. At this point, accounts begin to differ. According to the version presented by the Greek officers, the boat capsized by itself when there was a "commotion" that caused it to turn sharply and sink. Another version — based on investigations by several news outlets, human rights organizations, and investigative groups — concluded that the Greek Coast Guard had caused the *Adriana* to capsize when they tried to tow the boat (Martín and Jullien 2023). The boat capsized at 2:06 a.m. that night and sank shortly thereafter. No one on board was wearing a life jacket.

There is scant evidence of what happened that night. Greek authorities diverted Frontex's rescue assets (in this case, a drone) to another boat in distress elsewhere. The cameras on the Greek rescue boats were switched off. Crucial data from the hours that followed, including phone conversations, were also not recorded. In early 2025, the Greek Ombuds concluded that there were "serious and reprehensible omissions in the search and rescue duties on the part of senior officers" of the Greek Coast Guard and denounced the fact that "crucial evidence was not disclosed ... despite repeated relevant requests" (Greek Ombudsman Independent Authority 2025).

We must then rely on the accounts of the thirteen officers aboard the Greek Coast Guard patrol vessel and of the survivors of *Adriana*'s shipwreck to reconstruct the events that took place in the early morning hours of June 14, 2023. More than two years later, we do not even know with any certainty how many people were on board the *Adriana* (the boat carried somewhere between 500 and 750 passengers). At least 350 came from Pakistan: having been forced below deck by the smugglers, only twelve survived (*Al Jazeera* 2023a). Smugglers had also locked women and children in the hold (*France 24* 2023). All of them drowned. There were 104 survivors and 82 bodies were recovered. The rest, along with the boat, sank into one of the deepest sections of the Mediterranean Sea. The *Adriana* and its passengers are now approximately five thousand metres deep, much deeper than the *Titanic*'s wreck.

Why did the rescue operations of the *Titan* and the *Adriana* unfold so differently? The disappearance of the *Titan* triggered a rescue operation, while the sighting of the *Adriana* launched a law enforcement operation. The preventable loss of human life along the maritime border of the European Union today is a direct consequence of the tension between these two policy priorities: to save lives and to keep people out. To understand the difference between these two areas of policy, we need to go back in time to investigate how the history of government regulation on safety, control, and risk at sea informs the protection of life at sea today.

Three international conventions in particular are central to this discussion. The first is the Safety of Life at Sea (SOLAS) Convention, which defines safety requirements for vessels at sea. The second is the United Nations' Convention on the Law of the Sea (UNCLOS), which parcels the waters into different areas within and without states' zones of sovereignty and ownership. The third, the Search and Rescue (SAR) Convention, aims at standardizing procedures to protect human life at sea. The obligations and responsibilities arising from these conventions make it more challenging for EU member states to decisively end sea migration by any means necessary. But to understand how we got to this point, we need to return to where we began the chapter: four thousand metres under water, somewhere off the coast of Newfoundland.

THE SINKING OF THE TITANIC

The wreck of the "unsinkable" RMS *Titanic* has fascinated undersea explorers for more than a century. Owned and operated by White Star Line, the ship sank during its maiden voyage when she hit an iceberg in the North Atlantic Ocean near midnight on April 14, 1912. This tragedy was the deadliest wreckage of a single ship ever recorded at the time:[5] only 710 of the estimated 2,224 passengers and crew on board survived. Greed was the main cause of such a high death toll. The ship had enough davits (the cranes that project over the side of the ship and are used to support, raise, and lower equipment) to hold up to sixty-four lifeboats. But the *Titanic* only carried twenty lifeboats — enough for roughly half of the passengers on board. To make things worse, four of those were collapsible and impractical to use during an emergency evacuation on the open sea. Still, the *Titanic*'s safety equipment went above and beyond existing safety regulations at the time. This meant that, with the space saved from not carrying the extra lifeboats, the company was able to add cabins and suites for first-class passengers without breaking any rules.

As the *Titanic* advanced in the moonless night, the captain steamed on at full speed into an ice field, ignoring repeated warnings. When the *Titanic* hit an iceberg, the lack of sufficient safety equipment on board and an inefficient communication system contributed to the high death toll.

The similarities between the implosion of the *Titan* and the accident of the "unsinkable" *Titanic* are striking: both happened at the same place, and both accidents were caused and worsened by reckless business decisions. But while the accidents themselves were eerily connected, the aftermath was not. When the *Titanic* sank, rescue efforts were ad hoc and involved primarily private vessels who happened to be in the vicinity. This accident in fact paved the way for current global approaches to maritime safety.

There are innumerable books, songs, movies, radio programs, podcasts, paintings, and newspaper articles that tell the story of the sinking of the *Titanic*. Yet very few of them look at the profound impact it had on the way the world approached safety at sea moving forward. The tragedy is the foundation on which many of the life-saving measures we take for granted today are built, for example, that a boat will have sufficient safety equipment for all its passengers and crew, or that it will be able to communicate with emergency services on land.

The immediate response from US authorities was to require all US-flagged ships and those navigating to and from US ports to "carry sufficient lifeboats for all, be adequately manned with trained crewmen, and ... that lifeboat drills be conducted on every voyage" (Havern 2012, 12). The International Ice Patrol was created after the tragedy, leading to the first concerted effort to articulate co-operation among countries to improve marine safety. More broadly, the tragedy "jolted the maritime world towards internationally accepted safety rules" (Palmer 2005, 300) and was "a catalyst for governments to come together and create an international body, now known as the International Maritime Organization (IMO), dedicated to maritime safety, security, and environmental protection" (Lantz 2012, 4).

REGULATING SAFETY AT SEA

The International Maritime Organization (IMO) is the source of most regulations that apply at sea today, including the SAR Convention. Although its history is closely linked to the sinking of the *Titanic*, efforts to set up a body to address the needs of the shipping industry predate the 1912 tragedy, which made it all the clearer that a common set of rules was necessary to ensure higher profits from maritime commerce and increase safety during navigation.

The earliest records we have of any sort of international maritime law date back to the Roman legal code (the *Nomos Rhodios Nauticus*, or Rhodian Law). Much later, in the mid-nineteenth century, steamboats shook maritime transport: freed from the whims of winds that ruled sailing, the new technology was arguably the main driver in the integration of the global economy between 1870 and 1913. The maritime order that emerged during this period was a system intimately connected to the production and reproduction of capitalism, in which the sea was a crucial space for commerce, transportation, and communication. In addition, new technology offered great opportunities for the exploitation of natural resources that lie within and below the waters (Campling and Colás 2021). In short, wealthy nations saw collaboration as the key to greater riches. This early stage of international alliance-building led to the creation of the International Telegraph Union in 1865, the International Meteorological Organization in 1873, and the Universal Postal Union in 1874. These organizations were anchored in the belief that the emerging global economic system needed a set of common rules to flourish.

Throughout the twentieth century, the shipping industry remained suspicious of any attempt to impose rules that might infringe on its freedom. This did not stop countries from plowing through in their efforts to build multilateral co-operation. In a second and more intense wave of internationalization that took place between the beginning of the First World War and the establishment of the United Nations at the end of the Second World War, wealthy countries (often colonial or former colonial powers) pushed for the adoption of a number of international treaties. In their view, the only certain way to avoid another conflict among the wealthy nations of the world was to weave them into a system of political and economic interdependence. This led to the creation of the United Nations and a flurry of other organizations (often under the broader umbrella of the United Nations) such as the International Civil Aviation Organization (ICAO; 1944), the Food and Agriculture Organization (FAO; 1945), the United Nations Educational, Scientific and Cultural Organization (UNESCO; 1945), and the World Health Organization (WHO; 1947). The Inter-Governmental Maritime Consultative Organization (IMCO) was created at the 1948 Geneva Conference and became the IMO in 1982. Combined, these intergovernmental bodies led to the foundation of the modern international political system.

The IMO is a creature of this era, an institution central to the development of a common understanding of maritime safety. But, like many similar organizations, it was and remains a consultative and advisory body. In other words, the IMO lacks the power to impose its decisions, ensure that its members respect the terms of its conventions and agreements, or impose sanctions to those who do not. This lack of coercive power is one of the crucial aspects that explain what the IMO can and cannot do when it comes to enforcing the SAR Convention.

While the name, structure, and functions of the IMO have evolved over the last eight decades, its mandate has remained largely unchanged. In a nutshell, the organization's work focuses on promoting maritime safety, efficiency, and the removal of obstacles to free trade among its members. Today, one hundred states are members of the IMO. They collectively handle more than 98 percent of merchant marine tonnage worldwide. Throughout its lifetime, the organization has championed the adoption of over thirty conventions relating to maritime safety, marine pollution, and liability and compensation.

The IMO (in its different iterations) is responsible for two of the three international conventions central to the work of maritime rescue that will be discussed in this book: the Safety of Life at Sea (SOLAS) Convention (1974/1980) and the Search and Rescue (SAR) Convention (1979/1985). The third convention that frames maritime rescue, the United Nations Convention on the Law of the Sea (UNCLOS, 1982/1994), is under the purview of the United Nations. Not coincidentally, Spain began to build its rescue system in the late 1980s and early 1990s, coinciding with the negotiation and implementation of these conventions — as well as with the country's entry into the European Communities, later to become the European Union.

THE SINKING OF THE TITANIC AND THE SAFETY OF LIFE AT SEA CONVENTION

In November 1913, less than two years after the *Titanic* disaster, representatives from more than one hundred coastal countries came together to improve international ship safety norms. Following seven weeks of intense negotiations, the first version of the Safety of Life at Sea (SOLAS) Convention was adopted in London in January 1914 (International Conference of Safety of Life at Sea 1914). Although never implemented, the London Convention, as it came to be known, is generally thought of as "the key starting point in the history of international co-operation in developing maritime standards" (Palmer 2005, 309).

The adoption of the London Convention was a key development in Admiralty (or Maritime) law, the body of law that governs relationships among private actors operating at sea. This is different from the law of the sea, which falls under public international law. The traces of the *Titanic* disaster in the London Convention are obvious. The Convention defined minimum international standards for commercial vessels with more than twelve passengers travelling overseas (including to and from Colonies, Possessions, or Protectorates). It also included provisions on ice and derelict destruction, ship construction requirements, continuous radio communication, life-saving equipment and fire protection, and safety certifications. One of the Convention's objectives was to put in place a communication network between vessels travelling through the Northern Atlantic and equip those vessels with the material and personnel needed to prevent another tragedy akin to the sinking of the *Titanic*.

Over a hundred countries took part in the negotiations, which began with high ambitions just months after the tragedy. However, only thirteen countries signed the London Convention, and just five ratified it: Great Britain, the Netherlands, Norway, Spain, and Sweden. These were all wealthy European nations with a vested interest in the further opening up of the seas to facilitate sea commerce and resource extraction from other, poorer territories around the globe.

There was strong opposition to the text. Some of the resistance came from private merchant companies, who viewed the increased requirements as an unwelcome intrusion and feared it would reduce their revenue. Few of the countries who participated in the negotiations were satisfied, as is clear by the fact that only five of the more than one hundred states who participated in the negotiations ratified the final version. Those who withdrew from the negotiations agreed with the overall intent of the Convention but rejected the final document. Colonies and former colonies in particular saw the London Convention as a veiled attempt to perpetuate European plundering overseas: from the United States to Argentina, these countries viewed it as an effort to undermine their sovereignty and, by extension, their ability to use sea commerce to compete on equal terms in the global economy (*Safety of Life at Sea* 1914). This concern would resurface during the negotiations leading to the United Nation's Convention on the Law of the Sea (UNCLOS) decades later. In hindsight, these critics were proved right: international agreements like the London Convention and the UNCLOS have failed to level the playing field in terms of access to the ocean's resources. On the contrary, they have deepened existing inequalities among countries in the global arena, as we will see shortly.

A final group of people opposing the London Convention were the unions. Labour organizing among seafarers has always been challenging. This is a workforce always in movement, often away from land, and subject to multiple jurisdictions: that of the boat, that of the port, or that of their country of citizenship. Seafarers' unions have articulated their demands around the fact that their constant movement and circulation make their job very different from those that are performed on land.

The space of the sea shapes labour and labour organizing in various ways. For one, seafaring has been a globalized industry for most of history. Its workforce has always consisted primarily of poor men and included a strong component of racialized labour that has been (and, in some cases, continues to be) forced into exploitative work relations. Historians Peter Linebaugh and Marcus Rediker (2012), in fact, see the ship as a critical site of labour antagonism in the brutal expansion of capitalism during the seventeenth and eighteenth centuries. And, in their excellent historical overview of the relationship between oceans and the capitalist system, US-based scholars Campling and Colás (2021) talk about the ship as a "workplace in motion," the backbone of which has been the "deep-sea proletariat" who are often racialized men, always from poorer countries, without exception paid less than their white counterparts — if paid at all.

This was true when Andrew Furuseth founded the Sailors' Union of the Pacific in 1891, and it remains true nearly a century and a half later. Moreover, a ship is a mobile, self-contained workplace that crosses jurisdictions, where a captain is often more than just a boss — they are the king. Under these murky legal conditions, labour organizing is a formidable challenge. Throughout the centuries, seafarers have had to fight for every inch of progress in their working conditions. This perhaps explains why many seafarers saw the London Convention as a threat to the few hard-won gains they had made over the years. Their fear was that governments would define the lowest common denominator as the norm for salaries and working conditions on board.

The Labour Movement's Opposition to the London Convention

When the US Senate held hearings on the first SOLAS Convention, they called on Andrew Furuseth, a pioneering organizer of the American sea worker labour movement, to testify. Furuseth had been appointed by Woodrow Wilson, then president of the United States, to attend the negotiations where the London Convention was drawn up. But Furuseth resigned on December 22, 1913, arguing that the treaty was detrimental to both the political and economic interests of the United States and American seafarers. In the months and years to come, Furuseth continued to articulate his fury against the London Convention using his unique and sharp prose.

Let's stop for a minute here to appreciate the complex figure of Andrew Furuseth, a Norwegian American seaman and reputable labour leader nicknamed "the Old Viking" by his contemporaries (Weintraub 1959). Furuseth was a ferocious union leader. Calm and solitary in his personal life, he was a shrewd and belligerent negotiator who devoted his life to the improvement of sea workers' labour conditions in the United States. It is not an exaggeration to say that his work at the bargaining table has had an impact on the lives of all employed in the sector to this day. Furuseth participated in the creation of at least two maritime unions in the early twentieth century, the Sailors' Union of the Pacific and the International Seamen's Union. He was the key figure in the passage of the Maguire Act of 1895 and the White Act of 1898, which ended the common (and legal) practices of corporal punishment of sailors and their imprisonment in cases of desertion. Furuseth is also credited with drafting the Seamen's Act of 1915, commonly known as the Magna Carta of the Sea, and the Jones Act of 1920 on sailors' compensation rights. He drafted and pushed for the adoption of these new regulations, and followed through to make sure they were respected. These are the bright spots in the character of a man otherwise full of shadows: an open xenophobe, Furuseth was also a founding member of the Asiatic Exclusion League in 1905 and did not hesitate to advocate for white American sea crews while denigrating all others.

When arguing against the London Convention, Furuseth's main concern was about its potential negative impact on the labour conditions of US sailors in particular and, more generally, on the interests of sailors in countries that could not depend on a steady supply of cheap, unfree labour made available through colonial tools of indenture or enslavement.

It is hard to comprehend today the horrendous working conditions these men put up with at the time, even those who ostensibly freely chose this life and received relatively higher wages than their counterparts in the colonized world. There existed a centuries-old custom for ships to function in many ways as their own jurisdictions. Wages were negotiated either directly with the captain or, most often, through intermediaries called crimps. The employers charged exorbitant prices for sailors' room and board while on the ship, as well as outrageous interests on loans workers took on before their departure. If, upon arriving at port, a member of the crew wanted to quit or desert, the captain could send the authorities to fetch him. If a captain on another boat wanted to hire a runaway sailor, they had to pay a fine.

As an example, in his 1912 autobiography *My Life at Sea*, British Captain William Caius Crutchley recounts how, as a young man, he swam away from the schooner *Alwynton* "with irons on" in Adelaide, Australia, after the captain had put him in detention without food or water for days and whipped him along with his friend, who had committed the crime of having stashed love letters in his trunk. The captain asked the police superintendent to take Crutchley into custody, but the superintendent refused, considering the captain's methods excessive. Still, Crutchley and two of his sailor friends were ordered to return to work on the *Alwynton*. Fearing retribution, the young sailors swam away once again, and Crutchley eventually found a job on another boat, the *Troas*, whose skipper, "being badly in want of hands, agreed to see me through the police court and ship me as an ordinary seaman." When the court sentenced Crutchley with either a fine of £5 (more than $1,300 2023 Canadian dollars) or a month of detention, the new skipper paid the fine, "and I forthwith took up my berth in my new ship" (Crutchley 1912, 40).

Crutchley's experience was one among many and highlights sailors' dire lack of control over their working conditions. By 1914, opposition to the type of corporal punishment and bondage to a specific ship or captain that Crutchley had experienced in his youth was widespread. Furuseth was a staunch opponent of both, but he was not the only one. Around the same time in Brazil, a Black sailor named João Cândido Felisberto led the five-day long "Revolt of the Lash" in Rio de Janeiro to end corporal punishment. He paid dearly for it (Capanema P. de Almeida 2011). Furuseth led a similar effort in the United States at a much lower personal cost. Showing great determination, he led the passing of reforms that outlawed the customary corporal punishment of seamen and their imprisonment in case of desertion. But when it came to the London Convention, he saw it simply as a trick that would enrich boat owners at the expense of sailors.

In 1914, as he was drafting the Seamen's Act, Furuseth published an analysis of the London Convention's potential consequences on the American

Merchant Marine. As a labour leader, his main concern was the impact that further internationalization of sea trade could have on the wages of American seamen. He explained that "the merchant marine of the United States, a high-wage country, cannot compete, in the oversea trade, with the vessels of lower-wage countries." He explained that these lower-wage countries already benefited from "special privileges." In fact, foreign ships in US ports at the time were legally protected to "forcibly hold the crews secured at the lower-wage rates of foreign ports." Foreign ship owners could additionally request the assistance of the US police powers "to capture and return seamen who attempt to quit the service of their ships." For this reason, Furuseth argued, wages on these foreign ships were generally lower than those that would be accepted by US seamen in the country's ports (Furuseth 1914, 3). In his analysis of the potential impacts of the London Convention, he took issue specifically with the lower labour standards and salaries that "Mediterranean" and "Oriental" seamen were, according to him, willing to accept.

Furuseth believed that the London Convention was a smoke screen: under the pretense of improving safety, the agreement wedged an external interference into domestic matters, harming US seamen as well as the broader national economic and political interests of the country. He brought these and other concerns before the United States Senate during official hearings about the proceedings of the London Convention (*Safety of Life at Sea* 1914). Ultimately, Furuseth thought that improving safety at sea was a simple business that could be taken care of by the US government alone. In his view, each state could set their own standards.

The Long Life of the London Convention: Safety at Sea Today

Furuseth need not have worried. The First World War broke out a few weeks after the negotiations ended and the London Convention never came into force. Regardless, the Convention is, to this day, one of the most influential international texts in the history of maritime law. For one, it articulated, for the very first time, a global standard for maritime safety. In addition, the Convention was the catalyst for the creation of both the International Ice Patrol in the Atlantic and Arctic Oceans and what would become the International Maritime Organization (IMO). Both still exist today.

As maritime technology and labour standards continued to progress throughout the twentieth century, it became urgent to revisit the decisions made at the London Convention. A second version of the SOLAS Convention was signed in 1929, but this one, too, had to be put on pause during the Second World War and did not come into force until the spring of 1958. Two other versions were adopted in 1948 and 1960 (IMO n.d.). The current text was adopted in 1974 and came into force in 1980. Today, virtually all merchant ships in the world (in terms of gross tonnage) carry the flag of one of the 167 countries that are signatories to the Convention.

Throughout its many modifications to keep up with changes in practices and technology at sea and evolving labour standards, the rationale and principles of the Convention have remained the same. The Convention's primary objective is to define "minimum standards for the construction, equipment, and operation of ships, compatible with their safety" (IMO 1974). In this way, the SOLAS Convention is similar to regulations mandating minimal safety standards for vehicles on the road.

The SOLAS Convention was the first document adopted by the IMO to form a comprehensive regulatory framework of more than fifty conventions and protocols that create a common set of rules in the areas of international shipping "including safety, environmental protection, legal matters, technical co-operation, maritime security, and shipping efficiency" (Sekimizo 2012, 25). However, working conditions aboard vessels remain uneven across jurisdictions: human trafficking and forced labour at sea are not uncommon in certain fleets. Not coincidentally, exploitation at sea is more prevalent among racialized foreign workers from poor countries.

BOUNDING THE WORLD'S OCEANS

The SOLAS Convention (1974/1980) set the minimum safety requirements for vessels navigating the world's oceans. A few years later, the United Nations Convention on the Law of the Sea (UNCLOS 1982/1994) set out to clarify matters related to jurisdiction: who owns the waters bordering nations, who has the right to exploit the resources in the waters and the seabed, and where domestic laws do and do not apply. The UNCLOS is the core of the contemporary legal framework for all activities taking place at sea. Today, 169 countries and the European Union have ratified the Convention. The United States has not. Getting there was hard work though — a path paved with fights over political and economic power.

Issues of ownership and jurisdiction are central to contemporary conflicts between law enforcement efforts at the border and the duty to provide maritime rescue services. For example, by default, a country's territorial waters and Exclusive Economic Zone (defined in the UNCLOS Convention) are included in its zone of responsibility for rescue purposes, which tends to be much larger. However, domestic legislation about immigration, for example, does not apply in international waters. In other words: most border enforcement and migration control actions carried out in the waters surrounding the European Union are carried out in areas beyond states' jurisdiction.

Who Owns the Sea?

The adoption of the UNCLOS demonstrates the triumph of an understanding of the relationship between humans and the world's marine environment based on the principle of ownership. Many other principles could have been the basis of this relationship. Philip Steinberg (2001), among others, has looked at the way premodern societies have understood their relationship with the oceans. For example, he argues that societies living in the Indian Ocean region up until the arrival of Vasco de Gama in 1498 understood the deep sea as a "great void" located entirely outside of human society: a space for transportation that was not to be trusted or governed. The opposite was true for Micronesia throughout known history and until very recently. According to Steinberg, Micronesian societies saw ocean space as land-like: a space of connection in everyday life, where territory and resources could and were claimed and appropriated.

Mediterranean societies until 500 AD had a vision of the relationship between humans and the sea that was somewhere between those two: the deep sea was seen as a space beyond possession, but one that societies had the responsibility to steward to protect the abundance of resources (specifically fish) it provided. Political powers did claim sovereignty of the sea nearest the coast; beyond that, the ocean offered nations the opportunity to assert their political and military power, and, in general, allowed them to increase their influence in the region. This was particularly the case during the golden years of the Roman Empire. Steinberg (2001, 65) argues that the Romans "claimed *imperium* — the right to command — in the Mediterranean, but did not claim *dominium* — the power to own, use, enjoy, and dispose of property."

Later in history, the ocean occupied a central place in the colonial project. As such, it could no longer be outside the sphere of the social and the political. But to whom did it belong? Iberian powers (Spain and Portugal) dominated early colonial oceanic travels, with the Catholic Church playing referee to where and how far the two could extend their sphere of influence. Other European nations also had colonial ambitions. The struggle between the established and aspiring colonial powers over sovereignty and the rights of navigation on the high seas that began in the late sixteenth century would launch a new era of international law. The outcome defined the outline of ocean geopolitics for centuries to come, eventually leading to the ratification of the UNCLOS.

The Battle of the Books

The way sea space is imagined shapes how all activities taking place in it are regulated and governed, including rescue. Starting in the sixteenth century, the world's oceans were seen as a conduit for political power and economic domination.

The race for the ocean began in earnest after the English defeated the Spanish Armada in 1588. This defeat was a knife to the heart of Spanish military pride. It was also the beginning of the end of Iberian colonial dominance, with the Dutch and the English demanding a (bigger) part of the colonial cake. Pressure peaked in 1603. That year, a small fleet belonging to the Dutch East India Company raided a Portuguese vessel, the *Santa Catarina*, near Singapore (Chester 2009). The vessel and the cargo were taken back to the Netherlands and sold as a prize of war. But was this seizing legitimate? Was it even legal? Edward Gordon (2008, 254), co-curator of a 2009 exhibit on this issue, concludes that a "furious row erupted over the legality of the seizure, which struck many as immoral — in fact, scarcely distinguishable from outright piracy."

The episode that followed is known as "the Battle of the Books": a challenge to Iberian dominance of maritime commerce and, by extension, of Papal authority to decide on these matters. The *Santa Catarina* incident proved extremely controversial. Faced with enormous popular opposition and with shareholders threatening to withdraw their capital, the Dutch East India Company hired Hugo Grotius to defend their case. Grotius was only twenty-one at the time, but he was already a sort of celebrity known for his prowess on both Dutch politics and on European law. Years earlier, at the tender age of fifteen, Grotius had accompanied leading Dutch statesman Johann van Oldenbarnevelt to France as a diplomatic attaché. On that occasion King Henry IV of France had declared Grotius "the miracle of Holland" for his erudition on legal matters. Today, Grotius is considered one of the founding fathers of international law largely due to his work on maritime law (Gordon 2008).

To argue for the legality of the seizing of the *Santa Catarina*, Grotius set to work on his *Commentary on the Law of the Prize*. Only one chapter of his treatise was published during his lifetime, titled *Mare Liberum* ("The Freedom of the Seas"). Dated 1609, Grotius argued in this document that "[t]he sea is common to all, because it is so limitless that it cannot become a possession of any one, and because it is adapted to the use of all, whether we consider it from the point of view of navigation or of fisheries" (Grotius 1609, cited in Steinberg 2001, 91).

There was no ambiguity as to Grotius's ultimate goal to provide "a legal justification for the participation of the new [Dutch] republic and its commercial wing, the [Dutch East India Company], as equals in the lucrative world market that had been forged by Iberian imperialism after 1492" (Campling and Colás 2021, 73). However, his proposal for a deep sea common to all was influential well beyond the events of the *Santa Catarina*.

Grotius' argument faced significant challenges. Among the most notable was the response from English legal scholar John Selden, whose rebuttal to *Mare Liberum* became the most widely acknowledged. While not the only critique,[6] Selden's stood out for its stark contrast to Grotius's treatise and had a similarly lasting influence. Selden was a specialist of ancient English law who ventured into politics in his middle age. His piece would not be published until 1635, more than twenty-five years after Grotius's *Mare Liberum*. In it, he argued that states can own ocean space and treat it as part of their territory: the *Mare clausum* (closed seas) approach.

Although Grotius and Selden's arguments differed in many ways, they both advocated for the stewardship of the high seas, an idea that continues to shape legal decisions in this field. According to Steinberg (2001, 97), both jurists "propose systems wherein rights to private property are overlain with regulations forbidding usurpation of rights to common usage."

These arguments were not separate from the political developments inland at the time. While European lawyers and politicians debated the status of the world's oceans, a new territorial order was being forged. The new geopolitics of the continent were built upon an early version of the nation state, a novel way of articulating the relationship between secular political power, territory, and the resources and people that inhabited it. This new territorial order was written into the Treaties of Westphalia in 1648. Slowly and gradually, through the intervention of many other treaties over the next three centuries, this new invention reshaped the political landscape of Europe — and, through colonization and imperial domination, that of the world.[7]

Could this land-based view of the world be extended to the world's seas and oceans? In the end, the vision that prevailed in the post-Westphalian mercantilist era of the seventeenth century was a mix of Grotius's and Selden's. Selden's *Mare Clausum* became the norm in the waters closest to the coast under a regime of ownership that mimicked the land-based appropriation of space that defined the new political order of the nation state. Meanwhile, Grotius' *Mare Liberum* doctrine dominated when it came to the high seas, which (in this view) could not be owned, but were instead to be used as a space for resource extraction and transportation.

The early industrial era shook up that view of ocean geopolitics. The early nineteenth century brought with it a different view of ocean space as a great void — a space of the unknown, of danger, of freedom, and a source of power. The ocean remained the theatre of military strategy, the place where the fight over dominance, wealth, and influence among capitalist nations was fought (Campling and Colás 2021). At this time, the United States emerged as a strong player and challenger to British dominance. Some former colonial powers still clung to their former empires, but that was about to change: the twentieth century also brought with it the official end of European colonialism. This was also the era of a nascent global governance of the oceans. As we have seen in the previous section, many of the first international organizations were born at this time with the goal of standardizing the rules and regulations that applied to ocean space.

Fast forward to the periods during and after the Cold War and the advent of a new stage of ocean geopolitics. According to historians Campling and Colás, three factors shaped the new maritime order of the twentieth century — the (formal) emancipation of the colonies, a growing dependence on fossil fuels, and the development of the nuclear arsenal. The world's oceans were the new final frontier for resource extraction and a force-field key to the thriving capitalist system. It is in this context that the contours of today's maritime regimes finally took shape, leading to the enclosure of much of the world's oceans.

MARITIME SOVEREIGNTY AND JURISDICTION ACCORDING TO THE UNITED NATION'S CONVENTION ON THE LAW OF THE SEA

In its different versions, the main ambition of the United Nations' Convention on the Law of the Sea (UNCLOS) has been to provide a legal framework for all activities at sea. Before the mid-twentieth century, most nations abided by the twelve nautical miles rule to define their territorial waters — those that were an integral part of their territory. Beyond that lay the high seas, open to all. Many were the discontents in this system: it was clear that "the traditional legal order of the freedom of the seas had become obsolete for the satisfaction of the economic requirements of most of the world's states and for the protection of the marine environment" (Couper 1978, 303). The initial impetus for the Convention came from the former colonies in the period after the Second World War. Newly independent territories had an existential need to clearly define the new boundaries of their territory, both at land and at sea. They were committed to this goal and, perhaps more importantly, they also wanted to extend their claims over the sea so they could begin competing in the global market.

The United States made the first move. On September 28, 1945, President Truman issued two proclamations: the first regarding the country's rights to exploitation of natural resources on the continental shelf and the second the exploitation of fisheries in the high seas. The combined result was a vast expansion of the area of the ocean open for exploitation for the country's benefit. Other nations followed Truman's lead and declared control over all the natural resources found in the continental shelf attached to their land boundaries. This was the kickoff of the development of today's maritime order.

Two years later, in 1947, the United Nations established the International Law Commission (still functional) to encourage "the progressive development of international law and its codification" (OLA 2024). The International Law Commission struggled to bring countries together to agree on a new division of the oceans. But its work paid off: nine years later, the United Nations held its first Conference on the Law of the Sea in Geneva, Switzerland. Its members adopted four conventions that, combined, codified the rules of international law relating to the territorial seas, contiguous zones, and the high seas, and set the ground rules for the conservation of fisheries and other living resources. (Exclusive Economic Zones, or EEZs, were created in 1982.) Another achievement of the Convention was the adoption of an optional protocol for the settlement of disputes and nine resolutions regarding, among others, nuclear testing in high seas, pollution by radioactive materials, and multilateral conservation efforts.

Alastair D. Couper, a Welsh maritime historian, has argued that the United States and other Latin American countries were mainly responsible for the first and second UNCLOS conventions in 1958 and 1960 respectively. But behind the façade of success there were profound disagreements among the negotiating parties. In fact, only one quarter of the world's sovereign states that existed at the time ratified the conventions. Former colonies in particular were opposed to it, as were those (including some of those same former colonies) who saw the protection of a maritime commons as a waste. If the sea was the source of unending riches, why put a limit to its exploitation? Specifically, demand for oil increased dramatically after the Second World War at a time when technological advances permitted its extraction from the ocean's depths for the very first time. A race to claim jurisdiction over natural resources on the continental shelf and beyond had begun among coastal nations.

There is no doubt that the single most important outcome of the first UNCLOS Convention was the division of the ocean into territorial waters (equivalent to a state's land territory and including internal waters) and the high seas. But Couper insists that one crucial question remained even after UNCLOS II in 1960: how far into the sea did the right of states to extract minerals from their claimed continental shelf extend? Couper (1978, 302), who was present at the negotiations for UNCLOS III, had "concern over the possibility of creeping jurisdiction, and even wholesale colonization, of the seabed and surface." UNCLOS III sought to address these concerns. The consensus-building process took place between 1973 and 1982, with the Convention coming into force in 1994.

Successive versions of the UNCLOS conventions in 1958, 1960, and 1994 gradually imposed a land-centred vision of geopolitics onto the world's oceans, which policymakers seem to have imagined (and perhaps continue to imagine) as static and neatly divisible. But the reality is very different: the constant flow and circulation that define the ocean make it impervious to attempts to fence it in neat and distinct areas. In the middle of the consensus-building process for UNCLOS III in 1978, Couper (296) observed that:

> Debates as to how the ocean should be used are, to start with, the classically simple ones of who is entitled to what, where, how much, and when? But the answers to the allocational problems of maritime space and resources are far more complicated than the land divisions once made at the advancing frontiers of the newly opened continents [...] There is [...] often a gap between policymakers' perceptions of national interests in dividing marine space and resources and the realities of ecological and geographical unity of the oceans, and between traditional maritime customs and laws and the operational requirements and environmental consequences of a complex and rapidly advancing technology.

If we set aside these concerns, then the main outcome of the UNCLOS III (also known as the Montego Bay Convention) was to carve out the seas into neatly distinct areas with implications for ownership, exploitation, and jurisdiction. This division is still in force, resulting in three maritime areas. The area closest to the coast, the territorial waters, includes the territorial sea, that is, waters within twelve nautical miles of the mean low watermark or baseline. Thus, the territorial sea along with internal waters (those within the bays and above the baseline), and archipelagic waters (among close islands of an archipelago) are considered part of the country's sovereign territory. All resources found in this area in the sea and the seabed belong to the coastal state.

A state's jurisdiction (the right to apply laws and exploit natural resources) wanes as we move past the limit of the territorial waters. The next twelve nautical miles are known as the contiguous zone. States can enforce specific laws in this zone, namely those related to customs, taxation, immigration, and sanitary laws, but only if the infringement began or will continue within the state's territorial waters (a doctrine known as the right of hot pursuit). The contiguous zone is part of the Exclusive Economic Zone (EEZ), which extends two hundred nautical miles from the baseline. As the name indicates, states have exclusive rights to explore and exploit maritime resources located underwater, a fact that has made the defining of the bounds of the EEZ a contentious matter among neighbouring states at times. Beyond the twenty-four nautical mile line from the coast where the contiguous zone ends, however, domestic legislation does not apply. Past the outer limit of the EEZ or the continental shelf (whichever is greater and up to a maximum of 350 nautical miles), we are in international waters. Here, only international law applies (Figure 2).

There are at least two reasons why the division of the ocean into these distinct areas is relevant to understanding maritime search and rescue systems in Europe and, more specifically, in Spain in contexts of sea migration. First is the application of domestic law, and in particular immigration and border control laws and regulations. These laws and regulations only apply in territorial waters and the contiguous zone. With the folding of maritime rescue into border control, a de facto expansion of European states' sovereign area is occurring, at least for the purposes of migration governance. One could question, and perhaps should question, how legal it is for state security forces to be enforcing domestic laws and regulations in international waters.

FIGURE 2: Maritime zones recognized under international law

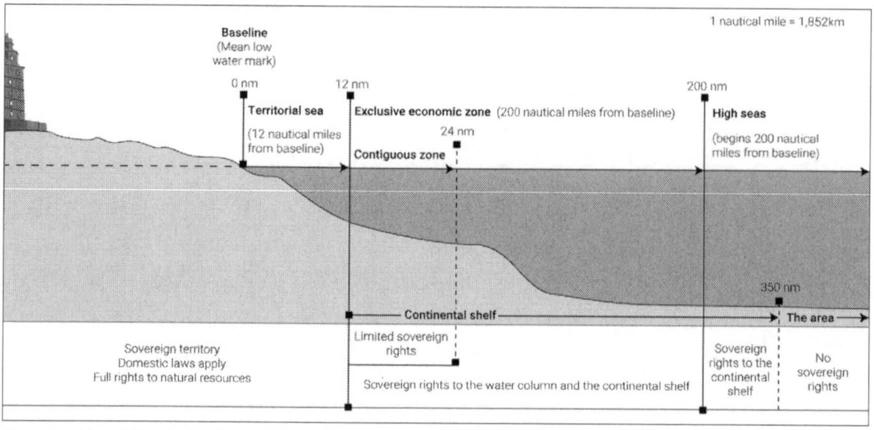

Created by Elizabeth Rose Hessek and reproduced with permission.

The second reason why these zones are important is that both the sea floor and migration have become lucrative businesses in recent decades. With the advancement of underwater mapping and resource extraction technologies, the sea floor under international waters is open for exploitation. Huge reserves of rare metals, oil, and other sought-after materials can be found there. It used to be that their extraction was too costly or simply impossible, but that has changed. Today, the oceans' resources are at the fingertips of both countries and private companies.

At the same time, the European Union has proven to be a generous negotiator when bargaining with countries of origin and transit for people migrating by sea — willing to give up some of its underwater wealth, even. These countries' co-operation is crucial to the success of current European approaches to migration control, which are based on the containment of people on the move outside its territory. The amounts of money that the European Union and member states are willing to shell out to keep people out are staggering: billions of euros are negotiated at the single brush of a pen — six billion for Türkiye in 2016, 7.4 billion for Egypt in 2024. In the case of Spain, the waters between the territory of the Western Sahara and the Canary archipelago in particular have been a chessboard on which sovereignty, jurisdiction, border control, and rescue responsibilities all blend in Morocco's long-term strategy to annex the Western Sahara's land and adjacent waters, as well as all the resources that lay therein. In other words, by accepting migration and border control responsibilities, collaborating countries like Morocco could gain leverage to make sovereignty claims, with significant political and economic consequences.

PROTECTING HUMAN LIFE AT SEA: THE SEARCH AND RESCUE CONVENTION

No matter who claims ownership, one thing is indisputable: the sea is a perilous realm for humans. Numerous incidents — shipwrecks, drownings, shark attacks — serve as evidence: depending on perspective, the ocean floor is either a site of treasure or a graveyard. Reflecting on the transatlantic slave trade, African American poet Amiri Baraka described it as a "railroad made of human bones" in the poem "Why's/Wise" (Mediasanctuary 2009). In her exploration of the misguided dreams of young African men migrating to Europe, Senegalese writer Fatou Diome (2003) painted the Atlantic as a ravenous beast.

Some of the greatest novels of the nineteenth and early twentieth centuries drew inspiration from the ever-present danger lurking in the waters and from a vision of the ship as a space out of place and time, a self-contained world far from human civilization existing among the waves. For example, the main character in Jack London's 1904 novel *Sea Wolf*, Humphrey Van Wayden, is swept away by a storm from his tame San Franciscan existence and ends up on a whaleship under the dominance of a brutal captain. His two lives, on land and on board, could easily have been set on two different planets. A real-life event inspired another one of the greatest modern fictions, Herman Melville's 1851 *Moby Dick*: the attack and sinking, thirty years earlier, of whaleship *Essex* by a vengeful sperm whale bull about two thousand miles off the coast of Chile. After the sinking, the crew split up. Some stayed in Henderson Island, while the rest of the survivors set off on three separate boats. After six weeks at sea a British ship, the *Dauphin*, came upon one of these boats. Horrified, the crew found the derelict vessel covered with human bones. Two men were on deck, barely alive: one on the stern and the other on the bow, both covered in sores, dehydrated, and sucking on the bone marrow of their shipmates' remains.

The story of the *Essex* became a tale shared around fires and taught in classrooms throughout the English-speaking world, but it would be a mistake to think the crew's encounter with death was exceptional. Just as the Safety of Life at Sea (SOLAS) Conventions tried to improve the safety on the vessels navigating the oceans, throughout the second half of the twentieth century other laws and conventions sought to make the seas less deadly. The goal of the SAR or Hamburg Convention (after the city where it was signed) was to standardize the widely different approaches to maritime rescue throughout the world. Or, borrowing from the text, to put in place an international search and rescue plan "so that, no matter where an accident occurs, the rescue of persons in distress at sea will be coordinated by a SAR organization and, when necessary, by co-operation between neighbouring SAR organizations" (IMO 1979). The SAR Convention was adopted in 1979 and ratified in 1985. By signing it, contracting states committed to creating national life-saving systems (similar to maritime firefighter or ambulance systems) and coordinate them both domestically and internationally through a network of national and regional coordination centres. This forced state signatories to the Convention, including Spain, to upgrade their legislation and rescue infrastructure.

While the SOLAS Convention sought to improve safety standards in commercial vessels and the UNCLOS clarified issues of jurisdiction and ownership, the SAR Convention defined states' responsibility to deal with emergencies at sea. All coastal EU member states have signed the convention. According to the European Commission (which operates as the European Union's cabinet government), this means that they are "obliged to develop maritime SAR services and to take any urgent steps to ensure that the necessary assistance is provided to any person who is, or appears to be, in distress at sea" (European Commission 2024).

In truth, while the SAR Convention may have been signed and ratified toward the end of the twentieth century, it simply regulated an age-old custom. Throughout history, seafarers and communities living off and by the sea understood that saving people whose lives were at risk in the waters was not a choice but a duty. This custom, known as the law of the sea (without capital letters) was in place for centuries before governments put pen to paper in Hamburg. This duty stands as an unshakable principle for those who labour at sea, far from the halls of power.

The Origins of Organized Maritime Rescue in Europe

This is a point worth repeating: seafaring communities have always understood their obligation to protect the lives of those at risk of drowning at sea. For most of history, these efforts were often improvised and involved getting into the sea with one's boat, throwing ropes at people struggling at sea, or providing clothes and food for survivors of a shipwreck. Sometimes, survivors were saved and freed, and other times, they were taken to make a profit through their labour, or worse. These, however, were usually spontaneous or one-off initiatives. More coordinated initiatives would not appear until the eighteenth century. In Spain, the first official rescue plan dates from

1773 (SASEMAR 2016). The *Instrucción sobre el modo y los medios de socorrer a los que se ahogaren o se hallaren en peligro en el río de Sevilla* (Directive on the Ways and Means to Assist Those Drowned or at Risk of Drowning in Seville's River) was ahead of its time: it included trained and uniformed rescuers, proper signalling, and the designation of a designated area at the local hospital to attend to victims of drowning.

If the 1773 *Instrucción* was exceptional in its foresight and thoughtfulness for the era, its emphasis on and approaches to resuscitation were very much attuned to was going on in other places in Europe at the time. Some of the methods this early document proposed included covering the person in ashes, rescue breathing through a pipe, body rubs with a mixture of alcohol and ammonia, or bleeding through the jugular. Other popular resuscitation methods throughout the eighteenth century included covering the victim's body with manure, hanging them by the feet, filling their mouth with vinegar or urine, tickling their noses, rolling them in an open barrel, or laying them down between two living, naked people. It seems the main goal was to shock the body back to life.

The gold standard for resuscitation at the time, though — the one put forward by the 1773 *Instrucción* and used by many medical doctors throughout Europe — was intra-rectal tobacco insufflation (Philippe, Saudamini, and Djillali 2019). The British Human Society started installing these resuscitation kits along the River Thames in the 1780s, and by the turn of the century smoke enemas were standard medical practice in several European countries. In France, the resuscitation kit was known as the Pia Box (after its inventor, Philippe-Nicolas Pia) or the *boîte fumigatoire*. The box contained a bellows and the different tubes needed to complete the procedure, which started by getting the person naked, then forcing air into their lungs through the mouth, then forcing tobacco smoke into their anus, and finally tickling their nose with a feather. This method was first promoted locally and then eventually adopted by ministerial decree in France and Great Britain in the second half of the nineteenth century.

As the Pia Boxes were at the peak of their popularity on shore, European governments became more proactive coming up with ways to assist those still in the water. Once again, Great Britain was a pioneer. The country had begun experimenting with unsinkable rescue boats in 1789, and in 1824 the British government created the Royal Institution for the Preservation of Life from Shipwreck, the first of such organizations in Europe. It would eventually become the Royal National Lifeboat

Institution, the organization responsible for most rescues in the British zone of responsibility today.

In France, volunteer-run local organizations known as Sociétés humaines et des Naufragés began keeping watch and accumulating (modest) rescue assets, mainly boats. The first organization of this kind in France appeared in Boulogne-sur-Mer in 1825 and remains active. The Société wanted to fill the gaps left by government intervention in the hugely popular seaside resort; clearly, more than smoke enemas were needed. The turning point was a sermon by Reverend M.A. Edge on September 11, 1825, where he expressed the community's concern. This sermon piqued the interest of Boulogne's Philanthropic Society, which sponsored a report prepared by English and French doctors. The report's proposals were basic by today's standards: to train rescuers ("swimming guides"), who "would be provided with floating jackets and ropes [...] and a wide, flat canoe like the Norwegians'" (Thierry 2020). Once onshore, the people rescued would be taken to the Société's premises, which would have "a furnace with a cauldron and a tap; a bathtub; a stove [...]; two sponges and two wool mittens [...]; a table six and a half feet long by three and a half feet wide. In the bedroom, bed and bedding, basin, syringe and medicine box." All in all, approaches to rescue had advanced precious little between 1773 and 1825.

A couple of months later, the French government formally authorized the creation of a Société humaine et des naufragés in Boulogne-sur-mer, led by a Franco-British board of directors. These sorts of local organizations were the harbingers of similar initiatives at the regional and national scale. The Société centrale de sauvetage des naufragés would be created forty years later in 1873, followed by the regional Société des hospitaliers sauveteurs Bretons in 1873. Both would eventually be absorbed and replaced by the Société nationale de sauvetage en mer (SNSM), created in 1967. The SNSM remains one of the key actors of maritime rescue in France to this day.

The French and especially British approaches to sea rescue became the blueprints for the Spanish strategy in this area. In 1859, Captain Miguel Lobo y Malagamba, widely considered the pioneer and founding father of maritime rescue in Spain, translated several of the founding documents used by the British and exhorted decision-makers in the country's main port cities to create a national rescue agency similar to the British Royal National Lifeboat Institution (Ocampo Aneiros n.d.; SASEMAR 2016).

Lobo must have been both very persuasive and extremely stubborn. Eventually, the Ministry of Development gave in, creating a proto–life-saving system in the main Spanish ports and ordering a first batch of seven self-righting rescue boats from the British. In 1880, four years after Lobo's death, the Sociedad Española de Salvamento de Náufragos began operations. As was the case in both France and Great Britain, the Spanish organization was staffed by volunteers and managed at the local level. Eventually, the armed forces assumed rescue responsibilities as well. Never a sufficient or fully integrated system, the early Spanish approach to sea rescue was left to flounder during the Spanish Civil War (1936–1939) and Franco's dictatorship (1939–1975). It was not until decades later (after Spain joined the European Communities in 1986 and ratified the SAR Convention in 1993) that the country would begin to seriously develop a national maritime search and rescue system. Even then, sea migration would not become a focus of the national rescue system until the turn of the twenty-first century.

Maritime Rescue in Europe: An Uneven Patchwork

Fragmented as these early efforts were, they all converged in their belief that a centralized and coherent system for the protection of human life at sea was needed. The SAR Convention codified an old custom and, specifically in the European context, created an environment where countries had little choice other than to coordinate their efforts. The Convention changed the world of sea rescue for three main reasons. First, it made clear that signatory states were legally and unambiguously obliged to put in place systems to protect *all* human life at sea. Second, it defined the basic components of a rescue system. Third, a country's rescue system had to be developed so that collaboration with neighbouring states was not only possible, but actively encouraged. All of this meant that many signatory states, Spain among them, had to overhaul their preexisting rescue systems or build them from scratch.

The first goal (to provide mandatory and universal rescue services anywhere and everywhere) required the partition of the oceans into thirteen large search and rescue areas, themselves divided into smaller zones of responsibility (known in the Convention as search and rescue regions or SRR) each under the management of a single national government. This way, the SAR Convention removed any ambiguity about who was responsible for coordinating a rescue operation.

The Convention invited neighbouring signatory states to agree on the boundaries of their respective zones of responsibility, but did not require it. In fact, the limits of a country's zone of responsibility are defined unilaterally by each state. This should be unsubstantial, as all boundaries and borders are rendered irrelevant by the letter and spirit of the Convention. Still, the absence of an obligation to agree on mutually exclusive zones of responsibility has led to a chart of rescue zones that is perhaps a bit more complex than the architects of the Convention had originally anticipated. For example, the Spanish and Moroccan zones of responsibility overlap in the Atlantic, with both countries claiming responsibility over the same area. In the Mediterranean, some countries have not signed the convention, have yet to communicate the boundaries of their zones of responsibility to the International Maritime Organization, or have not put in place a functional maritime rescue system; this is the case for Tunisia, for example. In some cases, governments have agreed to co-operate in areas where their zones of responsibility overlap, as in the shared zone of responsibility between Spain and Morocco in the Western Mediterranean. Finally, some countries' zones of responsibility are not recognized as legitimate by everyone; this is notably the case of Libya, who declared the creation of one such zone in 2020 using money from the European Union. But the country has not had a functional government since Gaddafi was killed in 2011, and some argue that what happens in these waters violates the principles of the SAR Convention and, therefore, the zone should not be considered a zone of responsibility as such (Migreurop 2020).

Also the territorial waters are a relatively small size compared to countries' zones of responsibility. As mentioned before, the boundaries of the zones of responsibilities are meant as guidelines to indicate which country bears responsibility for a rescue operation; they cannot be used to avoid the unambiguous legal duty of any capable party to assist everyone and anyone whose life may be at risk. Still, when it comes to sea migration, it is important to bear in mind that the zone of responsibility and the territorial waters and contiguous zones have different statuses in regard to the application of domestic law and border enforcement.

The second goal of the SAR Convention, to put in place a functioning maritime rescue system, created a number of obligations for signatory states. States had to acquire sufficient rescue assets such as boats, planes and helicopters. They had to put in place a communications network to allow for the transfer of information between rescue assets and the coordination centres. They also had to hire personnel to staff maritime, air, and coordination units. As they say, though, the devil is in the details.

While the SAR Convention outlined the basic elements of a search and rescue system, it did not define the minimum standards. There is, for example, no predefined number of rescue assets per area, no definition of what these assets should be, or how they must be distributed throughout the zone of responsibility. As a result, countries developed their own approaches to maritime rescue over time. The choices each nation made were shaped by existing institutions, past experiences with maritime rescue, and factors like institutional inertia and the unique political circumstances surrounding the initial allocation of rescue responsibilities.

The third goal of the Convention, to collaborate with neighbouring states, was easier than the other two goals from a technical point of view, but tricky in terms of the politics involved. We will see many examples of how this complexity continues to play out in this book.

It was thanks to and through the SAR Convention that maritime rescue was re-invented (and, in some cases, simply invented) in Europe in the late 1980s and early 1990s. This was particularly the case for the poorer countries along the southern border: Greece, Italy, Malta, and Spain. These countries signed the SAR Convention for two reasons: they had to if they were to join the European Communities (later, the European Union), and they saw the Convention as a way of protecting their fishing industry, including assets and crews working in the high seas. Perhaps this self-centred approach explains why, by design or by circumstance, the system that emerged in Spain had a decidedly universal vocation developed with the single goal of protecting all human life at sea, just as the Convention instructed countries to do. That universal vocation remained unquestioned for decades, until sea migration started to factor into political calculations.

THE POLITICS OF ORGANIZED ABANDONMENT AT SEA

The rescue operations that followed (or did not follow) the implosion of the *Titan* and the sinking of the *Adriana* were both framed by the same international conventions. These conventions have their origin in the emergence, throughout the nineteenth century, of technocratic international bodies, and were developed throughout the twentieth century. Combined, they form the foundation of the international maritime regime. The SOLAS Convention provided the first and most comprehensive definition of safety at sea. The UNCLOS established clear guidelines for sovereignty, ownership, and jurisdiction over maritime areas. Building on these, the SAR Convention assigned the responsibility of rescue among countries that had agreed on a common set of standards and protocols. The idea was that, had that vengeful whale attacked the *Essex* in the late twentieth century, there would have been a good chance that the survivors would not have had to resort to cannibalism and the fortuitous passing of another ship for survival. Instead, with the flick of a conveniently located and reliable radio beacon, the sailors could have requested and received timely assistance.

Of course, the mere existence of a rescue system does not guarantee survival: none of the *Titan*'s passengers survived, and very few of those aboard the *Adriana* lived. One of the main questions this book asks is why, when all wealthy countries with a coastline have a maritime search and rescue system in place, are some people's lives treated as more deserving to be saved than others? Why were no efforts spared to locate the *Titan* when it vanished in the depths of the North Atlantic Ocean, but Greek border guards stepped aside as the *Adriana* drifted and sank? There is a thread connecting the aftermath of the sinking of the *Essex* in the nineteenth century to these more recent events: racist discrimination played a role in ensuring that Black crew members of the ill-fated whaling ship were the first to perish. This was the result of a combination of factors: these men were already in worse physical condition due to poor nourishment, they were placed in the whaleboats with the least chances of survival, and they were the first to be sacrificed to feed the rest of the crew (Philbrick 2000).

However, the Conventions surrounding search and rescue in force today are universal by design. They are translated into domestic legislation and regulations that are also explicitly nondiscriminatory. In the case of maritime search and rescue, these conventions and legislation are applied in international waters, waters in which we are all foreigners in equal measure. And yet, as sea migration feeds into the anxieties and fears of Europe, and as rescue assets are integrated into a border designed to keep those from poorer countries out, member states' promise to protect human life at sea is increasingly flexible and dominated by political calculations. As time goes by, this promise has shifted from being a legal duty to assist those in distress at sea to an instrument for the control and punishment of illegalized human mobility.

This increasingly repressive and punitive approach to maritime search and rescue seems to be an article of faith in today's Europe. The logic goes as follows: sea migration must be stopped, rescue services are already there, therefore we should use those services to prevent migration, to detect and intercept irregular migrants, and feed them into a system that exploits, detains, and deports them. We seem to be becoming desensitized to the drama that unfolds at the watery gates of the Mediterranean and the Atlantic day in and day out. The dehumanization of the figure of the migrant on a boat has paved the way for a situation in which it seems acceptable for European countries to have a two-tier rescue system: one for migrants, and one for everyone else. That is a best-case scenario: in some cases, such as in Malta, migrant boats in distress are simply and systematically not rescued. How did we get here? How did we get from a Convention that makes it clear that rescue is universal and mandatory, to a practice where poor and racialized people are left to die at sea? Perhaps the pretended universality of the SAR Convention has always been a mirage. Even though racism and xenophobia are not explicitly written in to the pages of international conventions, these conventions contribute to the structural racism and racist violence that defines not just maritime rescue, but contemporary international relations as a whole.

Since 2018, Spain (who has signed the SOLAS, UNCLOS, and SAR Conventions) also has had a two-tier system, one for migrants and one for everybody else. As we move into the next chapter, we learn about an exceptional government agency at the centre of all the changes that have occurred in the world of maritime rescue in Spain: SASEMAR (or Salvamento Marítimo, as the agency is usually called). This government agency is exceptional in many ways, not the least because it has no border enforcement mandate or ambition. It is not an NGO, and it is also not a Coast Guard force: it is, quite simply, a maritime security agency run by the government. The agency was born in the early 1990s, which was an extremely exciting time for Spain: the country had just become a new member of the European project, fresh out of forty years of a brutal dictatorship; a place where immigration was so rare that there was not even a specific law to regulate it yet.

3

A Brief History of the Spanish Maritime Search and Rescue System

IN OCTOBER 1970, five years before Francisco Franco's death and the end of a forty-year military dictatorship, the fishing boat *La Isla* sank just a few metres off the craggy cliffs under the Tower of Hercules in Galicia. A heavy gale blew that night. The boat ran aground around 5:00 a.m. while nearby neighbours in the As Lagoas shantytown slept. Their slumber was cut short by the screams of the local fishermen aboard, who were trapped between the cold waves and the sharp rocks. "The sailors were shouting, crying and asking for help, but we couldn't do anything," recalled a neighbour. They frantically ran up and down the streets of As Lagoas and then woke up a local store owner, one of the few people with a landline at the time, to call the Naval Military Command. Minutes later, firefighters, police officers, and members of the Rescue and Lifesaving Federation, the army, and the Guardia Civil territorial command arrived (Mouzo 2015).

The problem, they soon realized, was that there were no boats and no helicopters, and nobody was trained to conduct a rescue under these circumstances. All they could do was look on helplessly as the fishermen struggled to stay afloat among the waves. This went on for hours. In their frustration, some young local men tried to jump in the water, but their older neighbours stopped them; others tried to throw ropes, but the ropes were not long enough. Fishing boats already at sea were asked to help. The men on those boats — neighbours, friends, and relatives of those in the *La Isla* — tried to help, but the storm made it extremely dangerous to approach the rocky coast. Members from a nearby flying club managed to get a light aircraft as close as five metres from the sailors, but the windows of the plane were too small to throw lifejackets or lift the men. Finally, another fishing boat, the *Segunda Isabelita*, was able to get close enough to the wreck. The sailors rescued the sole survivor and retrieved one corpse from the sea. The sailors retrieved one corpse from the sea and rescued the sole surviving member of the crew, who had spent six long hours holding on to a floating piece of wood. The bodies of the other fourteen men were never found (SASEMAR 2016).

The sinking of the *La Isla* was a tragedy for the local population. Such calamities were relatively frequent at the time, though, exposing the absence of anything that could be called a maritime rescue service in Spain. The SESN (Sociedad Española de Salvamento de Náufragos; Spanish Society for the Rescue of Shipwreck Victims), created in 1880, had worked relatively well until the beginning of the Civil War in 1936, and then was left to languish for decades. By 1949, the SESN owned twelve functional lifeboats and ran fourteen rescue stations so scarcely equipped they barely deserved the name. The Navy, with no vocation or means to do the job, took over as the main institution responsible for maritime rescue for a while. In 1960, when Spain signed the third SOLAS Convention, it finally felt like things were looking up. By signing the Convention, the country had formally committed to putting in place rescue assets, some basic infrastructure, and a communication strategy. On top of that, Spain joined the International Maritime Organization (IMO) in 1962. Alas, nothing changed except the fresh signatures on paper.

The 1960s brought about other important changes, though. After decades of isolation, the dictatorship allowed a slight opening to the outside world. The moderate economic development the country experienced during those years brought about a relative modernization of the fishing fleet. With more modern and safer boats, accidents involving fisherfolk became rarer. But at the same time other kinds of maritime traffic increased. There were more fishing boats, more merchant vessels, more oil tankers, and more recreational boats at sea. With more people in the water, the chances of something going wrong increased. This was especially true in areas with a high concentration of maritime traffic such as the coast of Galicia. Accidents clustered in the unforgiving area known as Costa da Morte (Coast of Death), which includes the port of A Coruña, one of Europe's major ports with heavy oil tanker traffic.

The same year that the *La Isla* sank, the tanker *Polycommander* ran aground in the Ría de Vigo, causing the biggest environmental catastrophe the area had known to date. Between 1976 and 1987, the oil tankers *Urquila* and *Andrios Patria* and the *Casón*, which carried chemical products, sank near the same section of the Spanish coast (Arbex 2001; SASEMAR 2016; Villa Caro 2020). Two later catastrophes involving the *Aegean Sea* and the *Prestige* (in 1992 and 2002, respectively) were crucial to the development of SASEMAR — an agency colloquially known as Salvamento Marítimo.

During the 1990s, Spain undertook the formidable task of building a maritime rescue system almost entirely from scratch. Immigration was not part of Spain's experience at the time — the country's history had been defined by emigration, not immigration — nor was it a consideration for the political class. Instead, Spain's entry into the exclusive European club and the rapid succession of environmental disasters were pivotal for the development of SASEMAR. This explains why the agency was, and remains, ill-equipped for law enforcement. In short, frequent accidents highlighted the dire state of Spain's system for preventing and managing maritime emergencies. These accidents primarily impacted the fishing and shipping industries, prompting local calls for action to prevent further tragedies. Meanwhile, migration was not even addressed in Spanish legislation: the first comprehensive immigration law would not be passed until 1985. Politicians showed little interest in merging rescue and border control until the turn of the twenty-first century.

PAVING THE WAY: RESCUE IN THE 1960s AND 1970s

Confronted with a steady succession of accidents at sea and unable to put off the creation of a national rescue system any longer, the Spanish government was at a crossroads in the late 1960s. Franco's government could try to revive the SESN, which some considered too far gone by then. Another option was to transfer the responsibility to the Navy, but the Navy was not particularly enthusiastic. The third option was to create an entirely new entity. This is how, in July 1971, the Red Cross of the Sea was born.

This new organization existed under the larger umbrella of the Spanish Red Cross. Across the globe, each national branch of the Red Cross operates independently. In Spain, it has always functioned, and continues to function, almost as a branch of the state. When the Red Cross of the Sea was established, the Spanish Red Cross was very closely aligned with Franco's regime — in fact, many considered it primarily a tool to spread the dictatorship's propaganda. The director of the Spanish Red Cross at the time and eventual founder of its sea section was Francisco Queipo de Llano y Acuña Álvarez de las Asturias, Grandee of Spain and Count of Toreno, cavalry officer, politician, and entrepreneur. Queipo de Llano was a recipient of the Imperial Order of the Yoke and Arrows (Orden Imperial del Yugo y las Flechas), the highest military and civil distinction awarded by Franco's regime.

Queipo de Llano's prominence and his vast network of contacts may explain why, instead of developing the rescue capacity of existing organizations with experience in maritime rescue, Franco opted to create a new one under his exclusive control and command. In the words of SASEMAR's historians, the SESN "self-immolated" so that the Red Cross of the Sea could be born (SASEMAR 2016, 34).

The Red Cross of the Sea joined a hodgepodge of insufficient, outdated, and poorly coordinated rescue infrastructure. The Navy was still at sea and had responsibilities in the areas of Spain's maritime border control and fishery surveillance. The Ministry of Defense also had its own rescue service. The National Marine Institute and the Spanish Oceanographic Institute had vessels to assist fishermen and conduct marine research. Customs and Civil Protection Services were also present at sea and in the estuaries. The main challenge for the government was to centralize and coordinate all the different actors with responsibilities directly or indirectly linked to maritime rescue.

A few months after Queipo de Llano created the Red Cross of the Sea, in 1972, a team prepared Spain's first National Rescue Plan. The French Société nationale de sauvetage en Mer (SNSM) and the British Royal National Lifeboat Institution (RNLI) were once again of great inspiration. The plan mainly sought to coordinate existing rescue actors and acquire assets. But with a budget much smaller than the French and British services (600 million pesetas, or about 60 million euros in 2024), its ambitions were much more modest, and in the end, its main achievement was to lay the foundation for today's rescue communication network. As for the rescue assets, the government acquired boats gradually. Starting with the cheaper units, the first boats to arrive were the Type C boats, small rigid-hull inflatable boats that allowed the Red Cross of the Sea to conduct beach surveillance and rescues near the shore. Then came Type B boats, comparatively larger self-righting rigid-hull inflatable boats that also could not venture far into sea. Finally, the hard-hull Type A boats, "self-righting and unsinkable," could act up to twenty-five miles from the coast. The Red Cross of the Sea was also assisted when and as needed by the Navy. The system was improving, but there were still important gaps.

Rescue operations remained patchy until 1979, when the arrival of democracy brought about a crucial change in the mandatory military service that gave the Red Cross an unexpected boon. Military service (colloquially known as the *mili*) had been compulsory for all Spanish men since the late eighteenth century. The *mili* lasted nine months, during which young men over the age of eighteen had to step away from their normal lives (their jobs, studies, friends, and family) and move to a barracks. But Spanish society was changing, and more and more young men declared themselves conscientious objectors. Starting in 1979, an agreement with the Ministry of Defense made it possible for young men to "volunteer" with the Red Cross of the Sea instead of doing the *mili*. Five years later, in 1984, the Socialist government passed legislation to establish the Prestación social sustitutoria (Ministerio de Justicia 1988). This "substitute social service" allowed more than one million conscientious objectors to do between nine and thirteen months of community service instead of the *mili*. Although not all of them chose the Red Cross of the Sea, between 1984 and 2001 (when the end of mandatory military training brought this agreement to an end), the bulk of the organization's rescue "volunteers" came via the substitute social service.

The agreement between the government and the Red Cross was a temporary solution, but it had the benefit of addressing three problems at once. First, it released funds that would otherwise be spent on personnel, allowing the government to acquire more rescue assets than would otherwise have been possible. Second, it bought the government time to replace the piecemeal rescue system with a sounder and more integrated rescue mechanism. Finally, it gave conscientious objectors an alternative to the mandatory military service. The agreement may have helped some find their professional calling: many of the older generations of SASEMAR's sea crews started their careers with the Red Cross of the Sea.

Listening to former volunteers share stories about their time patrolling the beaches, it is clear that the work was both fun and stimulating. However, staffing a life-saving public service with young and often inexperienced volunteers was less than ideal. Enric Tarrida, a Catalan sailor who joined the rescue service in the late 1980s, explained that, in some cases, the only person who had experience on the Red Cross of the Sea boats was the captain, who was also the only member of the crew who got paid. Moreover, the service was uneven: crews in certain coastal areas with strong fishing communities tended to be formed by youth with previous sea experience, while those in other locations were mainly staffed with young volunteers from cities in the interior who had little or no experience at sea. Enric told me that

> In places like the Bay of Biscay, the volunteers were sailors, fishermen. And maybe they did a fantastic job. But in other areas, people were signing up just to avoid doing the *mili* and they didn't necessarily have any experience at sea, so every nine months you had to train new men, and by the time they were trained, they were gone, and you had to start all over again.

This was no way to provide quality rescue services that were up to European standards.

And so, the 1980s found maritime rescue in Spain still a threadbare jumble of poorly connected services. Accidents continued, for the most part near Galicia and Andalusia, the areas with the heaviest shipping and fishing activity. Regional governments no longer had their hands tied, however: new democratic government was decentralizing services, meaning they were able to take some of their rescue needs into their own hands. "The regional government [of Galicia] commissioned a study of the situation and presented a plan in which it recommended the development of its own rescue service [a service that could attend to the fishing vessels, that was coordinated with the national services, and that had its own helicopters]," recalls naval engineering professor Raúl Villa Caro (2022). The Galician government created its own search and rescue service in 1989, more than two years before SASEMAR became operational, and other regions followed suit. This increased the overall rescue capacity in the national territory and nearby waters and allowed the regions to exercise their newly acquired competencies after four decades of almost absolute centralization during Franco's dictatorship. However, adding a new layer of actors went against efforts to integrate rescue services to create a coherent system.

What would compel Spain to put in place a cohesive national SAR strategy? At a meeting in the Basque Country in 1985, a group of specialists concluded that the development of a maritime rescue regulation was in a deadlock because the various actors involved could not agree on who should have responsibility for rescue operations. It was generally understood that the Navy was reluctant to relinquish control of Spanish ports. However, it also showed little interest in assuming responsibility for a national search and rescue system. After decades of military dictatorship, the armed forces were largely unwilling to cede power in critical institutions: it took decades for the Navy to cede the Marine Captaincies, the organs responsible for the coordination of sea navigation in key areas.

This group of specialists produced a report, which highlighted the lack of a nationally coordinated maritime rescue service as a major concern. Given Spain's economic reliance on fishing, shipping, and tourism, this was already a pressing issue. Additionally, with Spain on the verge of joining the European Communities, it was essential for the country to catch up in many policy areas, including maritime rescue. To avoid adding more confusion to the already labyrinthine distribution of responsibilities and assets, the panel proposed the creation of a new, single entity to take on this task.

Though the majority of the recommendations from the 1985 expert panel went unheeded, four years later, the Ministry of Transportation, Tourism, and Communication spearheaded the adoption of what is generally considered the first National Rescue Plan, which included the creation of the Servicio de Salvamento Marítimo y Lucha Contra la Contaminación (Maritime Rescue and Pollution Control Service, an early iteration of SASEMAR). The government acquired new rescue assets. The Red Cross of the Sea remained active on beaches, but it stopped doing rescues at sea. Its mandate and assets were transferred to a short-lived entity, the UVSE (Unidad de Voluntarios de Socorro y Emergencias; Aid and Emergency Volunteer Unit). In addition, between 1989 and 1993, the ministry created a limited number of new coordination centres, acquired some boats and helicopters, and started hiring personnel to staff the budding rescue system.

As part of a larger effort to mainstream rescue responsibilities, the ministry signed agreements with rescue actors such as the Red Cross of the Sea, the Navy, Customs, and the Guardia Civil, with regional governments who had already some rescue services in place, and, most importantly, with Telefonica, the then government-owned telecommunications company, which would be responsible for managing the communication network linking all the different actors and parts of the rescue system. The next few years were a frenzy. The first rescue boat of the Salvamar kind, the *Algol*, smaller than the ones of this kind in use today, was delivered in 1991. Progress was finally underway. Meanwhile, sea migration was beginning — slowly at first and mainly between northern Morocco and Andalusia in southern Spain. It would take years before policymakers started seeing it as a concern.

THE 1990s: A COORDINATED RESCUE SYSTEM IS BORN

Despite having signed the SOLAS Convention in 1960, despite having adopted two National Rescue Plans in 1972 and 1989, and despite the quick succession of catastrophes at sea, Spain was still very much short of rescue assets by the end of the 1980s. As a stopgap solution, the government outsourced some rescue responsibilities to a private company called REMOLMAR (Remolques Maritimos S.A., also referred to as REMASA). At the time, REMOLMAR had six operating control centres throughout the country and a fleet of tugboats used to clean up environmental disasters at sea, assist with rescue operations, and bring boats to port when and as needed. Other private companies such as Boluda and Nosa Terra signed similar deals with the government.

Even though these agreements allowed the Spanish government to increase its overall rescue capacity, in practice, the boats that they made available were either too big or too small for most operations. On the one hand, there were the boats left over from the Red Cross of the Sea and newly acquired government boats, all under fifteen metres long, unfit for rescues at a distance from the coast. On the other, there were private companies' tugboats which, at forty to sixty-three metres long, performed well in large accidents such as fires or oil spills at sea but were less than ideal as primary rescue assets in most other scenarios (SASEMAR n.d.b).

The gap between the growing demand for emergency services at sea and the means available to perform rescues grew each year. Juan Carlos Arbex, SASEMAR's director of communications during the first few months of the agency's existence, admits that rescue plans prior to 1993 all failed for the same reason: the Navy refused to give up control of the ports and the Captaincies of the Merchant Marine. But the early days of post-Franco democracy in Spain were most definitely not the right time to upset the armed forces; not everyone had come to terms with the loss of power after forty years of military dictatorship. In 1981, the military tried and failed to overthrow the government, proving how fragile the young democracy was. "The government saw clearly that they had to let the demons of the past quiet down before doing anything that might upset the Army," Arbex told me. "The 1980s were the years to let the new society settle in the new ways."

Time went by. As the new democratic reality strengthened, the sense of urgency at sea increased. The conflict between different and sometimes antithetical visions of what the new Spanish SAR system should look like grew. In Madrid, the tension in the hallways of different ministries was palpable. There was a desperate need for a national rescue system, but the question was who would be in charge of it. Money and prestige were at play, and various ministries and government agencies wanted to claim them. Internally, two main government ministries vied for it. One was the Ministry of Transportation, Tourism and Communication, headed by José Barrionuevo Peña and responsible for the first National Rescue Plan. The other vision was spearheaded by the Ministry of the Interior, and more specifically the director of the Guardia Civil, Juan Luis Roldán Ibáñez. Roldán was set on creating a Coast Guard with a rescue mandate similar to the ones that existed in places such as the United States, Canada, and Italy. In addition to this internal power struggle, there was also pressure from the European Communities, which did not dictate how national governments were to handle rescues at sea but were clear that every member state had to have a maritime rescue system that conformed to European norms and regulations.

The Guardia Civil was a strong candidate for leading these efforts in Spain. As part of his plan to create a Coast Guard with rescue responsibilities, Roldán had already set up a maritime unit within the force, the SEMAR. But without appropriate assets or personnel, Roldán's dream was not feasible. His plan was also short-lived for another reason: Roldán was soon found to be behind the greatest case of government corruption of the 1990s. The now-defunct newspaper *Diario 16* uncovered a scandal that had already been circulating in the halls of Parliament for months — the same months that the cabinet was discussing the best approach for a unified rescue agency. Eventually, Roldán would be sentenced to thirty-one years in prison for the crimes of embezzlement, bribery, fraud, and forgery against the Public Treasury (Rodríguez 2022). He committed most of these crimes in his capacity as director of the Guardia Civil. One of his many crimes was embezzlement: Roldán had stolen funds from contracts with shipyards and other companies providing rescue services. When his crimes became public, he ran from justice, spending almost a year as a fugitive before being detained in Laos (Hernández and Duva 1995). Roldán became a toxic political figure. Making the Guardia Civil responsible for the creation of a new and expensive rescue agency was simply out of the question.

Then, in the early 1990s, the vision of a government-run, civil rescue agency was transferred to the new super Ministry of Public works, Transportation, and the Environment, then in the hands of a young and promising politician, Josep Borrell Fontelles (who would, many years later, become the European Union's High Representative of the Union for Foreign Affairs and Security Policy). Borrell had inherited Barrionuevo Peña's vision and made it his own.

In 1992, the government finally passed a new Port and Merchant Marine Law. The new law regulated the creation of a proper national rescue system and at last transferred the authority of the Merchant Marine from the military to the new maritime Captaincies, under civil command, which would become the first rescue coordination centres (Arbex 2001). After a decade of Socialist government, the moment had arrived: the 1992 Law was the very push needed to help maritime rescue in Spain move forward. Shortly afterward, Spain ratified the SAR Convention. After decades of rescue plans that floundered without a clear direction and withered under the opposition of the army, Borrell plowed forward with a vision for a civil rescue agency that could coordinate the bulk of responsibilities related to making the oceans safer for navigation. It was as if Roldán's vision of a military rescue service had never even existed.

Is Roldán the reason why Spain is the only country in Europe without a militarized rescue service? We can not know, but there were other factors at play as well. During one of our conversations, Juan Carlos Arbex, who was present at the meeting where the newly created national rescue agency signed an agreement with the Guardia Civil's maritime unit, echoed a sentiment other people also voiced: the Guardia Civil was not ready to take to the sea. According to Arbex,

> They had these little flimsy boats and their men were not sailors, they had to learn even basic navigation skills. The maritime unit of the Guardia Civil was terrified the men would be put on the boats, they couldn't even moor a ship! The truth is, the Guardia Civil agents are like fish out of water when you put them on a boat.

In the end, perhaps the deciding factor as to whether Borrell's vision for a civil maritime rescue agency or Roldán's vision for a militarized rescue force would prevail had nothing to do with internal power struggles but rather with the catastrophic sinking of the tanker *Aegean Sea* near the coast of Galicia in the last days of 1992.

ENVIRONMENTAL DISASTERS SHAPED THE EARLY SPANISH SEARCH AND RESCUE SYSTEM

The *Aegean Sea*, a Japanese-built oil tanker flying a Greek pavilion, sank while trying to enter the port of A Coruña in late December, 1992. In his new role as head of SASEMAR's communications department, Arbex wrote a detailed account of the accident in the twenty-seventh issue of the magazine, *Marina Civil,* published jointly by the Ministry of Public Works and Transportation and the General Direction of the Merchant Marine. In over sixty-five pages, Arbex described every aspect of the accident and included pictures, graphs, maps, and plans of the tanker.

The *Aegean Sea* was about twenty years old. It had been filled with eighty metric tons of crude oil in the Scottish Shetland Islands and was on its way to a refinery in A Coruña. The tanker had the highest safety certifications for its class, had just passed two inspections, and was fresh from four months of routine maintenance at the shipyard. The weather as it approached the port of A Coruña was bad, but nothing out of the ordinary for that time of year in Costa da Morte. The tanker was told to wait for authorization in a mooring area nearby. Two days later, the *Aegean Sea* was told to enter the port, a manoeuvre assisted by the harbour pilot. By then, the wind gusts were up to one hundred kilometres per hour with waves three to four metres high. This was also something the tanker should have been able to handle, though. And yet, during the manoeuvre, the *Aegean Sea* rammed against the rocks at full speed and cracked open.

The disaster was the ultimate test for Barrionuevo Peña's 1989 National Rescue Plan and the young Servicio de Salvamento Marítimo y Lucha Contra la Contaminación. The emergency procedure kicked in immediately: under the command of the Operative Coordination Centre, civil and military assets came together. First, they removed all twenty-nine members of the crew as the oil gushed out, barely a few minutes before the tanker exploded in fifty-metre-tall flames. The flames and the thick black smoke blanketed the city of A Coruña, just metres away. Overall, the Operative Coordination Centre mobilized one other tanker, five rescue vessels, two barges, three rescue motorboats, five helicopters, and nine other boats to rescue the crew from the disaster, in addition to other assets used to clean the area. The cleanup lasted months and could not prevent the terrible environmental damage that followed. Still, five days after the *Aegean Sea* ran aground, the European Communities published a note praising the Spanish government's actions.

Borrell, then head of the ministry in charge of the emergency response to the *Aegean Sea* disaster, also praised the response by national and regional rescue services, which he described as "irreproachable" in the editorial that prefaced Arbex's account of the accident. But Borrell insisted that there was still more work to do: Spain needed and deserved an even better maritime rescue system, and it would get it within the context of the new 1992 Port Law and under his watch. He wasted no time. A few days after the accident (the day before Parliament adjourned for the Christmas holidays), Borrell announced the creation of the Sociedad Estatal de Salvamento Marítimo, or SASEMAR.

Things moved fast after the announcement. In an interview, Arbex recalled the inauguration of the Gijón Maritime Rescue Coordination Centre (MRCC) in Cantabria. The Coordination Centre was attached to the also newly opened Jovellanos Comprehensive Maritime Safety Centre, an institution created to train rescue personnel from different public emergency response units. Arbex remembered Borrell showing the Spanish King Don Juan Carlos around the facilities under the heavy rain that battered the northern Spanish coast the day the Centre was inaugurated: "Borrell was showing His Majesty the electronic equipment, the radars, the simulators, and he said, 'This centre cost the same as one kilometre of highway, wasn't it worth it?' And the King agreed heartily. 'This, your Highness,' said Borrell, 'is the jewel of the crown of the Ministry of Public Works.'"

However, not everyone was satisfied with the official response to the *Aegean Sea* disaster. Some commentators thought that if the military had spearheaded the rescue efforts, many of the losses could have been averted. Looking back at his short stint at SASEMAR from semi-retirement, Arbex recalls that bitter fights about this issue were constant in the months after the accident. "Those months were very intense and very tough," he told me. "The agency received no sympathy from the established institutions and power structures. All it had was enemies, because there were many other people who wanted to claim rescue services for themselves." Six months later, tired of the tensions, Arbex left SASEMAR and returned to his work as a journalist and author specializing in the sea.

Despite these fights, the *Aegean Sea* disaster had demonstrated the urgency of establishing a top-notch service to deal with maritime emergencies. There was no going back. Borrell encountered no resistance when he announced the establishment of SASEMAR. Perhaps concerned by the quick succession of accidents involving oil tankers in Spain and other parts of Europe, a few weeks later, on January 22, the European Transportation Council mandated that member states must "complete and modernize their rescue and contamination fighting infrastructure, resorting, whenever necessary and feasible, to the financial assistance provided by the newly created European Cohesion Fund" (Arbex 2001).

Spain's next two National Rescue Plans made use of the European Union's offer and cemented SASEMAR's role in the country's search and rescue operations. The 1994–97 Plan had a budget of 34 billion pesetas (about 400 million euros in 2024), almost seven times that of the previous plan. Of these, six billion pesetas (70 million euros) came from the European Cohesion Fund. This money allowed the government to open new coordination centres along the coastline, acquire rescue assets, and sign thirty-seven new collaboration agreements with other actors and agencies.

The next plan (1998–2001) consolidated the system. The government continued opening more coordination centres across the country, acquired more boats, helicopters, and small planes, and developed strategic bases equipped for environmental disasters and underwater emergencies. SASEMAR's regional coordination centres were also (finally) linked to the Global Maritime Distress Safety System (GMDSS), a set of interconnected emergency systems developed in the context of the SOLAS Convention, which meant that those coordinating responses to emergencies at sea had much better access to vital information in real time. The administrative status of SASEMAR also changed during this time: in 1999, the agency became an *entidad pública empresarial* (public business entity).

Meanwhile, far from the burning oil tankers in Galicia and the contentious ministry halls in Madrid, another change was brewing. In 1988, a local photographer snapped a picture of a shipwrecked migrant boat on a beach near Tarifa in southern Spain. This photograph became the first mediatized image of sea migration to Spain. But few people were paying attention.

The *Prestige* Disaster

On November 19, 2002, almost exactly a decade after the sinking of the *Aegean Sea*, the oil tanker *Prestige* broke in half in front of Muxía, Galicia, leaking 65,000 tonnes of heavy fuel into the ocean. The *Prestige*, an aging vessel, had been drifting for five days. The Spanish, French, and Portuguese governments had repeatedly refused to let her dock after the captain noticed a crack in the hull, perhaps hoping that the inevitable disaster would happen in somebody else's jurisdiction. The spill happened in the open sea, making it impossible to contain. The *Prestige*'s oil slick polluted over 2,300 kilometres of the Spanish, Portuguese, and French coasts. It was (and remains) the worst environmental catastrophe in Spanish history, and the worst oil spill Europe has known so far.

An epitome of today's globalized merchant industry, the *Prestige* had been built in Japan in 1976, but was registered by the American Bureau of Shipping, insured in the United Kingdom, exclusively owned by a Liberian company, operated by a Greek company under a Bahamian convenience flag, and carried high-density fuel oil owned by a Russian company based in Switzerland. Crude shipping may be the definition of a globalized sector, but the *Prestige* was no luxury tanker: after twenty-six years of service, it was battered. This trip was going to be its final voyage before being sent for scrapping.

During the ensuing legal case, it became obvious that the Spanish Ministry of Development had attempted to minimize the disaster all along. The government had gone as far as to hide information from the public to pretend the spill was under control. When the tanker sank, rescuing the *Prestige*'s twenty-seven crew members was the easy part; dealing with the oil spill was much more difficult. As the full dimensions of the environmental disaster became evident, the Spanish government tasked a publicly owned company with environmental conservation responsibilities (TRAGSA) to manage the cleanup. TRAGSA's efforts were not sufficient to address the gravity of the disaster, though (García Mira 2013). The oil slick and the *chapapote* (solidified oil) covered rocks and beaches, killing birds and fish. Social and political pressure mounted: people were angry. Public frustration grew with those who had played political ping pong with the damaged tanker as well as with those responsible for coordinating the emergency response immediately afterward. Frustrated, outraged, and overwhelmed, citizens in Galicia organized to create the platform Nunca Mais (Never Again). They had had enough with preventable accidents damaging the fragile coastal ecosystem and threatening their livelihoods.

The *Prestige* disaster marked a whole generation of Spaniards. Once again, an environmental disaster shed light on the limits of the still-nascent Spanish system to protect both humans at sea and the marine environment, and made clear that changes to the shipping industry could not wait any longer. But while long-term political change was important, cleaning the coast was urgent. Environmental organizations, student unions, and citizen groups organized cleanups along Galicia's coast in the spring of 2003. Volunteers worked together to manually remove oil and *chapapote* from the beach. The citizen response to the disaster was one of the greatest feats of grassroots organizing in contemporary Spanish history. Citizens from across the country boarded buses headed to the oil-soaked beaches of Galicia.

Aran Sol Juanola was one of the few hundred mostly university students who joined the cleaning effort. Originally from Barcelona and studying to become an aerospace engineer in Madrid, he told me that "We were at the dorm when I heard the news. It was all we talked about for weeks. And in class everyone was saying, 'Oh shit, we should go help with the cleaning!'" In the spring, he saw a poster in the cafeteria announcing that buses would be leaving to bring volunteers to Galicia and decided to go. "I couldn't stand it any longer, just watching the news with my arms crossed. I *had* to do something," he said.

The bus Aran boarded was headed to Costa da Morte, near the site most damaged by the spill. The volunteers knew that cleaning up a massive oil spill was not a job a bunch of twenty-year-olds could finish during a weekend, but they wanted to help. When they arrived at the village, they were overwhelmed by locals' hospitality. For two days, they slept on mattresses placed in an open-air area inside a municipal sports centre. Neighbours brought food for the volunteers and let them come into their homes at the end of the day so they could shower. Yet, when they arrived at the beach on the first day, Aran recalled feeling dismayed by the impossibility of the task:

> In the morning they gave us white coveralls and gloves and we went down to the beach to clean it. When we got there, the beach looked clean, but the *chapapote* was under the sand. The tides and the waves had covered the *chapapote* with sand. They gave us some garbage bags and a dumpster, and we started pulling out trays of tar. See, you put your hands under the sand, and they came out like trays. At first the trays were big but there were always little pieces left, so you tried to pick up as much as you could, but the pieces got smaller and smaller. When we left after two days of nonstop cleaning from sunrise to sunset, it looked as if we had done nothing.

On the last day, the volunteers were walking back to the village and sharing their frustration, discussing whom to vote for in the upcoming regional elections. For many, it would be the first time they were able to vote. Their overwhelming sense of helplessness and their frustration with the government's handling of the environmental disaster that they were literally touching and smelling weighed heavy on their conversation. As they walked up the hill from the beach, they came upon a journalist from the national public news channel and a camera crew. Aran recalled that "behind the journalist were two kids wearing our same coveralls, stretched out on their bellies on the beach, pulling little beads of *chapapote* the size of small fingernails out of the sand. And she was saying that the beaches were already clean!" The volunteers confronted the journalist: "We were livid!", he told me. "We had spent two days kneeling on the sand, two full days with little rest, and we had barely cleaned anything. The journalist was lying through her teeth, we got into a huge fight with her."

Arbex came to a similar conclusion regarding the politicization of the catastrophe, although he had a different perspective. The day the tanker split in two, he had been filming at the A Coruña Captaincy. According to Arbex, suddenly, someone "rushed in, yelling and screaming that there was a giant oil slick somewhere." Nobody at the coordination centre had heard anything — a surveillance plane had gone over the tanker just that morning and had reported that everything was fine. But the situation evolved quickly: "By the time they realized what was going on, politicians, harassed by the media and worried about the impact on the upcoming elections, went into hysterics, and the people coordinating the emergency response couldn't do their job: they knew what they had to do, but they were not allowed to do it." Pretending that everything was under control in the months before the elections was more important than mitigating the impact of the oil spill.

SASEMAR after the Prestige: 2002–2012

The *Prestige* environmental disaster shook federal politics. The Merchant Marine had adopted a National Contingency Plan for Accidental Maritime Contamination and was implementing a new National Maritime Rescue Plan at the time (2002–2005). The government wanted to acquire new boats, improve coordination, update technical equipment, start using the vessel Automated Identification System (AIS), and hire new personnel. But the budget allocated to this plan was just 295 million euros — not nearly enough to match its ambitions. When the tanker's hull cracked in two, SASEMAR office staff was just settling into their new permanent headquarters in Madrid. The sinking of the *Prestige* in late 2002 forced the government, and SASEMAR, to ramp up their plans — and their budget.

The *Prestige* disaster marked a before and an after in Spain's maritime rescue plans. By then, Borrell had made the jump to European politics, and Francisco Álvarez Cascos, then minister of development with a Conservative government, was in charge of SASEMAR. As a direct consequence of the disaster, the Conservative government of José María Aznar passed the Plan Puente in 2003 without waiting for the National Rescue Plan, which was still in force, to come to its end. The "Bridge Plan" was exceptional, and exceptionally financed. It injected 288.5 million euros into Spain's budget for developing rescue assets, effectively and unexpectedly doubling the budget of the 2002–2005 plan. That money brought the government closer to its ambition to making Spain a reference for maritime emergency response in Europe. This meant buying more boats and more helicopters, hiring more personnel, creating more strategic bases to fight against marine pollution, and improving coordination between the different rescue actors and parts of the system.

The fragmented approach that had defined the first decade of Spain's maritime rescue system evolved into a more cohesive operation after the

Prestige disaster. Oil spills underscored the value of the relatively modest rescue agency, proving it to be a worthwhile investment for both Conservative and Socialist governments. At the same time, sea migration had increased enough to warrant significant political attention. In fact, more than 817,000 people with precarious migration status became legal residents in two separate regularization campaigns in 2001 and 2005 (Serrano 2024). A small percentage of them had reached Spanish territory on boats. And yet, maritime rescue and migration remained two separate items in public debates and policy agendas.

How did this happen? At two critical moments in SASEMAR's history, when public concern might have turned toward sea migration, an oil spill dominated public attention. The *Aegean Sea* and *Prestige* disasters kept SASEMAR focused on big boats like oil tankers, drawing attention away from the little boats that had already become more frequent in the Mediterranean and would soon take to the waters around the Canary Islands. These two environmental disasters reinforced bipartisan support for SASEMAR, a backing that would remain strong for the next fifteen years — until the far right targeted the agency during the 2018–2019 electoral campaign, specifically because of its role in migrant rescues. In this way, the agency's mandate became an unlikely point of consensus between the Socialist and the Conservative parties.

Next came the fifth National Rescue Plan (2006–2009), which sought to rehaul SASEMAR's status within the government. This plan came into force during the first "*cayuco* crisis," when tens of thousands of young men from West Africa arrived in the Canary Islands in artisanal fishing boats. Boasting a budget larger than any of the previous national plans (more than one billion euros), the new plan sought to impose mandatory response times and acquire the assets that would make them possible. By the end of 2009, SASEMAR had acquired new multipurpose vessels and developed a maritime fleet of fifty-five Salvamares and four Guardamares. In the sky, the agency began renovating its helicopter fleet, replacing some of the old Sikorskys S-61N with the newer and more adaptable AugustaWestland AW139, still in use. Another breakthrough for the agency was that, for the first time, SASEMAR had its own planes. While the agency owned a growing number of rescue assets, it continued to outsource staffing and maintenance to other companies. Once the Red Cross of the Sea shrank its operations in 2002, SASEMAR's main partner at sea was REMOLMAR, the private towing company now operating with an exclusive mandate from the state to perform rescue missions. The 2006–2009 plan made no reference whatsoever to the growing demand to attend to emergencies involving migrant boats.

From 2006 onward, it became impossible to ignore the new realities of rescue in the Spanish zone of responsibility. Improvements to the safety standards of merchant vessels and oil tankers – and commercial activities at sea in general – meant that large environmental catastrophes such as the sinking of the *Prestige* were finally becoming rarer. At the same time, however, the presence of recreational boats at sea was booming, and the new popularity of maritime sports such as windsurfing meant that SASEMAR crews were being called to intervene in an ever-expanding number of scenarios. Moreover, sea migration had increased spectacularly in 2006, the year when more than thirty thousand people reached the Canary Islands by boat, overwhelming emergency responders in the archipelago. At the agency's headquarters in Madrid, the arrival of these migrant boats was treated as a short-lived event that would leave no lasting mark on SASEMAR's long-term mandate.

The following National Rescue Plan (2010–2018) made only a passing reference to migration, despite the agency being completely overwhelmed by the arrival of people by boat to the Canary Islands in the preceding years. This plan doubled down on the direction set in previous plans: it aimed to prevent environmental disasters, to improve the emergency response system, to engage in maritime safety research and development, and to create a new institutional framework that would enable the professionalization of personnel and coordination with European and international agencies. To do this, the agency had an average yearly budget of slightly more than 135 million euros.

There was a clear disconnect between the reality of sea migration and SASEMAR's official mandate. Still, in the formative period between 2002 and 2012, the agency continued to provide life-saving services to people on the move, becoming the service that it is today. The acquisition of REMOLMAR by SASEMAR in 2012 marked the beginning of a new era for the agency. REMOLMAR, initially a private company, had existed since the mid-1960s as a subsidiary of Transmediterránea, the most important shipping company in Spain at the time. After a significant expansion in the 1970s and some difficulties the following decade, Transmediterránea was partially nationalized in the mid-1980s to prevent its disappearance. This means that when Enric Tarrida (retired rescuer and former union representative) joined the rescue fleet in 1989, he was not hired by SASEMAR (which did not exist yet), but by REMOLMAR, which had begun its operations under the exclusive mandate of the state.

In 1992, when the Spanish government passed the new Port Law and created SASEMAR, the agency became REMOLMAR's main shareholder. The two remained separate entities for nearly two decades, during which SASEMAR's rescue crews were still employed by REMOLMAR. But the economic crisis of 2008 meant that the Conservative government of Mariano Rajoy had to find ways to save money. In 2012, the Plan for the Restructuring and Rationalization of the Public Business Sector effectively extinguished REMOLMAR, which was acquired by SASEMAR. Now in charge of REMOLMAR's rescue assets and personnel, SASEMAR became the sole agency responsible for the bulk of maritime search and rescue at the national level. This had a huge impact on sea crews. For decades, REMOLMAR and SASEMAR had had different collective agreements. As of 2012, however, Enric Tarrida and all the other rescue crews formerly hired by REMOLMAR became state employees. This change only applied to sea crews, though: air crews are still outsourced to private companies through public contracts adjudicated periodically.

THE CREATION OF A TWO-TIER RESCUE SYSTEM

From its creation in 1989 to the end of the sixth National Rescue Plan in 2018, SASEMAR's strategic planning overlooked the growing phenomenon of sea migration almost entirely. However, on the ground, the situation was quite different. During the first "*cayuco* crisis" in 2006–2008, the conservative government of José María Aznar had set up an informal structure to manage boat arrivals to the Canary Islands. This structure involved periodic meetings between the Guardia Civil and other frontline actors like SASEMAR, the Red Cross, regional emergency services, and child protection services. This structure was formalized and reinforced, with considerable public attention, in the Western Mediterranean in 2018. Then and there, a two-tier maritime rescue system was created in areas of the Spanish zone of responsibility where rescue needs and migration zones overlapped.

This happened specifically in August 2018, when the Socialist government of Pedro Sánchez announced the creation of the CCOE (Centro de Coordinación de Operaciones de Emergencia; Emergency Operation Coordination Centre). At its helm would be the MUO (Mando Único Operativo; Single Operative Command), a position filled by a senior member from the Guardia Civil. The CCOE would bring together different actors involved in migration reception and processing, including the armed forces, Frontex, the National Intelligence Service, the Guardia Civil, the National Police, the Customs Department, Maritime Captaincy, SASEMAR and the Red Cross. After some months of planning, on March 20, 2019, the CCOE and the MUO became functional. Both were integrated into the Coordinating Authority for the Control of Irregular Migration in the Strait of Gibraltar and depended on the Secretariat of Public Safety.

From that moment on, when SASEMAR received a distress call for a boat in the Western Mediterranean, two things could happen: if migrants were involved, the coordination of the rescue operation would be delegated to the military command (the CCOE and the MUO). If those at risk were not immigrants, then SASEMAR's civilian personnel would handle the emergency, with the military getting involved only in specific cases (for example, if SASEMAR's boats were not available). The implications of this two-tier system are discussed in Chapter 4.

The two entities (SASEMAR and the Guardia Civil) have always co-operated. Typically, this co-operation sought to provide protection for rescuers, civil servants who do not have training or equipment to impose order if things get unruly during a mission. Oriol Estrada, union representative and rescuer since the 1990s, told me that "the first protocols were triggered by the fact that some migrants could sometimes behave a little bit, I won't say aggressively, but they were not friendly either. And sometimes we found large knives and so we did not feel very safe. In those cases, we would request that a couple of Guardia Civil agents would come on board for our safety." Additionally, the Guardia Civil has operated their own maritime service for decades and has jurisdiction to intercept vessels at sea.

Nevertheless, for nearly three decades, the two government agencies were officially independent of each other. That changed officially in 2018 when SASEMAR's coordination centres in southern Spain started taking orders directly from the Guardia Civil. These changes were not reflected in the 2019–2021 National Rescue Plan, which mentioned migration only twice, even though more than 43 percent of the boats assisted by SASEMAR crews in 2020 were migrant boats. The annual budget barely increased during this period, remaining slightly less than 157 million euros per year.

The next National Rescue Plan (2022–2024) was slightly more generously funded. SASEMAR had 170 million euros at its disposal in 2022 and almost

190 million in 2023. Again, the plan paid little attention to migration, which it mentioned only three times in sixty pages. This is intriguing. For over fifteen years, the European Union had been trying to crack the black box of member states' multivarious approaches to maritime rescue precisely because of their potential to assist with the control of migration along its external border.

This concerted effort to standardize maritime rescue policy and practice was part of a broader goal toward integrated border management in the European Union. For example, the European Commission's Recommendation 2020/1365 sought to standardize the sharing of information on rescue operations, particularly those carried out by rescue NGOs. A year later, in 2021, the European Commission created the European Contact Group on Search and Rescue, "a platform allowing for a structured dialogue among EU countries and Schengen Associated States, and with other relevant stakeholders, on the implementation of the legal framework and the evolving practice of SAR" (European Commission 2020). More recently, the European Pact on Migration and Asylum of the European Commission doubled down on efforts to harmonize rescue practices at sea. As time goes by, the absence of references to migration in SASEMAR's strategic plans becomes more conspicuous. Yet, at least officially, the agency has somehow managed to keep its head in the sand, sticking to a mandate that has barely evolved since the 1990s.

While it is true that the majority of SASEMAR's work has nothing to do with migrant boats, why has the agency refused to acknowledge the impact that migration (a phenomenon which has become so central to its work and which is such an important topic for the European Union) has had on its daily work? And why has the European Union allowed SASEMAR to keep flying under the radar? A generous reading may suggest that the government remains strongly committed to the principles of the SAR Convention, a commitment that is, in fact, shared by the senior members of the Spanish Navy deployed across the Mediterranean that I talked to. It may also be that SASEMAR's senior personnel fear that being too closely identified with migration could put the agency's survival at risk, or that European policymakers are simply reluctant to tell other member states how to handle their own affairs. It may also be the case that, whatever the language used in its reports and Rescue Plans, and whatever policymakers in Brussels say on the record, the takeover of SASEMAR by the Guardia Civil is well under way.

This takeover may not always be as explicit as it was when the creation of a military authority in the Western Mediterranean figured prominently in the Socialist Party's 2018 electoral campaign. The militarization of SASEMAR can happen in subtler ways. For example, in 2023, a second "*cayuco* crisis" hit the Canary Islands, but there was no formal military infrastructure in place to manage the situation in the Atlantic region. Almost forty thousand people arrived by sea from southern Morocco, the territories of the Western Sahara, Mauritania, and Senegal that year, once again overwhelming migrant reception services.

In October of that year, the regional government asked Spanish President Pedro Sánchez to create a military-led entity similar to the one in the Western Mediterranean in the archipelago. In declarations to the media, regional MP Cristina Valido said that "a thousand people arrived within twenty-four hours," adding that her government could not be held responsible for coordinating with the different federal ministries involved in the management of irregular migration. She continued: "We have asked the President to create a Single Operative Command to coordinate the actions that need to be implemented in the face of the migratory crisis that we are experiencing" (Europa Press Nacional 2023).

The following month, the federal and regional governments signed an agreement whereby the governing party in the islands committed to supporting the upcoming state budget proposed by Sánchez's government in exchange for, among other things, the creation of a coordinating authority for the Canary Islands similar to that in the Western Mediterranean (*El País* 2023). Then, the national government announced the creation of an Interministerial Immigration Commission (La Moncloa 2024). This Commission was fundamentally different from that of the military Coordination Centre in the Western Mediterranean, however. For one, its focus was to increase the reception capacity of the islands (or facilitate the transfer of migrants who arrived by sea to mainland Spain) and to increase co-operation with countries of origin and transit of sea migration. There was no mention of the new military coordinating authority being in charge of the Commission.

Why is there such differences in approaches in the Western Mediterranean and the archipelago, two areas that are both within the Spanish zone of responsibility? In fact, as we have seen, a subtler version of the military coordination centre was already managing rescue operations involving migrant boats from their headquarters in Gran Canaria in 2006. The military organized monthly meetings with other agencies and organizations in the islands to coordinate a common response to the arrivals. Many of those sitting around the table were the same that participated in the military-led Coordination Centre in the Western Mediterranean: the Red Cross, the National Police, the regional government, and the local and regional emergency services. However, in 2006, the government was fresh from a national election and the far right was weakened. They did not need to make a spectacle of the militarization of migrant rescues in the Canary Islands. This stealth militarization seems to have resulted in a gentler splitting of rescues at sea. Years later, in 2023–2024, during the second "*cayuco* crisis," members from the Alarm Phone network covering the Atlantic zone still reported that, in their experience, emergency services in the Canary Islands tended to be more proactive and less militarized than in the Mediterranean.

SASEMAR TODAY

In the late 1980s, when Enric Tarrida first started working for a private company tasked by the government to implement Spain's first maritime search and rescue plan (REMOLMAR), Spain had "just a few small fibreglass boats" to cover the huge surface of the Spanish zone of responsibility — which, at roughly 1.5 million square kilometres, is three times Spain's landmass. Thirty-five years later, SASEMAR has a world-class training centre in Gijón, twenty coordination centres, six strategic bases for marine pollution, seventy-six boats, and fourteen air units. The company directly employs 1,500 people, including five hundred rescuers on the sea units. Air rescue crews are still contracted out through private companies that also maintain the planes and helicopters. As the number of assets and staff has grown to face the challenging task of keeping the Spanish zone of responsibility safe, the structure of the company has become more sophisticated.

At its core, the SAR Convention requires national rescue services to include three key elements: a network of coordination centres, sea units, and air units. SASEMAR has one National Rescue Coordination Centre (NRCC) located in Madrid that centralizes all activities and nineteen regional Maritime Rescue Coordination Centres (MRCCs) that are located in coastal areas. It may seem peculiar that SASEMAR's headquarters are located inland, as far from the coast as it is possible to be in Spain. The question comes up so often that one of the first episodes of a new podcast made by the agency's in-house communication team is entitled *Salvamento Marítimo in Madrid?* In truth, less than 10 percent of personnel are based

FIGURE 3: Map of the Spanish zones of responsibility in the Western Mediterranean and Canary Islands

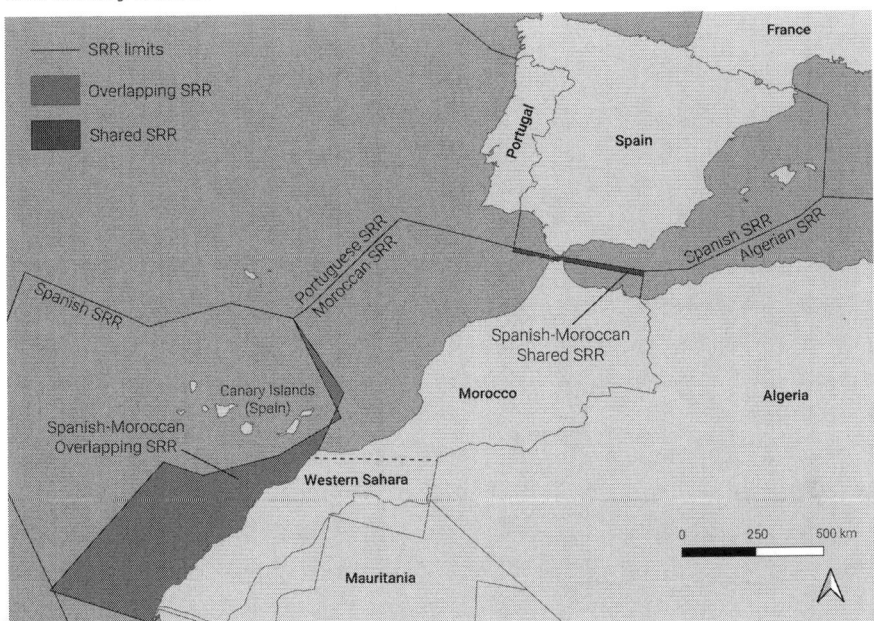

Source: IMO. Map created by Elizabeth Rose Hessek and reproduced with permission.

at the national centre. This staff manage the company's human resources, administration and finances, information technology, and operations departments, among others. When needed, they direct emergency calls to the appropriate MRCC, run marine security campaigns, communicate with the media and other state institutions, and detect illegal dumping in Spanish waters. These are important functions, but they can be fulfilled from anywhere. At the end of the day, the main reason SASEMAR's headquarters are in Madrid is probably because the Spanish government retains a highly centralized structure.

By contrast, SASEMAR's nineteen regional coordination centres are located along the coast. While the National Coordination Centre in Madrid handles the big picture, the "towers" (as the MRCCs are often called) coordinate rescue operations, mobilize assets and personnel, and make most of the decisions. The staff's proximity and detailed knowledge of local assets and conditions means shorter response times to emergency situations. In addition to the MRCCs, six strategic bases provide additional support. These bases have highly specialized personnel and equipment that can be deployed in particularly challenging situations: rescue divers, underwater remotely operated vehicles (ROVs), side-scan sonars, etc. (SASEMAR n.d.a). Their main mandate is to assist in complex operations such as oil spills.

The sea units are another crucial piece of SASEMAR's work. Today, the fleet is much more diverse than in the early 1990s. In addition to the forty-two rigid-hull inflatable boats that the Red Cross of the Sea still operates along the coast, SASEMAR has four kinds of rescue vessels. The Salvamares are fifteen to twenty-one metres long and can reach speeds of over thirty knots. Rescue crews of three to four people per boat maintain and adapt these small crafts to the specific conditions at each port, adding extra storage for lifebuoys in migration areas, for example. Salvamares are fast and versatile, but they have limited capacity and no berths: even common areas tend to be used to store rescue equipment, leaving little space for rescued people to come aboard. The number of Salvamares (the main type of boat used for rescues) almost tripled between 2008 and 2023.

Next come the Guardamares, the newest addition to the fleet, at around thirty-two metres long and slower than the smaller boats, reaching a maximum speed of thirty knots. These boats have three main advantages compared to the Salvamares. The first advantage is the cabins for the crew, who live on the boat during their month-long shifts. The second is a higher rescue capacity, since they can carry more people. The third is greater autonomy at sea: the Guardamares can travel longer distances without having to refuel.

Tugboats and multipurpose boats are larger and slower and rarely get involved in rescue missions in areas of migration. Some of the tugboats are still the ones inherited from REMOLMAR. They are between two and three times the size of a Salvamar (forty to sixty-three metres long) and are designed for the heavy lifting involved in pulling boats and cleaning up debris at sea. The largest rescue boats SASEMAR operates are multi-purpose vessels, much slower boats up to eighty metres long that tend to work as support platforms for other units at sea. Nowadays, SASEMAR owns the entire fleet, and the agency now directly employs its maritime rescue crews.

Finally, the Spanish rescue system would not be what it is today without its air units, helicopters and small reconnaissance planes. SASEMAR owns eleven helicopters, nine AugustaWestland AW139 and two Airbus Eurocopter EC225 Super Puma, in addition to three medium-range twin-engined planes (all CN-235-300). These units are invaluable for locating vessels at sea at any time of day and night and rapidly extracting those in need of emergency medical attention. From the deck of a boat, visibility across the sea is limited even in the best conditions. Additionally, boats move and drift, and their exact location can change relatively quickly. Helicopters and planes travel faster than the boats, covering more ground in less time. This means that, typically, sea crews depend on the "eyes in the sky" that planes and helicopters give them. Otherwise, a rescue boat must either happen upon a boat in distress by chance, or know exactly where and when it left the coast, its intended route, and the direction and strength of the winds and currents in the area.

SASEMAR's Rescuers at Work

Let's take a typical rescue operation involving one or more boats carrying people on the move. Usually, when there is a distress call, the plane or helicopter will leave the base first. The helicopters deployed along the southern Spanish border in the Western Mediterranean and the Atlantic are the AW139. These helicopters typically carry a four-person crew: the pilot and the co-pilot sit in the cockpit, while the winch (or crane) operator and another rescuer travel in the cabin with the equipment. Unlike most helicopters used by regional rescue services, SASEMAR helicopters have technology that permits them to work during both day and night.

On-board technology also allows control of the craft to be transferred back and forth between the cockpit and the cabin during the course of a rescue. For example, shortly after leaving the base, the pilot will activate the thermal camera, which translates infrared energy (heat) into an image or shape on the screen. The thermal camera is operated by the winch operator, who shares the information with the pilot and co-pilot through a "fifth screen." When they arrive at the site of the emergency, three very powerful lights illuminate the area to evaluate the situation. If there is no exposure (that is, no one's life seems to be in immediate danger), the helicopter transmits the coordinates of the boat in distress back to the regional coordination centre and either remains in the area or (more often) returns to the base, since these crafts have a limited autonomy of about three and a half hours in fair weather. If an immediate intervention is needed, however, because there are people in the water or there is a medical emergency, the pilot transfers the control of the helicopter to the winch operator, who has a better visual and is in charge of hoisting the rescuer and the rescue equipment (typically a basket, stretcher, or harness) to lift the injured person or persons.

Even when a rescue is warranted, there are important differences depending on whether those who intervene are sea or air crews. For example, those working on boats are mandated to remain on board at all times. This means that all these rescuers can do is transfer people between boats or throw lifesavers to people who are in the water, hoping to bring them closer to the boat so they can lift them on to the lower rescue area. Boat crews also use a thick net both as a ladder for people to climb onto the boat and to "catch" the bodies of those who have died at sea. By contrast, helicopter rescuers jump into the water frequently. "The problem," one winch operator said, "is that often the tower operators don't really know what we are going to find, and so we leave the base without a good idea of the equipment we'll need." An experienced helicopter rescuer describes the situation they may encounter when arriving at the site of an emergency in which an overcrowded boat with migrant people is involved:

> Imagine being lowered into the water at night in the middle of a storm, maybe twenty metres plus the three or four between the high and the low of a wave. Once you are in the water, people think you are going to save them, and so they climb onto you. They are frantic, they push you under water. Someone either turns off or grabs your headlight — either way, suddenly you see nothing. You know there is a baby on what is left of the boat, because you have seen it from the helicopter. Your thoughts go instinctively to the children first, you can't stop yourself from wondering if they are ok. You are pretty certain there are people with severe hypothermia and maybe a couple of cardiac arrests. But you are under the water, and at that point you do not even know if you are going to make it. You swim away, you get some air. In the dark, in the waves, against the wind, somehow you manage to calm them down a bit. You put the harness on one that seems to need help and when you begin the ascent back to the helicopter, you may realize that there are two, three, four people grabbing onto the two of you. Eventually they fall. You get back to the helicopter, then back down, and next thing you know you have three [people with] cardiac arrests and a dead child in the cabin, and the red light is blinking because the helicopter is running out of fuel. So, you go back to base and hope that the boats will get there in time.

Of all the SASEMAR crews, helicopter pilots are possibly the most thoroughly trained, the most exposed in a rescue operation, and the most precariously employed. This is because SASEMAR does not hire air crews directly. While the planes and helicopters are owned by the agency, the personnel are subcontracted through a private company chosen through public tender every few years. In 2024, that contract was awarded to Avincis, the largest provider of emergency air services in Europe, for 305 million euros. Like the previous contract holder, Babcock, Avincis has similar contracts with regional rescue services. For this reason, staff in the aerial units often alternate between SASEMAR planes and helicopters and those operated by regional rescue services.

However, two main factors make the national agency the primary provider of emergency services at sea for people on the move. The first one is that regional rescue services generally stay within twelve miles of the shore, that is, in Spain's territorial waters. Only SASEMAR crews have a clear mandate beyond that point. The other one is that SASEMAR helicopters are always fitted with equipment to perform rescues at night at sea. Or, as a pilot working with the Canary Islands regional rescue service explained, "We always see the coast and we work from dawn to dusk. Beyond those parameters, you call SASEMAR."

Rescuers in the Air and Rescuers on the Waves: Two Solitudes

The contractual difference between staff in the aerial units (who are contracted out) and the towers and boats (who are government workers), along with the fact that boat crews work at port and air crews are based at the airport, means that there is very little contact between those working on boats and those in the air units beyond the mandatory trainings. Helicopter crews and boat crews know each other, respect each other, and depend on each other during an operation, but there is a sense of strangeness between the two. It does not help that air rescue crews feel that they are treated as secondary actors within the agency.

Undoubtedly, working conditions contribute to sea crews having a stronger sense of collective: they work together, often far from their families, for weeks at a time. They either lodge in the boat itself during their month-long shifts (in the case of Guardamares and bigger rescue vessels) or are locals who live near the port (in the case of Salvamares). They also have a strong labour union to represent them.

Air crews, on the other hand, are weakly organized, and they are about a fifth the size of sea crews, with roughly one hundred people in 2021. They also do not have a large union to protect their interests. They may have long-term contracts, but these can be cancelled if their direct employer fails to renew their contract with the central government. Because air crews do not have a specific collective agreement, their working conditions may change at any point, including their salary. For example, in 2014, the government awarded the contract for aerial services in maritime rescue to Babcock, an Irish multinational corporation that specializes in the provision of public services. By 2018, helicopter crews employed through Babcock (later bought by Avincis) had a maximum base salary of 1,800 euros per month (CGT 2019). But then, citing low company revenues, in the summer of 2019, the company announced it would reduce workers' wages by up to 30 percent. In an unprecedented move, air crews mobilized to protest. The main union representing sea crews (CGT SASEMAR) supported their direct action, and in the end, the campaign was successful: after a brief strike, the company reversed the salary claw back. However, the mobilization brought to light the somewhat uneasy relationship between the two fleets as well as the differences in their labour organizing strategies.

The division between sea and air crews is imposed by the structure of SASEMAR, but there are also important differences in the institutional culture of both crews. According to some interviewees, air personnel (in particular pilots) are often former members of the armed forces, bound by a different way of seeing the relationship between the work that they do and their employer — which is, ultimately, the government. Some air personnel may see themselves as an elite force with little in common with the sailors. This does not mean they do not support each other; rather, it highlights the fact that they approach their work and collective bargaining from fundamentally differing perspectives.

Among sea and air crews, those who have been with SASEMAR the longest consider that the national agency made great advances in its first decade and a half but has fallen short of its mandate since the early 2000s. Some consider that in some parts of Spain, regional rescue services are surpassing SASEMAR in terms of protecting life at sea. For example, a helicopter rescuer that alternates between SASEMAR and a regional rescue agency in northern Spain reasons that the national agency needs to start providing emergency medical services and not just medical transport. He said that,

Given the kinds of situations we find on a daily basis, we should be considered an emergency medical service, like an ambulance, but the truth is that neither SASEMAR boats nor the helicopters do this. We just move people around. At present we don't function as an emergency medical service, but as a medical transportation service. If any of us has emergency medical training, it is because we have acquired that skill elsewhere.

Rescue and Migration in the Spanish Zone of Responsibility

In addition to the MRCCs, the boats, the planes, and the helicopters, the Guardia Civil's SIVE (Sistema Integrado de Vigilancia Exterior; Integrated System for the Surveillance of the External Border) system is also essential to Spain's rescue infrastructure. The SIVE is an interconnected network of radars, sensors, and other devices used to detect migrants and prevent criminal activities along Spain's external maritime border. This surveillance system was initially implemented in southern Spain at the turn of the twenty-first century and has gradually expanded to other sections of the coast, such as the Canary Islands. Even though Guardia Civil agents often boast about the system, SASEMAR workers are not so sure about its utility. One Guardamar captain felt the SIVE camera's resolution was so poor that it rendered the tool useless. Another, who has been working on a Salvamar for almost a decade, is certain that "the radars only detect boats that are between twelve and fourteen nautical miles from the coast," a somewhat disappointing result for a system with a biannual maintenance cost of over 27 million euros (Dirección General de la Guardia Civil 2022).

Despite the growing involvement of other actors and agencies, SASEMAR remains the cornerstone of a world-class search and rescue operation that integrates and coordinates diverse actors to protect life at sea. Traces of the long road that led to today's well-oiled rescue machine are still visible in the agency's day-to-day operations. As mentioned above, when Spain's mandatory military service was eliminated in 2001 and the subsidiary social service disappeared with it, the rescue mandate of the Red Cross of the Sea and its little semi-rigid rescue boats was significantly diminished. However, Red Cross volunteers and coordinators still collaborate closely with SASEMAR. As long-time rescuer Oriol Estrada explains, "We have been working together for so long, we are friends. At port, we are just a few metres away. The red blankets we carry on the boats, they give them to us. And when we get to port after a rescue, they are there, making sure that people get whatever primary medical care they need." In other words, SASEMAR's work is still embedded in a broader network of rescue actors and organizations that includes the Red Cross, the Navy, the Guardia Civil, Frontex, and the regional rescue services.

THE END OF AN ERA: RESCUE BECOMES ENTANGLED WITH MIGRATION CONTROL

In the last days of 1992, when Borrell walked between the two lions that flank the main entrance of Spain's Parliament building in Madrid after the last session of the year, his main concern was probably to contain the damage that the *Aegean Sea* environmental disaster could have had on the general elections that were just around the corner. He was, after all, the Minister of Public Works and Transportation. His position, and the re-election of his party a few months later, depended on his handling of the crisis. The creation of SASEMAR that day marked an important stage in the development of Spain's maritime sector as the country moved to join the European Union. After decades of isolation and the climbing human and environmental costs of accidents at sea, the moment was long-awaited. There was still a long way to go to catch up with other member states. Internal power struggles, corruption scandals, and the urgent challenges of a quick succession of environmental disasters made SASEMAR what it is today: an anomaly in a European context where maritime rescue responsibilities fall mostly upon the military or militarized agencies. By contrast, for most of its history, SASEMAR was an agency fully independent from the Ministry of the Interior whose public image was primarily focused on the protection of the marine environment.

With democracy and membership in the European Union came prosperity and political stability, both factors that turned Spain into a country of destination for people on the move and a stepping stone for those headed toward other places in Europe. Meanwhile, the agency stayed on course, responding to the increase of sea migration without drastically changing its approach to maritime rescue. This was possible because the SAR Convention gave free rein to individual countries to organize their rescue system as they saw fit and because, for more than twenty-five years, the support of Spain's two main political parties kept SASEMAR safe from partisan attacks. For these reasons, Spain's maritime search and rescue system has remained remarkably ill-suited for law enforcement. Instead, and in contrast to its European neighbours, Spain's approach was perfectly designed to realize the ambitions of the SAR Convention: to protect the marine environment and *all* human life at sea.

This changed as migration became first politicized and then identified as a threat to Spain's national security. SASEMAR's single-minded commitment to providing a universal life-saving system could not survive in a context where sea migration, a small but extremely visible form of arrival for thousands of foreigners, had become a central topic in regional and national elections. The increase in arrivals by sea has changed the work SASEMAR does and the day-to-day activities of rescue crews in the sections of the Spanish zone of responsibility that overlap with routes favoured by people on the move. Most importantly, migration has brought SASEMAR to the fore of public discourse — it's work receives more attention now than ever before from the media and policymakers.

The next two chapters examine how the phenomenon of sea migration has transformed the work of the agency since its creation, sometimes forcing it to take sharp turns. I analyze the circumstances foregrounding the evolution of SASEMAR's role along the external maritime border of Spain and, by extension, of the European Union. Rescuers' work is being scrutinized and criticized; they are being accused of facilitating irregular migration and even benefiting from it. In the Mediterranean and the Atlantic, the Guardia Civil is taking over the coordination of rescue operations involving migrant boats.

Developments in the Western Mediterranean and the Canary Islands highlight the ongoing tension between human safety and national security, which is ostensibly threatened by sea migration. Throughout Europe, we appear to be moving away from a previous approach that offered the pretense of humanitarianism, which some scholars have called "the humanitarian border"[8] and which exposes the fragile balance between the logics of care and control along the external limit of the European Union. Here, agencies like Frontex and national coast guards reclaim and reframe the language of humanitarianism to justify increasingly coercive border policies to "both effectively manage disaster and to secure imminent mobile populations — as potential subjects of harm and potentially harmful" (Pallister-Wilkins 2018, 993). Repression is thus presented as a strategy to dismantle criminal networks that exploit the suffering of people on the move.

The dichotomy between national safety and human security is a false one, and the tightening of borders only exacerbates the vulnerability of those already in distress. Nevertheless, European policymakers have embraced this repressive logic unquestioningly, doubling down on a vision of sea migration as a threat that needs to be contained elsewhere. This has led to the militarization of the sea border and the outsourcing of rescue responsibilities to countries of origin, transit, and destination outside of Europe. This approach forestalls a complex but potentially more fruitful conversation: why do people migrate in the first place? What can be done to address the root causes of their migration, or, at the very least, manage human mobility without turning the borderlands into zones of violence and death? Instead of engaging with these fundamental questions, current policies transform the Mediterranean and the Atlantic into graveyards.

4

The Spectacle of Militarization and Abandonment in the Western Mediterranean

ON FEBRUARY 6, 2014, two hundred young Black men stormed the eastern section of the fence surrounding Ceuta, a Spanish exclave in North Africa (Martínez Escamilla 2020). Just under half of them managed to avoid Moroccan forces deployed along the outside perimeter and reach the coast. The beach here is split in half by two fences separated by a roughly twenty-five metres "no-man's land" that is supposedly Spanish territory, but that has become a legal void. The migrants swam around the first fence, rushed through the gap between the fences, and got into the water to swim around the second fence hoping to set foot on Spanish territory.

The sixteen Guardia Civil agents on site that day had received orders to stop people from entering Spanish territory. They used riot control weapons — fifteen smoke canisters, 145 rubber bullets, and an unknown number of blanks — on the approximately ninety people who were struggling in the water. Panic ensued. Some were wounded or killed by the agents' gunfire, while others drowned after being pulled under by people trying to stay afloat. The events of that day have come to be known as the Tarajal massacre. Of the roughly ninety men who waded into the sea that day, twenty-three were summarily deported back to Morocco and fourteen bodies were recovered. The other fifty-three remain unaccounted for.

Three organizations (CEAR, Coordinadora de Barrios, and Observatori DESC) brought a legal case against the Spanish government in February 2015 (CEAR 2024). In the years since, the case has been closed and reopened several times.

On one of the occasions when it was reopened, in 2018, a Cameroonian man named Hervé, who had survived the massacre, testified in the case. He could not swim, but he had a lifejacket. In his testimony, he recalls: "We were screaming from the water, screaming for help, and when we saw Guardia Civil agents approach us, we thought, 'It's going to be ok, they are coming to rescue us, they will get us out of the water and rescue us.' But then I saw that the agents were hitting those who were nearest to their boat" (Araque Conde 2018).

No charges have been laid yet. A year after Hervé testified, a judge condemned the agents' actions. "While it is true that measures to protect the border are activated during attempts at illegal entry," the judge wrote, "these measures cannot give rise to the assumption, even remotely, that borders or the spaces between them are zones of exception in relation to human rights" (CEAR 2024). She then indicted the sixteen Guardia Civil agents who were present at the border that day arguing, among other things, that they could have helped the people in the water but "had abstained from doing so without cause justifying their omission." The agents positioned at the fence shot at the migrants in the water and continued to do so even when they saw some were drowning. They had the legal obligation to call SASEMAR to prevent drownings, but they chose not to do so. Even though this legal decision was released in 2019, it was never implemented; the case was filed for a third time. A group of pro bono lawyers led by Patricia (Patuca) Fernández swore to exhaust all legal avenues to get a resolution on the case. In February 2025, more than ten years after the massacre, they were still fighting to have the case reopened.

During the commemoration of the events in 2024, at the round table before the march from downtown Ceuta to the beach of Tarajal, Patuca Fernández argued that the cruellest act that day ("Not the gravest: that was the killing") was the disrespect of the bodies of those who died. She recalls that in one of the recordings shared during the trial, an agent from the GEAS (Grupo Especial de Actividades Subacuáticas; elite underwater unit) of the Guardia Civil said to another agent, "There are three bodies floating here." His superior answered, "Let them be." And so, they did.

What prompted the agents to use excessive force against that group of men on February 6, 2014? They certainly had orders to use whatever means necessary to prevent their entry. But even then, why did they refuse to call the rescue services?

The Tarajal massacre was a shifting point in the handling of migration by land and by sea in the Western Mediterranean: the events that day led to the official normalization of "express mass deportations" (known in Spanish as *devoluciones en caliente*) and opened a new era in Hispano-Moroccan relations. In this chapter, I focus on the impact these changes had on maritime search and rescue and on the lives of the people who leave northern Morocco on a flimsy boat, their eyes fixed on the other side of the water.

CEUTA

Ten years after the Tarajal massacre, I am participating in an homage to the victims. A group of human rights defenders have organized a 24-hour blitz of protests to mark the anniversary of the events, some in the gated city of Ceuta. I am part of a group of about thirty people leaving from the city of Granada in southern Spain. I arrive at the meeting point a little before 5:00 a.m. and wait, chatting with four other participants until the bus arrives. The rest of the demonstrators join us over the next half hour and then we leave. It is still dark outside. Three hours later, we pull into Algeciras, the city across the bay from Gibraltar, where we board a ferry with about a hundred people from other Spanish towns and cities. On the ferry, people dance to the music blasting from a boombox someone has brought for the ride: they are playing "Ouvrez les Frontières," the open border anthem by Ivorian reggae singer Tiken Jah Fakoly.

The seas are rough and I spend the two-hour ride on the deck with other activists. The Strait of Gibraltar is only fourteen kilometres wide and, when the weather is clear, looks more like a wide bay than the economic, social, and political chasm between two continents that it has become (Figure 4).

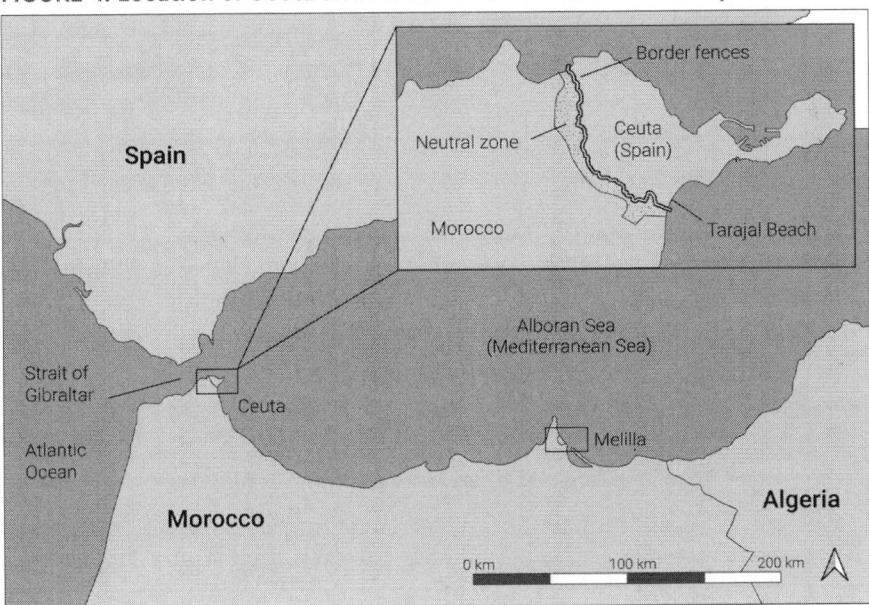

FIGURE 4: Location of Ceuta and Melilla in relation to mainland Spain

The inset map shows the location of the border fences between Ceuta and Morocco that extend into the sea. Created by Elizabeth Rose Hessek and reproduced with permission. Source: Google Earth 7.3 (2023)

In the thick fog, from the ship, I can barely make out Europe on one side, Africa on the other. On a sunny day, one can see the cars travelling on Moroccan roads, the boats coming and going, the seagulls flying back and forth over this narrow strip of blue. But today is not sunny. After two hours of lurching over the choppy waters, drenched from the sea spray, we arrive at the port of Ceuta, a city in North Africa that has been part of Spanish territory since the sixteenth century.

Fresh off the boat and on the way to the meeting point at a local high school, we pass a statue of two Guardia Civil agents wearing old uniforms from Franco's era. The two are on alert: one agent keeps an eye on the mountains, the other on the beach. I learn later that it is one of several military-inspired statues in the city by Spanish sculptor Luis Martín de Vidales Gómez. We also pass by a statue of Hercules — a giant, bearded man pushing two columns apart. One of these columns is said to represent Calpe Mons (Gibraltar), the other Monte Hacho (in Ceuta). According to the myth, Hercules made the Strait as he crashed through the Atlas Mountains (which were not yet a range) on his way to see the Hesperides in their garden. Hercules kept the two continents apart with his superhuman strength.

The statues of the two watchful agents and the colossus embody two aspects of the city's spirit. First, Ceuta feels very much like a city on the defensive. With 3,000 military personnel in a population of less than 83,000 people, the percentage of military workers is three and a half times higher than the national average. This has long been the case, as Ceuta remains a contested territory claimed by Morocco as part of its national domain. The presence of state security serves to reaffirm Spanish sovereignty in the exclave.

Secondly, much like Hercules straining to keep the two continents apart, Ceuta seems to exist as a sentinel of Europeanness south of the Strait of Gibraltar. This is no small feat, given its location in Africa and the fact that between 30 and 40 percent of its population is Arab, Muslim, or both (*Ceuta Actualidad* 2019). The city feels like a militarized stronghold where the essence of two continents, two identities, two religions, and two worldviews have been locked in a centuries-old struggle.

These are big ambitions for a small place at the very edges of Europe. In terms of size, Ceuta is relatively small: only a third of the size of the island of Manhattan. Small and peripheral, perhaps, but for centuries a thorn in the side of Hispano-Moroccan relations. The city is one of the Spanish "cities, islands, and rocks" (to use official language) claimed by Morocco in North

Africa. They are tangible traces of Spain's colonial history in the region. Morocco aims to eventually recover these territories and fulfill what the Kingdom considers the country's "territorial integrity." Ceuta and Melilla (the other exclave of Spanish citizens in North Africa, some four hundred kilometres east of Ceuta by road) are the only European territories with a land border in Africa. This makes these two cities a magnet for migrants wishing to travel north. With time, the cities' borders have become more and more fortified to stop and contain them. The fences are visible from many parts of the cities. They crawl over the mountains and jut out a few metres into the water: a tantalizingly short distance for people on the move waiting to reach European territory from Morocco.

Swimming around the fences is not generally considered a route in its own right but perhaps it should be. The day before the tenth anniversary march that I attended, the Guardia Civil stopped two people who were trying to swim around the fence. Fewer than twenty-four hours after our group left Ceuta, three others were stopped and sent back to Morocco. People use anything from pool toys (which can easily be pushed away by the wind) to empty bottles of water tied around the body as a sort of improvised floating device to scuba gear to swim or dive around the fences.

Even though the distance is short, swimming around the fences can be very dangerous. The currents are strong and the military is ever present on both sides, which means people are more likely to get caught. Tarajal beach is the site of frequent summary deportations where migrants are sent back to Morocco by the Guardia Civil, who simply open a gate in the fence and push people through without bothering to determine if they belong to a vulnerable group such as unaccompanied minors or asylum seekers. These are known as *devoluciones en caliente*: hot expulsions, or pushbacks.

Following the Tarajal massacre, the Spanish government tried to legislate mass expulsions into existence. At first, it seemed clear that these expulsions were contrary to Spain's legal obligations. However, in 2020, the European Court of Human Rights (ECHR) changed the tide of the conversation by siding with the Spanish government (Ayuso and Brunet 2020). Ruling on a separate event in which a group of migrants was summarily deported from Melilla to Morocco, the ECHR's decision blamed migrants for putting themselves in a position of illegality through their behaviour. According to this ruling, asylum seekers should have followed proper procedures to apply for international protection, and thus their mass expulsion was justified.

Spanish and European NGOs bitterly criticized this decision, which set the stage for mass expulsions at land borders and at sea. They argued that Spanish policy effectively barred people from seeking refugee protection from outside the national territory, leaving them with no legal avenue to appeal to. As a result, crossing the border illegally was the only way they could claim asylum.

The case of Basir, a Sudanese refugee who had been on the run since he was a minor, demonstrated this point (Martín 2024a). Basir, a Christian, had left his home country after his father and other members of his family were killed for their religious beliefs. He lived in Egypt, Libya, and Algeria before he reached Morocco and set his sights on Melilla. He tried, once, to reach the gated city, and was pushed back to Morocco in 2022 during the "Melilla massacre," where at least twenty-three migrants died as a result of police brutality at one of the checkpoints in the city's fence (Sapoch et al. 2022). After Basir's summary deportation, Arsenio G. Cores, a volunteer lawyer with the human rights group DEMOS, took on his case. He wanted to demonstrate that Spanish policy was designed to keep everyone out, even those with a clear need for international protection who followed regulations scrupulously. The main problem, he argued, was that asylum seekers had to enter Spanish territory to be able to make their claim. Spain could choose to accept such claims in its embassies and consulates in Morocco but generally refused to do so. Basir's case was clear-cut: Sudanese nationals' asylum claims are accepted almost universally in Spain. And yet the government refused to respond to his demands.

In March 2024, more than a year after forcing the Spanish Embassy in Rabat to accept his claim but having received no answer, Basir's lawyer succeeded in having Spain's Supreme Court demand that the government allow the young man to move to Spanish territory. Two months passed without receiving an answer. Not until May 2024—a decade after running away from Sudan and eighteen months after making his claim at the Spanish Embassy — was Basir given the green light to enter Spanish territory (Martín 2024b). If it was so hard for Basir (a person in such clear need of international protection, who had the support of an entire legal team free of charge, and whose plight had received so much media attention) to obtain refugee status, was it fair to blame people for attempting to reach Spanish territory illegally to make their claim, as the ECHR had done in 2020?

Not all people migrating by sea are asylum seekers, but some are, and they get on a boat because they see no other way to reach the safety Europe offers.

As I march toward the sea in stride with the other protesters determined to pay homage to those victimized and killed during the Tarajal massacre, I reflect on how the recent history of maritime rescue in the Mediterranean is woven into the ECHR's decisions and other policies and regulations meant to keep migrants at bay. Standing there with the other protesters, the connection between the land border and the sea border is clear and jarring. Both at land and at sea, border control and rescue fuse through two crucial and interconnected strategies. The first strategy is externalization, or the delegation of maritime rescue responsibilities to Morocco. The second is militarization, or the victory of militarized logics of control over the moral and legal obligation to protect human life at sea.

BORDER CROSSINGS AND CO-OPERATION IN THE WESTERN MEDITERRANEAN

Morocco is a stepping stone in the trajectory of Europe-bound people from Africa, and also a key partner for Europe in its attempts to stop those people. As such, EU policymakers consider it a country of both transit and origin of migration by land and by sea. What often gets lost in this Eurocentric account is that, since Morocco is relatively wealthier and offers more job opportunities than its neighbours, the country is also a destination of choice for many people on the move. Still, its role in the European border regime is undeniable, but not new. Migrant people started leaving Moroccan shores bound for Europe in the late 1980s — timidly at first, and more decidedly since the early 2000s. As Spain became more integrated into the European Union and its economy improved, the social, political, and economic rift between the two countries and the two continents grew. Spain became a more attractive destination both as a stepping stone in journeys to other European countries and as a place to settle.

From a European vantage point, Morocco falls into the same category as Algeria, whose beaches are also an important space of transit on the trajectory of sea migrants headed toward the Iberian Peninsula and the Balearic Islands. From west to east, there are three main "routes" in the Western Mediterranean: the Strait of Gibraltar, the Alboran Sea, and the Algerian route. To seal these sections of the maritime border, Spain and the European Union have sought co-operation with these two countries, with differing results.

NGO workers in Morocco and Spain often define Algeria as "one big black box." When it comes to migration, we do not know what happens there

— how many people leave, what the government does to stop them (or not), or to save them (or not) when their boats run into difficulty in the Algerian zone of responsibility. On the other hand, co-operation between Spain and Morocco dates to the early 1990s. For decades, Morocco has been taking back both its own nationals and other African migrants — those deported at the land border, rescued at sea, or captured in raids. Often, authorities take the latter to the heavily militarized desert area near its border with Algeria (Salmi 2014). There is evidence of the Algerian army firing shots warning people on the move to return to Morocco, and Moroccan forces doing the same to force them back to Algeria. Some people spend weeks trapped in this perverse ping pong game in this border area, some of them eventually perishing from hunger and thirst on the sand.

Through these actions, the externalization of European anti-immigration policies and Morocco's own form of anti-Black racism intersect perversely.[9] Put differently, the European Union's focus on stopping migration legitimates the targeting of an already vulnerable population. Black Africans in Morocco are often seen and treated by locals and state authorities alike as undocumented people in transit, regardless of their actual migration status. A shocking example of this indiscriminate targeting was the experience of Timothy Hucks, an African American US citizen who was working as an English teacher in Rabat in 2020 (Martín, Hierro, and Stacey 2024). One night, Hucks left his apartment with just enough money to buy a bottle of wine at a corner store nearby. Just a few metres from his building, he was stopped by Moroccan authorities, who assumed he was a migrant headed for Europe simply because he was Black. Despite his insistence that he was a US citizen working legally in the country and his pleas to be allowed to retrieve his documentation and cellphone from his apartment, Hucks was arrested, detained, and put in a van with other Black men. They were taken to Beni Melal, a city three hundred kilometres from Rabat, and left to fend for themselves. Eventually, Hucks was able to reach Rabat and return to the United States.

Hucks was far from the only Black person treated this way. Black Africans are an easy target for Moroccan authorities. Similar forced displacements, in particular, have been thoroughly documented. Often, the means used in these operations are purchased with European funds or directly donated by EU member states (Bulman et al. 2024). These forced displacements keep people on the move in a situation of extreme vulnerability and allow the Moroccan government to use migration control as leverage in negotiations with European governments.

Whereas Algeria is an unreliable partner for Spain and the European Union, Morocco has proven a willing, if demanding, ally along the land and sea borders. This is all the more remarkable given the long-standing territorial disputes between the two countries over the "cities, islands, and rocks" that remain under Spanish control in North Africa, on the one hand, and the administrative status of the Western Sahara, on the other. These disputes have a direct impact on migration and border governance as well as on co-operation on maritime rescue. The foundation for all agreements between the two countries is the long-standing yet sometimes volatile partnership along the land border — that is, along the fences of Ceuta and Melilla.[10]

Like Ceuta, Melilla is also relatively small. It counts fewer than 100,000 registered inhabitants and occupies an area about the size of London Heathrow Airport. Both cities are surrounded by the sea on one side and a fence separating them from Moroccan territory on the other. The fences are relatively new, but their histories are long. The first barrier the Spanish government built goes back to 1971; it was a one and a half-metre tall vehicle fence around Ceuta, meant to stop the spread of cholera from Morocco. Soon after Spain joined the Schengen area that allowed for the free movement of people inside the European Union in 1995, the government built the first chain-link fence.

The period between 2006 and 2017 saw the biggest investment of Spanish and European funds in the construction and maintenance of the fences. Between 2006 and 2007, Spain added a second fence, a sort of "razor wire trap" between the two fences, and new surveillance technology. Following criticisms, in 2019 the Spanish government removed the razor wire, only for Morocco to install it on top of its fence shortly afterward. A few months later, Spain replaced some sections of the fence with a border wall similar to some of the designs considered by Donald Trump along the southern border of the United States in 2017. Despite the scaling up of the fences and other surveillance technology, Spain's far right political party has been persistent in its demand that the wall replace the remaining fences along the entire perimeter of both exclaves (Carvajal 2019).

This quick overview of almost six decades of walls and fences separating Spain and Morocco highlights the fact that the two countries have collaborated to control movement on land for more than half a century. Besides the fences and the beaches, which Moroccan agents monitor to prevent departures, co-operation also focuses on repatriations — both resulting from pushbacks at the border and from formal deportations from

Spanish territory. It is often forgotten that the two countries signed the first repatriation agreement between an EU member state and a Third Country in 1992; this agreement has been modified and updated multiple times since. Yet, collaboration between the two countries on the waters between them, east and west of the Strait of Gibraltar, only began in earnest in 2018. From the outset, this collaboration at sea had an immediate impact on maritime rescue, eventually extending its influence to rescues in the Atlantic section of Spain's zone of responsibility.

The Strait of Gibraltar

The shortest crossing between Europe and Africa by sea is the Strait of Gibraltar. The distance is short, but currents are strong, and the crossing is closely monitored. Migrant boats with different degrees of floatability also contend with one of the densest concentrations of marine traffic in the world, which includes enormous tankers and container ships. Next to these giant vessels, migrant boats look like tiny pins floating in the sea.

SASEMAR has the reins of the Maritime Traffic Separation System in the Strait of Gibraltar. This system has a mandate similar to traffic control at airports: its role is to coordinate the trajectory of boats in the Strait of Gibraltar to prevent accidents. The task is crucial. About 10 percent of all international maritime traffic in the world passes through this fourteen-kilometre-wide strait (Salama 2020), with 110,000 boats per year, or over 270 per day on average, one every five minutes (Endrina et al. 2018; South Pacific Logistics 2024).

Container ships and oil tankers that are between three and four hundred metres long coexist with industrial and artisanal fishing boats of various sizes and tonnages as well as recreational boats such as luxury yachts, sail boats, and catamarans, ro-ro ferries for passengers and vehicles, and military vessels of various kinds. Unaccounted for in these statistics are military boats that do not have the obligation to declare their presence in the waters, as well as migrant boats and speed boats belonging to drug trafficking *narcos* who are trying to pass, quite literally, under the radar. There are also windsurfers, kite surfers, scuba divers, tourists and children on inflatable toys, and yearly competitions of any given sea sport. The place is teeming and the chances of something going wrong are high.

Some of this activity is new, but there is also a long history of human mobility written on these waters. The Strait is the original crossing route from North Africa to Europe; the movement of populations between North

Africa and southern Spain goes back to the first settlements in the region. Even before the rise in sea migration in the early 1990s, people arrived regularly by boat from Morocco, though in small numbers. Spain was poor, had not yet joined the European Union, and was fresh from a forty-year-long military dictatorship. It simply was not an attractive destination for people looking to improve their lives. But as the country joined the European club, things shifted. A very significant change was the creation of the legal figure of the immigrant, which appeared for the first time in the country's legislation in 1985. Up until that point, from a purely legal perspective there were only "foreigners" or "tourists" on the one hand, and "Spaniards" on the other.

Having an immigration law was a requirement to join the European Communities (an early iteration of the European Union). But with a foreign population of less than 2 percent and zero public conflict on the issue, Spain's passing of one of the strictest immigration laws in Europe at the time was a political choice (Agrela Romero and Gil Araújo 2005). Another important transformation was the injection of European structural funds into the Spanish economy and the country's entrance into the common European Schengen area, which brought an end to internal border checks. Borders between Spain and other countries within the European Union virtually disappeared. Economic growth, political stability, and free intra-European Union movement made Spain an attractive destination for international migrants. The shift from a country of out-migration to in-migration happened very rapidly. In some cases, these migrants only passed through Spain while on their way to other European destinations. Although still only fourteen kilometres wide, the social, political, and economic gap between the countries on either side of the Strait of Gibraltar grew exponentially in the years following the end of Franco's dictatorship.

It was at this time, in the late 1980s and early 1990s, as international migration entered the political debate, that images of sea migrants arriving in southern Spain began to emerge. The first published picture of a shipwrecked *patera* (the kind of boat that migrants coming from Morocco sometimes use to reach the Spanish coast) was published in the Spanish media in late 1988. The black and white image was taken by local journalist Ildefonso Sena near Tarifa on a windy winter morning. It showed a man lying on the beach with the *patera* in the background among the waves.

The image shocked Spain. In an interview thirty years later, Sena talked at length about what had happened that day (Ramajo 2018). After being dispatched by a local newspaper to find out why the Guardia Civil was at the beach, he unexpectedly became the translator, acting for both the agents and the survivors. He learned that the migrants had left Tangier at midnight. It was a pitch-dark, moonless night. Halfway through the Strait, the wind picked up: "They got scared and wanted to jump into the water, thinking they were a few metres from the shore, thinking they could already walk to the beach. But the boat capsized, and all twenty-four fell into the water. They heard cries for help in the darkness of the night." Of the eighteen missing, nine bodies turned up in the following days. "The Strait looks very small on a map," added Sena, "but it is not that small, and it is very dangerous depending on the winds."

Shaken by this experience, Sena would spend the next few years trying to understand who these people were. He learned that Moroccan men decided to get on *pateras* to reach their own version of the "European Dream"—one they could almost touch with the tips of their fingers in the stories they heard when their compatriots returned from Europe for summer vacation. "People at that time thought that Europe was paradise," he said. "Not Spain: Spain was just a transit country. Almost all those who crossed had friends or relatives in France, Germany, Italy, or other countries." Back then, the journey was organized rather informally, mainly by fishermen. The boats arrived undetected: "Spain and Europe did not pay attention to what was going on in the Strait of Gibraltar. But from that day on, everything changed" (Ramajo 2018). Indeed, starting in the mid-1990s, *pateras* became a common occurrence on the beaches of Andalusia.

Oriol Estrada, a rescuer who had been working for SASEMAR since its creation in 1993 and was posted in southern Spain in 1996, agreed: "The first migrant boats I saw, I saw them in '96, '97. They were wooden boats and they carried Moroccan citizens, and whenever one came, we were like, 'What the heck? A boat with Moroccans just arrived?! What are they even doing here?' But it just grew from there," he told me.

Today, Moroccan migrants still figure prominently in the Strait, although people from all over Africa use this route. On occasion, when wars have erupted elsewhere, there has been a surge of people coming from Pakistan, Afghanistan, Syria, and even farther beyond. Geographic proximity and overlapping responsibilities in the area mean that rescue duties along the Strait are somewhat blurry. Historically, SASEMAR has tended to act throughout the area, from the port of Ceuta through the shared responsibility zone with Morocco and across to Gibraltar itself (which, it should be noted, is British territory).

The boats these migrants use to cross the Strait can be anything from small, low wooden or fibreglass boats with a typically low horsepower engine (the original *pateras*) to pedal boats and other floating devices. For example, the SeaHawk4, an inflatable raft with maximum capacity for four people that costs two hundred euros online, is quite common among people on the move trying to cross the Strait of Gibraltar. According to José Maraver (Operations Director for SASEMAR in Tarifa), smugglers use this raft because it is cheaper and smaller, thus more difficult to detect by the radars installed in the area. However, these inflatable toys are wholly inadequate for crossing the Strait, and migrants often lose or break the flimsy paddles early in their journey (Camacho 2013).

Neither these nor the majority of other inflatable devices used by people are suitable for navigating the treacherous waters of the Strait of Gibraltar. Why do people use them, then? Perhaps the short distance offers a false sense of security. Others try to cross the Strait as stowaways in the many boats that cross it daily, hiding among circus equipment, inside car bumpers or seats, or even inside bus engines. These people are usually (but not always) detected by the increasingly sophisticated technology used at the border designed specifically to deter this kind of movement across the Strait.

Those risking the journey on boats must deal with the treacherous currents and heavy maritime traffic and avoid surveillance by Moroccan and Spanish security forces, and, increasingly, by drones deployed by Frontex. The surveillance infrastructure is thorough. This is the original location for the SIVE (Sistema Integrado de Vigilancia Exterior; Integrated System for the Surveillance of the External Border), managed by the Guardia Civil: originally deployed in the Strait in 2001 to deter and catch *narco* boats, this system also detects other boats, including migrant boats, and is at the origin of the European Border Surveillance System (the EUROSUR), established in 2013. Despite all these obstacles — currents, traffic, surveillance — the Strait remains active as a migration route and, as we see later, rescue operations are frequent.

The Alboran Sea

A bit farther to the east is the Alboran Sea, the westernmost portion of the Mediterranean Sea. Crossing this sea involves a longer trip (about 180 kilometres, depending on the points of departure and arrival). People on the move started using this route when the waters of the Strait became more heavily surveilled with the deployment of more Guardia Civil agents and the

SIVE at the turn of the twenty-first century. The boats in the Alboran Sea are, by necessity, more seaworthy than many of those found in the Strait. No pool toys, homemade floating devices, or diving gear would be sufficient to travel such a distance, even though currents here are weaker, and the space is generally less crowded than in the Strait of Gibraltar.

There are other advantages to this route. A much larger surface means that states (primarily Spain) have a harder time closely monitoring this zone. The oil tankers and container ships that are on the way to the Atlantic are more spread out and easier to avoid. Also, the Island of Alboran is approximately halfway between Morocco and Spain, offering relative safety to precarious boats in the vicinity.

Moroccans and citizens of other African countries use this route, although there is a division in terms of the types of vessels they use and the conditions of the journey. According to people on the move and rescuers, the trip is typically organized by Moroccan smugglers who reserve the best, least crowded boats for people of their own nationalities. On the other hand, Black people are often put in more crowded boats with worse floatability and older engines. This, of course, means that Black people on the move are more likely to run into difficulty or lose their lives at sea. Still, in 2023 this was the least deadly of the three Western Mediterranean "routes." According to Caminando Fronteras (2023), thirty people died or disappeared in this area, while 147 were lost in the Strait of Gibraltar and 434 along the Algerian route. These are not official figures, but they give us a sense of how the routes may compare in terms of the relative danger they pose to human life.

The number of people crossing the Alboran Sea by boat to reach Spain has fluctuated over time. The year 2018 saw the highest number of those who took this route. Not only were there more boats, but the boats were more crowded — there were more people to rescue in each operation. This is a key difference in the Strait route, and one that has important implications for organizing rescue operations, for it implies the possibility of a mass rescue. What this means in practice is unclear, as there is no official number above which a rescue operation is defined as a "mass rescue." The International Maritime Organization simply states that these are operations that surpass the rescue capacity of the agencies involved. As boats became more crowded in the Alboran (particularly among boats carrying Black migrants), SASEMAR's capacity to adequately respond to a capsized boat diminished. Manuel Capa, who has worked as a sea rescuer in several of

SASEMAR's rescue boats since 2012, remembers seeing boats carrying sixty, even eighty people. These numbers were frequent in the Canary Islands, but not in the Alboran Sea.

Crowded migrant boats also meant that rescue boats themselves were becoming dangerously crowded. Capa — who is also a spokesperson for the main union representing rescuers deployed at sea — estimates that the maximum carrying capacity for the agency's rescue boats may be around thirty people for the Salvamares and one hundred for the Guardamares. Higher numbers compromise the security of both the people being rescued and rescue crews during mild to severe weather events. Nevertheless, with increasing frequency SASEMAR captains were fitting up to 170 migrants in the smaller boats, and close to three hundred in the larger boats, putting both the stability of the rescue boats and the safety of everyone on board at risk.

The Algerian Route

The third route is the newest route in the Western Mediterranean, but also the deadliest as of 2024. Navigating from Morocco or Algeria to the Levante region or the Balearic Islands is a much longer journey (roughly 850 kilometres from Algiers to València). Broadly speaking, the Spanish Levante begins east of Cabo de Gata, a cape in eastern Andalusia, and ends around the Balearic Islands. The boats tend to leave mainly from beaches near the city of Oran in eastern Algeria. Algerian nationals are the main group using these routes, although this is changing: in recent years, Moroccan nationals have also been using this route to avoid the heavily monitored beaches of their own country.

Another recent development in sea migration practices in this area is the branching out of drug dealers into migrant smuggling. *Narcolanchas* are rigid-hull inflatable boats fitted with two to four powerful outboard motors, which tend to be priced at around 25,000 euros each. These *narcolanchas* can reach speeds of over one hundred kilometres per hour, or fifty-four knots. These boats typically carry marine radars (Garmin GMR 18 or similar) that cost up to 2,000 euros. These radars are used to detect other traffic in the area. One would imagine this helps them avoid crashing into other boats when they are cruising at high speeds in different kinds of weather and light conditions, but also (and crucially) it helps them stay clear of patrol boats in the area.

The rigid-hull inflatable boats make quick trips to a larger vessel that remains stationary somewhere in the middle of the sea. The larger boat functions as a sort of temporary storage spot — it receives drugs from smaller rigid-hull inflatable boats coming from Morocco or Algeria, and passes them on to other, similar boats delivering them to southern Spain. The business is dangerous but lucrative. Speed boats can do the round trip and transport large amounts of drugs and other illicit goods to mainland Spain in three to six hours.

In the past, these *narcolanchas* were concentrated within the Strait of Gibraltar. However, the deployment of special operations to crack down on criminal networks — who were, in this area, primarily focused on hashish traffic — led to the spread of the business. Today, *narcolanchas* are present everywhere along the southern Spanish shore; in fact, the Guardia Civil and the Policia Nacional have been playing a game of whack-a-mole with the dealers for decades. Their presence, as mentioned earlier, was the main reason for the launching of the first iteration of the SIVE in 2001. Along with illegal border crossings, drug dealing was the cause of a major internal restructuring of the Guardia Civil in 2004 that made it possible for the force to tackle its growing responsibilities at sea (Gabella Maroto 2004).

Until recently, hashish dealers tried to keep a low profile, but they have grown increasingly brazen. Some have even become TikTok influencers, posting videos of themselves during their sea crossings. They appear unfazed by state security forces, sometimes even being defiant and openly aggressive toward them. For instance, one night in February 2024, four *narcolanchas* rammed into two much smaller and less powerful Guardia Civil zodiacs near the port of Barbate, not far from Gibraltar. After toying with and intimidating the agents for some time, the traffickers, either intentionally or by accident, ran over one of the government zodiacs and killed two agents (López-Fonseca and Viúdez 2024). Similar incidents have become more frequent in recent years.

The presence of these criminal actors in the area interferes with sea migration and rescue for several reasons. First, it puts rescuers and migrants in harm's way. More than once, the SIVE radars have detected an unidentified object in the water, but to determine exactly what it was, they had to send someone to the site. Rescuers are not part of the state's security forces; they are not armed, and do not want to be armed. There have been close encounters with *narco* boats, and in some cases, rescuers have requested that Guardia Civil agents accompany them on board for their own protection.

Second, drug dealers have branched out into migrant smuggling. Realizing that tighter controls also mean a larger profit margin in the smuggling business (since they can charge more for moving people across a heavily guarded border), dealers are now picking up both people and drugs along the route. The *narcolanchas* have become *narcotaxis*, transporting both types of merchandise. Their engines, much more powerful than those used by Guardia Civil boats, make *narcolanchas* hard to detect and (especially) to intercept. The *narcotaxi* trend picked up in 2023, when almost two hundred such boats were detected along the southern shores of Spain (Martín and Cañas 2023).

Reports and videos emerged of smugglers using violence to force migrants (who had paid hundreds of euros and in some cases could not swim) off the boats, metres from the coast. At least five people drowned this way in the Strait and in the Levante region of Spain in 2023 alone, with SASEMAR unable to get to the sites fast enough. Similar to the attack on the Guardia Civil boats near Barbate in 2024, incidents involving *narcolanchas* require an urgency of response that SASEMAR is unable to offer. As the Algerian route has become more popular, and with the near total absence of collaboration on the part of the Algerian government, rescue operations tend to crowd very close to the beaches of southern Spain, while nobody really knows how many have drowned along the way or entered Spanish territory undetected.

A TURNING POINT IN THE MILITARIZATION OF MARITIME RESCUE IN THE WESTERN MEDITERRANEAN

Like union representatives Oriol Estrada, Manuel Capa, and Ismael Furió, many other rescuers sharpened their professional teeth in the context of a sea teeming with all kinds of activities, boats, and people. One day, for example, they would leave port only to find a windsurfer who had been taken by the wind; the next, they would assist a fishing boat with its hull pierced by a rock hidden under water; another night, they might find themselves facing a fast boat with armed criminals. Time went by, and more and more of the emergency calls they answered involved dangerously crowded boats carrying people on the move. As the reality of their job evolved, they went from carrying out their work in relative obscurity to having cameras and microphones waiting for them at port. Their comings and goings even became the subject of heated debates in the seats of regional governments and in Madrid.

At first, these debates in the Spanish Parliament had little impact on rescue operations. Migration numbers soared and the routes multiplied. So did Spain's rescue capacity, but there seemed to be a disconnect between these two developments. One could, in fact, be forgiven for thinking that not much changed in terms of how maritime rescue was done in the twenty years that passed between the day journalist Ildefonso Sena took the picture of the migrant on the beach and the year 2018. Also, as noted earlier, the sea border remained stubbornly out of the negotiations between Spain and its closest neighbour and ally, Morocco. For almost three decades, co-operation between the two countries on matters related to migration stood firmly on the shore and along the fences separating them — always on land. Meanwhile, at sea, the gap between the rescue capacities of the two countries widened.

Morocco did have its own national maritime rescue system, at least on paper. In 2002, the Moroccan government created a National Commission for the Coordination of Search and Rescue at Sea and established that all rescue operations should be accounted for in an annual report. The National Rescue Plan included the creation of a National Coordination Centre (NRCC) and four regional rescue coordination centres (MRCC) supported by eight subcentres and six intervention units. It also included a strategy for the smooth communication between the different rescue actors, which included the Ministry of Fisheries (in charge of the newly minted coordination system and responsible for handling communication with foreign governments and rescue actors) and the Royal Marine (who owned the rescue assets and managed the operations). Twelve years later, in 2014, Morocco had seventeen rescue boats and ten lifeboats it could deploy for emergencies near its coastline. The Royal Marine's patrol boats, the Air Forces' planes and helicopters, and the Gendarmerie's and Civil Protection services' resources and assets were also available as needed. Although the plan looked good on paper, most of it never materialized. Only one annual report was published in the period between 2002 and 2024 (Département de la Pêche Maritime 2010). Furthermore, these resources were very rarely used for the rescue of people on the move.

Given the state of the Moroccan maritime rescue system, and in full compliance with the SAR Convention, it became customary for Spanish rescue boats to act in the shared responsibility zone and even in Morocco's exclusive zone of responsibility. A typical operation would be triggered when a relative or someone physically on a boat in distress called either the emergency services, Caminando Fronteras, or AlarmPhone. Either way, the call would eventually wind up with emergency services, which, in turn, would call the coordination centre who would launch an operation. When the tower had an approximate location for the boat in distress, they would send out the helicopter and the rescue boat at the same time. That way, by the time the boat was in the vicinity, the helicopter had already given them an exact location. This strategy reduced the response time significantly, sometimes by hours. When the boat was in the Spanish or shared zone of responsibility, there were no additional steps. When it was in the Moroccan exclusive zone of responsibility, the coordinator would contact its counterpart in Morocco to ask for authorization to act. But this was a mere formality. Morocco routinely allowed entry to SASEMAR boats.

As a result, by 2018, more than two thirds of SASEMAR rescue operations took place in the shared and Moroccan zones of responsibility (Galán Caballero, Grasso, and Catalán 2019). That year, almost 50,000 people tried to cross the Alboran Sea by boat, a 167 percent increase from 2017. Additionally, this number only counted those who were apprehended by the authorities. Those who succeeded in reaching Spain undetected and many of the people who drowned at sea were not part of the official count. With the numbers soaring, negotiations between Spain and Morocco began to turn to the sea.

SASEMAR carried out the bulk of all rescue operations, which worked just fine for Morocco, who had no interest in or motivation to develop its own rescue capacity to address emergencies involving migrant boats. However, constant interventions in the Moroccan zone of responsibility to save the lives of people who were then taken to Spanish ports (again, in full compliance with the SAR Convention) were becoming expensive — both financially and politically — for the Spanish government. To contain the damage caused by the instrumentalization of sea migration by the far right, in the last months of 2018, the government imposed a gag order on SASEMAR workers: if they wanted to speak to the media or to researchers, they would have to obtain an authorization from the agency. SASEMAR also stopped publishing updates on rescue operations involving people on the move in their social media accounts. Those in charge were perhaps hoping the media attention would die away.

If that was their goal, they failed. Much like in other EU countries (notably Italy), the far right was quick to accuse SASEMAR of facilitating illegal entry into the country. In March that year, the extreme right party Vox put forward a non-legislative proposal in the Andalusian Parliament where they blamed the increasing number of migrants in the Western Mediterranean on the presence of rescue boats at sea (Parlamento de Andalucía 2019). In their view, the presence of rescue assets made migrants feel safer, encouraging dangerous journeys by sea — a point disproven time and again by research (Martínez Escamilla 2019). But Vox went even further. In their inflammatory intervention, they compared SASEMAR rescue fleets to "taxis with agreed-upon pickup points" and accused them of "inappropriate behaviour" (supposedly, charging migrants to transport them to Spanish ports). This was the first time that the rescue agency was openly attacked by politicians.

Enric Tarrida, one of the original crew of the rescue fleet and former union representative for the section of the main union representing boat crews (CGT SASEMAR), sat in the balcony of the Parliament listening to the debate. He could hardly believe his ears. Vox's discourse was a carbon copy of Salvini's a little more than a year earlier, when he accused rescue NGOs acting in the Central Mediterranean as "taxis" and charging migrants.

The Andalusian Parliament was quick to reject Vox's motion, but the damage was already done. In the arm-wrestle between border control logics and rescue practices, something had to give. By the time Enric left the Parliament and headed to a nearby coffee shop to digest the news, the job of the rescue fleet had already taken a turn. Their actions were scrutinized, their motives questioned. The debate that followed shed light on the paradoxes plaguing the work (and existence) of SASEMAR in the context of a European Union where rescue services were increasingly used to detect, repel, and even deport people on the move who were using the Mediterranean to reach Europe.

A few months later, at the fisherman's bar in the port of Almería where crews sat to chat between operations, a group of rescuers discussed possible long-term scenarios for SASEMAR, from the plausible to the far-fetched. For how long would the rescue fleet be allowed to consider the SAR Convention as their primary reference in their daily work? Would they be forced to carry weapons, to ask wreckage victims for their passports before rescuing them, to act as gods among the waves?

Sarcastic comments could barely hide their incredulity at being caught in this net of political machinations. "I am taking bets!" said one of the rescuers. "Who thinks they will paint our orange boats green like the Guardia Civil's, and who thinks they will end up blue, like Frontex's?" The joke hit too close to home. Around the table, the men looked at their hands, uncomfortably. Most of them were on temporary contracts and had families to take care of. If it came down to them becoming border guards, did they really have a choice?

Back in Madrid, the government was also sitting on hot coals. With the closely called general elections just a few months away, decision-makers had to act swiftly and decisively to put this new "migration crisis" behind them before it was too late. Sea migration had been on the table for decades by then. Placing the presence of SASEMAR and, more generally, maritime rescue on the negotiating table, though, was something new. The rescue crews were at a loss. "We were the jewel in the crown in the 1990s!" said Furió, then General Secretary of the main labour union representing the sea crews. "We saved the Socialists, we saved the Conservatives, with the *Prestige*, with other accidents. For the longest time nobody would dare criticize SASEMAR. But the winds have turned."

So they had. In 2018 and 2019, the Socialist government engaged in a frenzy of policy changes and diplomatic activity that would alter how maritime rescues have been done in the area ever since. Two interconnected developments marked the shift in maritime rescue wherever migrant boats were involved. On the one hand, the creation of a militarized authority for the coordination of rescue operations involving migrants. On the other, the transfer of rescue responsibilities to Morocco.

DOING AWAY WITH UNIVERSAL RESCUE: THE BIRTH OF A TWO-TIER SYSTEM

On August 3, 2018, the Spanish government announced the creation of the CCOE (Centro de Coordinación de Operaciones de Emergencia; Emergency Operations Coordination Centre). In charge of this coordination centre would be a senior member of the Guardia Civil, who would hold the title of MUO (Mando Único Operativo; Single Operative Command). This person, through the resources the CCOE made available, would coordinate interventions involving migrant boats in the Strait of Gibraltar and the Alboran Sea and "optimize the [use of] resources destined for border control and the attention of migrant persons in the area" (La Moncloa 2018). At sea, the CCOE brought together the Armed Forces, Customs, Frontex, the National Intelligence Service, the Marine Captaincies, and SASEMAR. The CCOE would gather information on departures, communicate with foreign governments, and take control of rescue operations involving migrants. Once at port, the MUO's job was to create a space where all the ministries and actors involved in the detection, reception, and processing of migrant people could come together. Upon arrival, the MUO and the CCOE would work with the Red Cross and national, regional, and local actors involved in the provision of services migrants may require, such as Youth Protection Services.

The CCOE became operational seven months later. It was housed in a nondescript building a few hundred metres from the ferry terminal in the port of Málaga, halfway between the Strait of Gibraltar and the eastern limit of the Alboran Sea, where the bulk of migrant rescues were concentrated at the time (Sánchez 2019). Its launch transformed rescuers' daily work in several ways. Suddenly, all rescue operations involving migrants were put under military command, whereas all other emergencies remained within the hands of SASEMAR's nonmilitarized structure. The first change then was that suddenly there was a two-tier national rescue system where there used to be one. This sorting of emergency cases at sea depending on whose life is at risk is contrary to the universal, nondiscriminatory spirit of the SAR Convention.

The creation of the military command also impacted the way operations were carried out. Rescue crews were not privy to the decision-making processes behind rescue operations — they went where the coordinator told them to go through the radio and followed instructions. But the impact of military involvement in their day-to-day work in the Western Mediterranean soon became obvious. "Before, the helicopter would leave the airport and the boat would leave port more or less at the same time," the captain of a Salvamar deployed in the area told me in the summer of 2019. "By the time the helicopter had a location for us, we were halfway there," he continued. That summer, however, he noticed that the order to leave port was not sent out until the helicopter had already located the boat in distress. That could add up to four hours to the operation. "In a situation where the boat's floatability is compromised," he said, "where people are already in the water, even a few minutes can make a difference, so now when we get there, it is more likely we will find situations that are extremely complicated."

Finally, the rescuers noticed that, after the CCOE took over operations involving migrant boats, they often found themselves in the vicinity of patrol boats from the Moroccan Royal Navy. This was new, and perhaps unsurprising — after all, one of CCOE's objective was to coordinate with countries of departure. At sea, this coordination meant that more and more often the Moroccan military was called to do the rescues in the Moroccan zone of responsibility while SASEMAR boats dispatched to address the emergency were told to stand by. The crews wondered: was this a rescue operation or a pullback? The line was blurring. The rescues, if that is what they were, happened in international waters — waters where Morocco had no jurisdiction, but where it had acquired the responsibility to protect human life. SASEMAR boats crossing the boundary of Spain's exclusive zone of responsibility along parallel 35° 50' were suddenly in an uncertain place. Rescuers did not feel personally threatened, but they were shocked and more than a little confused by this development.

Often, the tower would instruct rescue crews to go to the site where the migrant boat was in distress and wait for the Royal Marine military patrol. Their orders were to stay a few hundred metres away and to not intervene unless the boat capsized. The rescuers followed orders and waited, despite the desperate pleas of the people on a sinking boat. At this point, the transformation of their profession became clear to the rescuers. Some kept a close watch while others tried to keep busy and think of something else — teeth clenched, knuckles white on the handrail, trying to block the sounds and their own feelings out. "Once I kept thinking there was a kid that must have been the age of my own kid. I kept looking and wondering if it was my kid, I felt I was going crazy," a rescuer told me. The cries only intensified as the Moroccan boat approached and they had to turn away and head back to port. "The way they treated those poor people, I am not even sure they made it to land alive," said another, shaking his head. Union spokesperson Manuel Capa, with twelve years of rescue experience under his belt, also found those rescues disturbing: "It goes against every fibre of you," he said, shaking his head despondently, "it goes against everything you are as a human and everything you have learned as a rescuer. But you are told to leave, and so you do." For the first time they were not allowed to rescue, but they were not border guards either. What were they, then, and what were they doing out there at sea?

DEVELOPING MOROCCO'S RESCUE CAPACITY

Capa knew that, as part of the government machine, political considerations could sometimes take over SASEMAR's daily work and mandate. The timing of the increase in sea migration in the Western Mediterranean was extremely inconvenient: the government was in the midst of an electoral campaign. With the far right instrumentalizing sea migration, President Sanchez's plan hinged on Morocco developing its own rescue capacity, allowing SASEMAR to withdraw from Morocco's zone of responsibility. In other words, the goal was to let the Moroccans retrieve migrant boats before they crossed the imaginary line between the two zones of responsibility.

To deactivate migration in the electoral campaign, this had to happen fast. Throughout 2018 and 2019, the European Union and Spain provided powerful incentives for Morocco to invest in rescue assets and put those assets to use. They transferred funds, trained personnel, purchased equipment, offered preferential trade and temporary migration agreements. This built on decades of co-operation between the two countries, but Spain's push for Morocco to build up its rescue game at sea was both new and resolute.

In April 2019, Spain's Ministry of Development (within which SASEMAR was placed at the time) put all its cards on the table. "The [Spanish] government has offered to provide Morocco with boats, training on rescue tasks, computer and telecommunication resources with the aim of curbing the arrival of migrants to Spain," reported the media (Muñoz and Moreno 2019). During this visit, newspapers quoted José Luis Ábalos, the Minister of Development at the time, as saying, "I brought it up with the [Moroccan] President … [that] we would like to collaborate in the implementation of a maritime rescue service like the one we have in Spain."

The MUO and the CCOE were beginning to stand on their own two feet as Ábalos uttered those words. The timing was no coincidence. The transfer of rescue responsibilities to the Royal Navy in Morocco's zone and the Guardia Civil's takeover in Spain's were two interconnected parts of the same strategy. SASEMAR directives added that Spain would train "Moroccan military personnel" under the auspices of both the Spanish government and Frontex. In other words, the Moroccan maritime rescue system would be like the one in Spain but militarized. It would serve to rescue, but also, and perhaps mainly, to control migration. The logics of rescue and control had merged somewhere along the way. The Director General of the Merchant Navy, who also took part in the negotiations, said exactly that: "the operative philosophy in the southern border has changed," he declared, because "the best way to avoid deaths is for people not to leave Morocco." This is the humanitarian border in action.

Transfer packages paved the way, although not all of them were disclosed. In two years, Morocco went from third to first recipient of Spanish funds destined for border co-operation and migration control. Spain's annual budgets between 2017 and 2019 show sustained commitment to developing the Moroccan national border surveillance system through transfers listed under the rubric of international co-operation (budget line 494) and police international co-operation (budget line 794). These expenses included transfers to Morocco's state security forces to cover recurrent expenses (such as salaries), equipment (for example, vehicles), and training related to migration control. Combining this with information obtained through questions to Parliament and Freedom of Access to Information requests, it emerges that Morocco went from receiving minimal transfers in 2017 (126,000 euros) to receiving a whooping 32 million euros in 2019. This transfer is nothing compared to the six billion euro deal the European Union made with Türkiye in 2016, but it is still a significant expense. In addition, Spain transferred 2.5 million euros to Morocco to purchase police vehicles in 2018.

The European Union topped these transfers up. Most of the European money came from the EU Emergency Trust Fund for Africa and was aimed at integrating border control and the repression of irregular EU-bound migration. The European Union invested 179 million euros in Morocco's border management development between 2015 and 2021 (European Union 2023), and earmarked an additional 140 million euros in 2018–19 to increase Morocco's border and migration management capacity. Of these, 40 million euros were specifically earmarked for the acquisition of maritime, aerial, and terrestrial equipment to enhance border control (Statewatch 2019). Among other things, the Moroccan government bought new patrol boats "for the rescue of migrants in the Mediterranean."

In a significant, and perhaps symbolic shift, for the first time these boats came not from French shipbuilders, as had traditionally been the case. Instead, the ships came from Spain's shipbuilder Navantia. Each boat had a price tag of 260 million euros and included a contract for continued maintenance. At eighty metres long (more than twice the size of a Guardamar, and almost four times bigger than a Salvamar), these were boats designed more for military patrol than for rescue.

During these months, the King of Morocco also bought the seventy-metre *Badis I*, which had a price tag of US$100 million and annual running costs of around US$10 million. On the ground, people joked about the fortunate timing: barely a few weeks had passed between the signing of the deal and the purchase of the King's new boat!

But the matter was serious and the question about the purpose of the funds transfer remained: did Spain and the European Union seek to develop Morocco's rescue capabilities, its capacity to stop migrants from reaching European territory, or both? And what would it mean to merge the logics of rescue and control at sea? Perhaps if rescue data for Morocco were available, we would be able to answer those questions. But that information simply does not exist. The only detailed information about sea rescues available

FIGURE 5: Heat map of SASEMAR rescue operations involving migrants in the Strait of Gibraltar and the Alboran Sea between 2015–18 and 2019–23

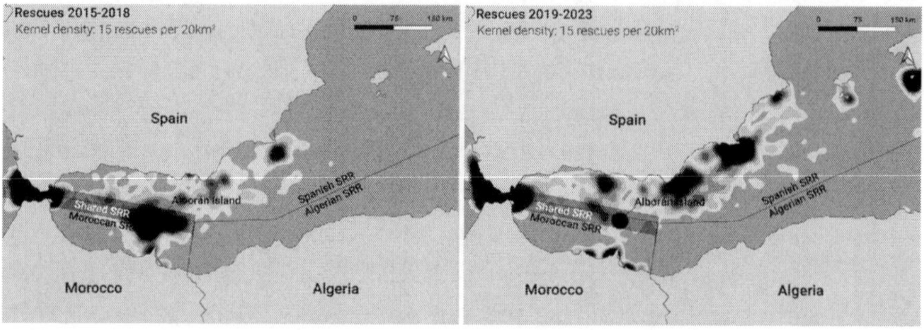

The black lines represent the boundaries between Spanish, Moroccan, and Algerian zones of responsibility. The grey area represents the shared responsibility zone between Morocco and Spain. Darker areas indicate a higher concentration of SASEMAR rescue operations. Source: Banos et al. 2024. Map created by Elizabeth Rose Hessek and reproduced with permission.

is provided by SASEMAR. Though they offer an incomplete picture of the situation in the waters between Spain and Morocco, SASEMAR's data include a stunning amount of detail: the latitude and longitude for each individual rescue operation, the reason for the rescue (with "precarious vessel" recently becoming the code for what used to be labelled "migration"), the number of people on board, the number of people rescued, and the number of corpses recovered. Using this information and comparing the periods before and after 2018, we see the emergence of a boundary at sea for rescue operations where there used to be none — and where, according to international law, there should not be one.

Using these data, it becomes clear that by 2019, SASEMAR had all but disappeared from the Moroccan zone of responsibility in the Western Mediterranean. Only three hotspots of intervention remained: the zones around the ports of Ceuta and Melilla and the Island of Alboran, all Spanish territories. In the Strait of Gibraltar (which is within the shared zone of responsibility), the rescue operations moved westward, to the Atlantic side, perhaps as a consequence of tighter surveillance around the areas near Ceuta's fences. Following this tightening of controls in Morocco, departures moved east, toward Algeria. The Algerian route, longer and more dangerous, became popular after 2019. But since Algeria does not collaborate with Spain on matters related to migration, those boats were only detected farther north, close to Spanish shores (Figure 5). This corroborates the impression of the captain quoted above, that the people they encountered at sea had been travelling longer and were in worse condition in 2019 than in previous years. This change was not a coincidence but a direct result of policy change.

As a whole, after 2019, SASEMAR rescue operations moved farther north. Rescue operations moved closer to the Spanish coast, triggering a "border effect" for rescues. Over the course of a few months, the 35°50' north parallel (the symbolic line that divides rescue responsibilities between Morocco and Spain) became a "real" border, determining who would conduct operations and where (Rodrigo 2021). It is important to remember once again that, according to the SAR Convention, borders (be they the limits of territorial waters, exclusive economic zones, zones of responsibility, or others) should not interfere in rescue operations when human life is at risk. There are no qualifications to this obligation to rescue, which applies regardless of the nationality or migration status of those in danger. Furthermore, since most rescues take place in international waters, domestic legislation does not apply. The emergence of a border at sea is problematic, particularly when there is no trace of the people rescued at sea by the Moroccan Royal Navy after (and if) they reach a safe port.

European and Spanish funds served both to develop Morocco's rescue capacity and to motivate the Moroccan government to intervene where it had not typically intervened before: at sea. This shift was also linked to broader geopolitical events and a growing awareness among countries of departure of the value of using migration control as leverage in negotiations with European powers.

MIGRATION, RESCUE, AND GEOPOLITICS IN THE WESTERN MEDITERRANEAN

It is impossible to quantify the actual number of deaths caused by the emergence of the "border effect" in this area. The NGO Caminando Fronteras (2023) estimates that more than 3,600 people drowned in the Western Mediterranean between 2018 and 2022. The attempts to seal this border at any price have turned migrants into an exchange currency, a source of political clout (and money) for countries of origin and transit.

This was the topic of heated debate at an internal meeting organized by Alarm Phone in the fall of 2023. Alarm Phone is an international activist network whose main mandate is to receive calls from migrants in distress at sea and force governments to launch a rescue operation. They organize several meetings a year (some in Europe, some in Africa), where they share knowledge, offer additional training to volunteers, and discuss their objectives as an organization. This time the meeting was in Morocco.

At the meeting, I met Cons, a man in his mid-thirties from Cameroon. I was invited to the meeting as an expert on the Spanish maritime rescue system, and Cons and his two Rastafarian friends were there to share their lived experiences as Black migrants living in Morocco. Cons had lived in the forest near Ceuta's border for ten years, waiting for the right time to jump the fence (jokingly, he added: "Ten years without a shower!"). Four times he had managed to cross over into Spain, and four times he had been pushed back to Morocco. He had also attempted the journey by sea unsuccessfully. When we spoke, he lived mostly in Tangier, although he moved around a lot — not because he wanted to, but because the Moroccan police would round up Black migrants (even those with a permit), put them in buses and move them around the country.

The other Black migrants attending the meeting (some of them women with young kids) confirmed that the Moroccan government kept moving Black migrants around. "They don't deport us to our countries," one of them told me, "because it is better to move us around, that way they can bring us to the border and use us as a threat whenever they have to negotiate with the European Union on border issues."

Research shows that these are not isolated incidents. Black people were deliberately targeted by Moroccan authorities, relocated across the country, and used as pawns in negotiations with European partners. But it should be noted that Morocco also did not hesitate to exploit its own poor population to achieve its geopolitical goals. Just a couple of years earlier, in the spring of 2021, nearly eight thousand migrants crossed the land borders of Ceuta and Melilla in a forty-eight-hour span (Martín 2021a). Some of these migrants were Africans from other countries who had come to the border by their own means following rumours that the Moroccan border police had stopped preventing border crossings. About two thousand of those who crossed during those two days were Moroccan minors that the government had picked up from other parts of the country and brought to the border on buses (Martín 2021b). At the border, Moroccan border guards stood back and watched as some jumped over the fence and others swam around it, doing nothing to stop them.

Many of these crossings happened at Tarajal beach, the site of the massacre seven years earlier. The media reported that some of the children had gotten into the buses fleeted by the Moroccan government to run away from violence at home. In the confusion, a mother got into the water with an infant strapped to her back. The baby, a small girl not two months old, slipped.

A diver from the underwater unit of the Guardia Civil jumped in the water without hesitation and emerged with an almost blue baby still wearing a bonnet and pink mittens. She was unconscious, but alive. Talking about the experience a day later on the radio, the agent's voice broke. "There were so many kids, so many babies, but not only, there were also older people who were having difficulty in the water. We … we lost one person. We tried so hard, but when someone is drowning everything happens so fast. We tried to get the kids and the babies out of the water first. We were trying to get them out as quickly as possible, but we lost one person. We lost one person." (Herrera 2021). Neither SASEMAR nor the Red Cross were called to assist those in the water.

In fact, the 2021 episode was a warning. The events took place soon after Spain had quietly provided medical care to Brahim Gali during the COVID-19 pandemic (Peregil and González 2021). Gali was the leader of the Polisario Front, the independence movement in the Western Sahara, and he lived in exile in Algeria at the time. Reports that Gali had been secretly flown to Spain and hospitalized there were seen as an affront by the Moroccan government, and the situation triggered the greatest diplomatic rift between the two countries in recent times. Asked to explain why the Moroccan forces did nothing as thousands of people crossed into Ceuta, the Moroccan ambassador to Spain gave a clear and succinct response: "Actions have consequences" (*El País* 2021). It was widely recognized that Morocco had leveraged both some of its poorest citizens and Black foreigners to pressure Spain into scaling back its support for the Western Sahara national liberation movement.

Things quieted down afterward. Moroccan border guards went back to controlling the fence. The adult migrants were deported back to Morocco, who accepted them. The minors, being protected by Spain's legal obligations and national legislation, could not be so easily deported. Barring some who were also pushed back at the fence amid the confusion, the rest were placed in overcrowded, closed facilities and some were eventually sent back (Fundación Raíces 2021; Martín 2021b). Meanwhile, the Moroccan government kept busing Black migrants around the country: to the south, where the *pateras* were departing; to the north, near the fences of Ceuta and Melilla, where they were most visible; and to the east, near the border with Algeria, in the desert. The bodies of Black people (sometimes migrants bound for the European Union, but not always) had become bargaining chips in negotiations with a Europe fixated on halting undocumented migration at any cost.

RESCUE AND MIGRATION IN THE WESTERN MEDITERRANEAN: A VIEW FROM TARAJAL BEACH

Late in the afternoon on the tenth anniversary of the Tarajal massacre, we arrive at the beach where it had all happened. I stand on the sand surrounded by other protesters as the organizers read the names of those whose bodies were recovered, including one person whose name we do not yet know (Figure 6). In the speeches, they ask for "truth, justice, and reparations" for the victims and their families, and then for a moment of silence. I try to picture the situation in my mind. The ninety who swam that day, and other days. The thousands of minors swimming in these waters in 2021. I remember the picture of a boy of about fourteen that appeared in the media; he had been sobbing unconsolably, surrounded by a couple of Guardia Civil agents. The boy sat on the sand a few metres from where I am standing now. He could not swim, so he had tied empty water bottles around his chest to stay afloat.

In a silence broken only by the rhythmic lapping of the waves, I raise my head and I see one of the women from our group. She is standing by the fence close to the water and staring at a police agent. She is in her seventies, white-haired and fragile looking — she appears perfectly harmless. The woman is standing next to a hole in the fence. She puts one foot through the hole and removes it when she sees the policeman motion in her direction. One arm in, then back to the right side of the fence. She does this several times while smiling innocently at the policeman. Eventually, he stops paying attention to her and the old lady bores of the game. Would he have shot at her if, instead of an old white woman, she had been a young Black man? Would her body have been left to float away, preferably to the other side, the Moroccan side, so that someone else had to deal with it? Would her family still be begging for a visitor visa to come retrieve her remains so that, ten years later, she could finally be put to rest?

For more than three decades, Spain and the European Union have been trying to seal their southern border. They have employed multiple strategies to achieve this objective. European countries have externalized the surveillance of the border to countries of origin and transit and encouraged those countries to integrate European anti-immigration efforts into their own legislation. They manage this through a combination of direct money transfers and development aid conditional on collaboration in the "fight against illegal migration." Spain and the European Union have created and actively sought ways to deport those who manage to cross the border — not

FIGURE 6: Gathering to commemorate the tenth anniversary of the Tarajal massacre in Ceuta on February 3, 2024. Photo by the author.

just to their countries of origin, but to any country willing to take them: Senegal, Mauritania, Morocco, Libya, Türkiye. These countries have put militaries and private military companies in charge of the border, and now of rescue too. These include the Moroccan Royal Navy, the Turkish Coast Guard, and even the so-called Libyan Coast Guard, which is involved in selling rescued people to criminal networks who exploit them as slaves (*Al Jazeera* 2023b; Hegarty 2018). As the European Union and member states continue to tighten the border, the legal obligations toward people on the move seem to be little more than an afterthought. Apparently, as long as migrants' rights are violated outside of European territory, anything goes. As a result, a growing constellation of deathscapes trace the external borders of the European Union today. Tarajal beach and the waters of the Western Mediterranean are part of that sad constellation.

Europe and Spain have justified the iron fist at the border on the principle that people on the move must use legal channels if they want to migrate to Spain. But do these channels exist? Temporary migration programs are informative: where Canada (population 40 million) offered visas to 500,000 temporary workers annually between 2018 and 2024, the entire European Union (population 447 million) offered 154,993 temporary visas in 2022, and Spain (47.2 million) offers approximately 15,000 seasonal worker visas annually to specific nationalities depending on economic and political need (Eurostat 2023).

The point is not that Canada's programs are progressive — many are not. For example, in 2024, the United Nations published a report detailing the many ways that temporary foreign workers were routinely exploited in Canada, including wage theft, lack of protective equipment, long work hours with few breaks, and physical and psychological abuse (Obokata 2024). According to Special Rapporteur Tomoya Obokata, this program — which has been in place since the early 1970s — was "a breeding ground for contemporary forms of slavery." The point is that other countries like Canada have opened up channels for people on the move to enter their national territory legally, either as temporary workers, as permanent residents, as asylum claimants, as refugees, or as all of the above. This option simply does not exist in most European countries, and certainly not in Spain. Applying for international protection (asylum) in Spain from Morocco is simply not possible, as NGOs and the Defensor del Pueblo have repeatedly denounced. Among other things, people cannot physically reach the spaces where they would be able to request international protection; to reach these spaces, they need to cross the border illegally first. This point is crucial: after all, the ECHR argued that mass deportations at the border were acceptable because migrants had put themselves willingly at risk even though there were ways for them to claim asylum from Morocco. This argument is void from the moment that possibility ceases to exist.

If there are no safe and legal ways to reach EU territory over land or by plane, then the only option available is the sea. The recent and ongoing weaving of the Spanish maritime rescue system (by definition, a tool to save lives) into this constellation of deathscapes is paradoxical, but not surprising. The creation of a two-tier system where some lives are worth saving and others not is consistent with the European Union's decades-long approach to migration and border control elsewhere along its maritime border — an approach that, regardless of the money poured into it, has proven inefficient and deadly. And still, along the Western Mediterranean and Atlantic regions, there is a sense of inevitability that there is no way to manage the border except with an iron fist, and that rescue assets should be brought into the fold of border control. Along the way, migrants (sea migrants in particular) have become pawns in a much larger political chessboard where other economic and geopolitical interests are playing out. Their lives, as racialized poor "others," have a merely transactional value for the powers at play. This is true in the Western Mediterranean, and it is increasingly true in the Atlantic, where similar developments are taking place.

5

The Canary Islands: A Stealthy Takeover of Maritime Search and Rescue by the Military

ARGUINEGUÍN, LA RESTINGA, LOS CRISTIANOS — the ports that SASEMAR's boats return to with dozens, sometimes hundreds, of exhausted people rescued at sea are also top tourist destinations. This is true for the ports in Andalusia as well, but here in the Canary Islands, the contrast is particularly jarring. In 2023, more than fourteen million tourists visited the Islands and thirty thousand people on the move arrived by sea.

I am pondering the magnitude of these numbers in the port of Arguineguín, in Gran Canaria. It is a sweltering February afternoon, and I am sitting in the Fishermen's Guild bar waiting for my drink. It is a placid sunny morning in a quaint fishing harbour turned tourist destination. However, evidence that this is one of the main ports of disembarkation for rescued sea migrants is hidden in plain sight. The Salvamar *Macondo*, bright orange under the blinding sun, is docked a few metres away. On the other side of the *Macondo*, almost invisible, an empty *cayuco* rocks gently in the waves — the remnants of yesterday's work (Figure 7). Judging from its build, this one came from Mauritania. The dinghy is in a section of the dock that is off-limits, behind a

FIGURE 7: The Salvamar *Macondo* in the Arguineguín harbour. In front of the *Macondo*, behind the fence, there is an empty blue *cayuco*; a white Red Cross container used for the initial interviews with migrants sits to the left. Photo by the author.

chain-link fence and a no trespassing sign. That section is where SASEMAR crews offload people rescued at sea, either from the Salvamar or directly from the dinghy. A container with the Red Cross logo also betrays the fact that this dock is more than a background for tourists' pictures. In late 2020, this was known as *el muelle de la vergüenza*: the dock of shame.

It was the early days of the global COVID-19 pandemic. That year, the Canary Islands re-emerged as the epicentre of sea migration to Europe. In August, when arrivals began in earnest, the Red Cross set up a temporary structure in the port of Arguineguín to protect migrants freshly off the rescue boats from the sun and rain as they waited to be processed by the authorities and receive the results of their PCR tests. The *cayucos* piled up by the hundreds across the port in what would come to be known as "the *cayuco* cemetery." Migrants were supposed to remain in the cordoned-off section of the port for seventy-two hours at most. This was above the legal limit, but most people agreed that circumstances obliged — it was a global pandemic, after all. However, by October, the migrant reception system on the islands had collapsed: there were simply no spots available for those arriving by sea. People were stuck on the dock for weeks on end, standing, crouching, sitting, or sleeping on pieces of cardboard or on folding beds typically used for disaster evacuation. Installed at regular intervals between the edge of the dock and the tents, a row of overflowing portable toilets leaked onto the pavement. There were no showers. At one point, over 2,500 people were crowded into 3,600 square metres of asphalt (equivalent to three Olympic-sized pools) in a temporary facility with a capacity for approximately four hundred people (Naranjo 2021). Still waiting for my drink, I try to visualize the number of people in such a small space for hours, days, weeks. I touch the asphalt with my hand. It burns.

The chaos was such that, at one point, a minor vanished. The boy, a teenager, had survived a gruelling journey during which sixteen of his twenty-five travelling companions had died, including six of his cousins. For nine days, nobody knew where he was. Workers and Red Cross volunteers going through the lists of migrants for food distribution assumed he had somehow managed to escape the heavily guarded dock. But he had not moved. A newspaper article explained that "he stayed in a little corner, on the asphalt, under a Red Cross tent and in a state of shock, for nine full days." An anonymous worker added that "someone must have fed him and given him water, because he sure wasn't able to move. He could have died there in the middle of the crowd, like a dog" (Vargas 2020a). The mayhem was extreme, and certainly not conducive to the respect of the strict public health directives in place to prevent the spread of COVID-19.

The Defensor del Pueblo (a figure akin to an Ombuds) would later describe the situation in Arguineguín as "the most obvious mistake" the government made to manage the "migration crisis" during this time (Martín 2020). After months of complaints on the part of, among others, NGOs and the Defensor del Pueblo, the Spanish government created a network of temporary facilities farther away from the eyes of tourists and journalists. Migrants moved from the "dock of shame" to a network of "warehouses of shame" (*las naves de la vergüenza*) and other centres placed throughout the islands (Lo Coco et al. 2022).

Northeast from Gran Canaria, in Lanzarote, the new space where migrants were sent was an isolated former bus depot where the chemical toilets leaked out of the warehouse and onto the road some thirty metres away (Vargas 2023). After a few months, the government closed the warehouse and opened a CATE (Centro de Atención Temporal de Extranjeros; Temporary Holding Centre for Foreigners), where migrants were kept while their files were processed by the police (Irídia and Novact 2023). Images shared by lawyer and activist Loueila Sid Ahmed Ndiaye showed migrants sleeping on the oil-stained floor on thin mats almost touching, puddles of sewage seeping from the chemical toilets mere metres away. Some had the thin red blankets provided by the Red Cross crumpled nearby. For most people, these are too small to cover both their feet and their shoulders at the same time; but far too often, this is the only blanket they receive.

In Gran Canaria, temporary accommodation for migrants rescued at sea and disembarked in Arguineguín was in an industrial area (Vargas 2020b). When the Defensor del Pueblo paid a surprise visit, he was horrified: the warehouses did not meet even the minimum sanitary requirements (EFE 2020). He asked the government to make sure that basic precautions were put in place to prevent the spread of COVID-19 among the people who were kept there in excessively close quarters. The Defensor del Pueblo also pointed out that people were not getting enough food or water; that toilet paper, soap, and towels were in short supply; that there were far fewer toilets than the regulations required; and that the government had yet to install showers in the facility. His shock was apparent in the tightly worded letter he submitted to the government.

People continued to arrive in the Canary Islands. Slowly, the docks and warehouses were replaced by more permanent structures, often far away from public view on property owned by the military or the police.

The government also opened new temporary holding facilities (CATEs), closed centres increasingly in the form of tents in walled-off lots nearby or connected to police stations. Former military barracks and buildings on the mainland were also rehabilitated into open centres for those who were relocated from other islands. A steady flow of flights began taking migrants to mainland Spain and, sometimes, back to their countries of origin. The tents on the docks reappeared sporadically when arrivals peaked. This multilayered system of open and closed centres, transfers, and deportations was still in place in the summer of 2024. These facilities all carried the word "temporary" in their names, revealing the government's refusal to articulate a durable institutional solution to a phenomenon that had long been structural. Here again, the framing of migration as a crisis (an exceptional and short-lived event) imposed itself despite all evidence to the contrary.

THE MANY DEADLY ROUTES OF THE ATLANTIC ZONE

Earlier, I argued against using the term "routes" to describe the maritime spaces migrants move through in the Western Mediterranean and around the Canary Islands. Like the Eastern and Central Mediterranean, these are zones traversed by many different routes, with flexible points of departure and arrival that evolve to respond to changing circumstances. For example, migrants travelling from West Africa, the Western Sahara, and southern Morocco heading to the Canary Islands might depart from points two thousand kilometres apart and arrive on completely different islands. These points of departure and arrival evolve to reflect broader events such as natural catastrophes, wars, and other geopolitical developments. Furthermore, migrants use different kinds of boats depending on where they leave from, who is organizing the trip, and who is travelling.

SASEMAR rescuers often classify the routes in the Atlantic zone in two broad types: short routes (one or two days long) and long routes (over two days). Shorter routes have points of departure in the Western Sahara or Morocco, some 109 kilometres or 60 nautical miles to the closest islands if leaving from Tarfaya, Morocco, and 241 kilometres or 130 nautical miles if leaving from Cap Bojador, Western Sahara. Those using these shorter routes often use rigid-hull inflatable boats and wooden or fibreglass boats. Rigid-hull inflatable boats are more stable but sometimes puncture at sea or during the rescue operations. Also, the boats' inflatable tubes tend to separate with excessive weight, so smugglers have begun to use belts to reinforce the structure and fit more people into the boats. These trips are typically organized by professional smugglers who stay on land. Compared to the boats they use for transporting Moroccan nationals, those used for smuggling Black Africans are in worse shape, have less powerful or older engines, and often depart with barely enough fuel to complete the journey.

Longer routes start off in Mauritania or Senegal. In Mauritania, the main points of departure are Nouadhibou, just south of the limit with the Western Sahara, and the country's capital, Nouakchott, farther down the coast. In a straight line, boats must travel between 500 and 800 kilometres to the Canary Islands, or between 270 and 430 nautical miles. This makes rigid-hull inflatable boats impractical. Instead, smugglers use wooden fishing boats and fibreglass vessels. As in the case of those leaving from Morocco and the Western Sahara, these migrants often travel with satellite telephones widely known as Thurayas (after their main manufacturer). The presence of these phones is one of the reasons it is often believed that the same smuggling networks are involved along the coast from southern Morocco through southern Mauritania. In addition to the navigational tools that other GPS-enabled devices also offer, satellite phones allow remote communication via satellite for calls and texts when deep at sea, in areas where cellphone coverage is poor or non-existent. According to some activists, the use of this technology has made sea migration safer, as migrants can reach relatives and emergency services at any point during their journey. However, satellite phones remain expensive and illegal in some places. In Morocco, possession of a satellite phone can be (and according to activists, has been) an incriminating piece of evidence in human smuggling cases. A migrant will almost certainly be accused of human smuggling if caught with one near a beach or on a boat.

Those who leave from Senegal and The Gambia must travel ten times the distance as those leaving from Morocco, between 1,300 and 1,700 kilometres (over 900 nautical miles) to reach the Canary Islands. Migrants departing from Mauritania or Senegal typically use large traditional wooden fishing boats known in Spanish as *cayucos* and as *pirogues* in French. Although not made for such long, demanding journeys, the build and structure of *cayucos* make them almost unsinkable. While SASEMAR rescue crews describe rigid-hull inflatable boats as the least safe type of vessel used in sea migration, they identify *cayucos* as the most seaworthy, and pateras as somewhere in between. In addition to the relative safety that these boats offer, *cayucos* leaving from Senegal often carry fishermen from coastal communities who have at least some seafaring experience. This is a marked difference from other routes in the Atlantic zone. Trips leaving from Senegal also tend to be organized by people from the same community with little or no intervention from criminal smuggling networks.

Some of the defining characteristics of the Senegalese route are changing, however. For example, the craftsmanship of the *cayucos* has declined, with some clearly built specifically for a one-way smuggling journey. Also, while in the past members of seafaring communities dominated on this this route, today there are more people from cities and from the interior (including other countries such as Mali) with no seafaring experience leaving from the Senegalese coast.

Even when experienced sailors are present and the boats are well built, this is a long and dangerous route. According to data from the organization Caminando Fronteras, in 2023, ten times more sea migrants died in the Atlantic than in the Western Mediterranean. Increased surveillance of waters near the African coast means that *cayucos* nowadays venture deeper into the ocean, a dangerous environment where currents and winds are ready to snatch them and bring them into the open ocean. The Canary current, as it is known, flows south, passing the archipelago, and continues toward South America. In 2021 alone, the current carried at least seven *cayucos* from West Africa to the Brazilian coast. These *cayucos* were either empty or carried the corpses of migrants who had missed the islands on their journey to Europe (Brito and Dana 2023). In 2024, a *cayuco* that had departed from Mauritania was found near the coast of Brazil with twenty corpses inside (Rodríguez 2024), and two more boats were found in the first few weeks of 2025 (Martín 2025). There is little doubt that others have gotten lost in the immensity of the ocean.

A crucial difference between the longer and shorter routes that lead to the Canary Islands is the absence of satellite phones. The routes from The Gambia and Senegal may be longer and riskier, but a prohibitive price tag means that satellite phones are rarely used by sea migrants leaving from these countries, who, in turn, typically organize themselves without much outside intervention and face at least a week of open ocean navigation in areas that are (so far) less heavily controlled by authorities. SASEMAR rescuers have observed that there are often "buckets full of batteries for GPS devices" at the bottom of the boats they bring to port, "but no satellite phones." In some cases, migrants throw the satellite phones into the sea to get rid of incriminating evidence, but most often these devices are simply not used.

Understanding that some people will leave regardless of the risks, some Senegalese activists are trying to promote the use of satellite phones to make the journey safer. One of them is Saliou Diouf, a trained naval technician I met in 2023. Four years earlier, Saliou left from southern Morocco on a rigid-hull inflatable boat, but one of the inflatable tubes exploded halfway through the journey. It is a small miracle that he and his companions survived. He returned to Senegal and created Boza Fii, a community organization that denounces the consequences of the European Union's border regime for Senegalese youth. According to Saliou, migrants leaving the Senegalese coast "use a GPS device, and when they lose signal, run out of batteries, or both, they use a compass. And if they are experienced sailors, they can also use the stars." But he finds this strategy extremely risky. Part of his activism involves making sure young people know what they will be facing at sea. "We are working on an intervention plan in the Atlantic zone, and one of our goals is to raise awareness among those who want to leave about using Thuraya phones to ask for help if they need it." The problem, of course, is the price of these devices: 350,000 CFA francs, or 550 euros (about 800 Canadian dollars).

THE ATLANTIC ZONE OF RESPONSIBILITY: TWO DECADES OF ARRIVALS AND EXTERNALIZATION

The Canary Islands have been a popular destination for migrants for decades. The first *patera* arrived at the archipelago in 1994, touching land on the island of Fuerteventura with two young men from the Western Sahara. They had followed a route known to local fisherfolk, completing their journey in less than twenty-four hours. Throughout the 1990s, a handful of *barcos chatarra* (rusted, derelict metal boats) used the same route, carrying more Sahraouis as well as nationals from India and Pakistan (Castellano 2014). Despite these arrivals, sea migration to the Canary Islands remained minimal compared to southern Spain until around 2002. By 2010, however, the Canary Island routes had become the primary way for people on the move to reach Spain by sea, consistently accounting for more than half of all arrivals. The shift was gradual at first. Then, in 2006, more than 31,000 people reached the Canary Islands by boat — 81 percent of all arrivals to Spain by sea that year, marking a five-fold increase from the previous year (Ministerio del Interior 2007; Figure 8). That was the beginning of a three-year period that would be known in Spain as the first *"cayuco* crisis" (*la crisis de los cayucos*).

FIGURE 8: Sea migration to Spain by year in the Western Mediterranean and the Canary Islands (2001–2023)

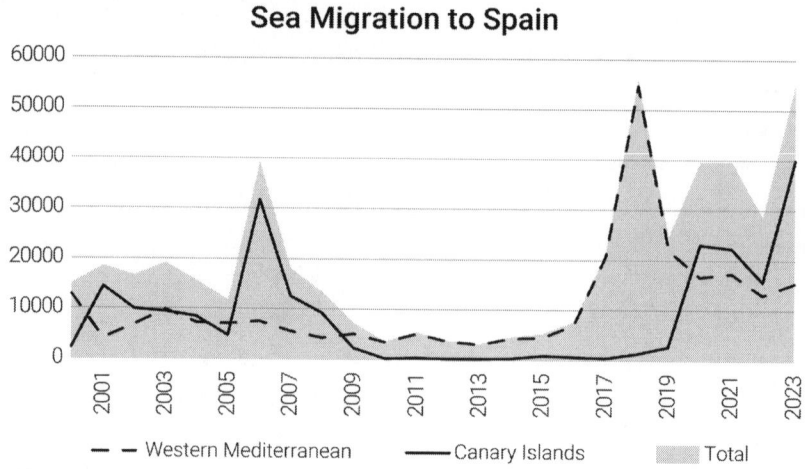

Graph prepared by Elizabeth Rose Hessek with data from the Spanish Ministry of the Interior. Reproduced with permission.

In Senegal, the country from which most of these migrants came, graffiti bearing the motto "Barça wala barsakh" peppered poor fishing communities, from Saint Louis in the north to Ziguinchor in the south. Barça (a reference to the Barcelona soccer team) symbolized the dream of reaching Europe and moving up in life; *barsakh* (which means "death" in Wolof) underscored the very real risks of the journey. Barça or death, then: the rallying cry of a desperate generation: we are willing to risk our lives to triumph or die trying (Boza Fii 2023). For the young men getting on the *cayucos*, staying in Senegal was simply not an option.

The 2006 "*cayuco* crisis" triggered a new era of co-operation between Spain and West African countries (Senegal in particular). Up until that point, Spain's relationships in Africa were a continuation of the country's colonial history in the region and involved four main partners: the Western Sahara (which the UN still considers a non-self-governing territory), Morocco, Equatorial Guinea and, to a lesser extent, Mauritania (Hernando de Larramendi and Planet 2007). However, after the number of boats started to increase, the Spanish government understood that it would have to ramp up its collaboration with African states that were countries of origin and transit if it wanted to stop sea migration.

The previous chapter showed what that looked like in the Western Mediterranean starting in the nineties, a place and time when Morocco was the primary partner. In the Atlantic region, the years following the "*cayuco* crisis" were crucial. The Spanish government adopted its first-ever Africa Plan in 2006 (Dirección General de Comunicación Exterior 2006). This became the main framework for Spain's international relations with African countries south of the Sahara. The Africa Plan focused on development aid, but it also established migration and border control as "top priority issues." For this reason, the 2006–08 Plan identified Senegal, Mali, and Mauritania as instrumental partners. Squarely on the tracks of the European Union's Cotonou Agreements (European Commission 2000), Spain's successive Africa Plans have made development aid conditional on collaborating in the "fight" against illegalized migration by land and, particularly, by sea.

Initially, Spain's strategy depended on a series of interdependent preventive and defensive initiatives. Preventive strategies sought to provide incentives to potential migrants to stay in place. For example, early in their collaboration, Spain transferred ten million euros to Senegal in the context of the REVA (Retour vers l'agriculture) Plan, which aimed at modernizing the agricultural sector and creating employment opportunities for young people. There is no evidence that the Senegalese government spent any of the money invested in the program to achieve these goals. Despite the failure of the REVA Plan, similar programs seeking to create employment opportunities for young Senegalese men in the fishing industry and in the trades were generously funded by Spain and the European Union in the years that followed.

These programs failed to give youth the capacity to obtain jobs that would allow them to make ends meet and therefore stay in Senegal. But did these programs really fail to achieve European objectives? In fact, they succeeded in establishing a working collaboration between Senegal and Spain, and they paved the way for the defensive measures that sought to "repel and expel": push back migrants at the border and deport those that managed to reach Spanish territory. The externalization of Spanish and European policy priorities in the area of migration and border control was key in Spain's and the European Union's strategy and took several forms. For example, soon after sea migration to the Canary Islands began in earnest in 2005, Senegal passed a new law criminalizing human smuggling. This law was the result of months of lobbying, cajoling, and negotiating on the part of Spanish government officials. Yet sea migration continued to increase in the months that followed.

In August 2006, Senegal agreed to let Spain post two Guardia Civil patrol boats and a helicopter within its territory. There were similar units already in Mauritania, a country that received and continues to receive important sums of development funds to keep migrants in the region (for example, in early 2024 Spain and the EU promised Mauritania a 500 million euro transfer to stop boats from leaving its coasts; Cué 2024). The presence of Spanish security forces, and their collaboration with local counterparts, sought to detect migrant boats before they left Senegalese and Mauritanian jurisdictional waters, that is, within twenty-four nautical miles from the coast (Arencibia 2020). Additionally, Spain deployed military personnel to train Senegalese forces on border control, and the two countries signed preferential trade agreements. Daily interactions were so frequent that, in 2010, I interviewed Senegalese border guards *in Spanish*: they had learned the language during the trainings.

In practice, initiatives to prevent departures were never fully independent from Spanish defensive initiatives at the border — initiatives that included the deployment of military personnel and equipment such as radars, but also migrant detention and deportation to countries of origin and transit. For example, as we saw in the previous chapter, in 2006 the Spanish government offered Senegal a few hundred temporary work visas in exchange for the repatriation of men who had arrived in the Canary Islands in *cayucos* earlier that year.

The program was based on a well-established annual program with Morocco and eastern European countries. But this was a new initiative in Senegal, and it was extremely rushed. A senior Spanish government official who was involved in the selection of the first group of workers jokingly reminisced about the madness of the program's early days: "We were told by the Minister himself that we had to try really hard to speed up the visa procedure because they were negotiating the forced return of some Sub-Saharan [Black] migrants who were in the Canary Islands and these visas were part of the negotiations."

The personnel at the Ministry of Labour and Immigration worked at a breakneck pace during the last couple of months of 2006, but their Senegalese counterparts did not seem to be in a hurry. By late December, they had still not submitted the documentation for the selected workers. Then, on the day everyone was getting ready to start their Christmas break, the Minister called. In an interview, a senior public servant at the ministry told me that the Minister "said it *had* to happen that day. So, we sent the applications to the police, and in an hour they had processed them all! Then we had to hire a private courier, because the visas had to be ready before the end of the year and we were going on holiday that afternoon!" And so, the visas were sent. Almost immediately, the Senegalese government approved the arrival of the first-ever deportation plane from Spain.

The frantic activity and generous funds made available to encourage Senegal and Mauritania to stop departures from their beaches and pull back those who were still in their waters are a textbook case of externalization of migration and border control responsibilities. It was the first time that this approach (nowadays routine) was tested in the European Union, and was, in some ways, an expansion of similar experiences of externalization that had taken place earlier in the Western Mediterranean. The main difference was that, in the Western Mediterranean, Spain had partnered only with Morocco (Algeria being unwilling); whereas Spain's main collaborators in the Atlantic were Senegal and Mauritania. The sea was a prime site for intervention in West Africa from the beginning of such collaborations.

It was problematic for the Spanish government to proudly hail Mauritania as an exemplary partner, however. The country has a one-party government, and human rights abuses are widely documented (particularly against Black people). The collaboration between the two countries was, as a result, rather secretive — but it happened, and it continues to happen. For example, in 2009, one of the main detention centres for people on the move in Mauritania was a former primary school that had been refurbished for its new purpose using Spanish development funds. Years later, in 2024, the Spanish Development Agency announced the renovation of two other detention facilities for migrant people in Mauritania, one in Nouadhibou and the other in Nouakchott. The projects, which had a cost of 4.5 million euros, were funded by the European Union's Emergency Trust Fund for Africa (FIIAP 2024).

Senegal, seen as a beacon of democracy and political stability in the continent, was different. In 2007, a Spanish government official described the Senegalese government to me as an "ideal partner." Over time, these partnerships with Mauritania and Senegal had a ripple effect that changed who travelled, how they travelled, and who provided (or did not provide) rescue services in the waters where they travelled.

The People behind the Numbers

In 2008–10, when the first "*cayuco* crisis" was in its last throes, I was in Senegal. There, I met several people who had taken or captained a *cayuco* to the Canary Islands. One of them was Modou, an underwater fisherman in his fifties. Modou was a Lebou man from Thiaroye-sur-mer in Dakar's metropolitan area, a fisherman from an ethnic group defined by fishing living in a fishing community. His whole existence was shaped by his relationship with the sea. But despite all his hard work, he could not manage to feed his family. The fishing stocks in the waters of Senegal had been depleted by industrial fleets from other countries (including Spain). Traditional fishermen like Modou simply could not compete with industrial fishing boats.

Young men knew this. As they contemplated their choices for the future, it was clear to them that they could stay in Senegal and keep hustling in poverty, or they could get on a boat and maybe make it to Europe. Youth from Thiaroye-sur-mer and other fishing communities all along the Senegalese coast, from Saint Louis to Casamance, organized themselves. They took the same boats they used for fishing and kept going and going, until (if they were lucky) they reached the Canary Islands. As Modou said, shrugging his shoulders, "It is the same trip, just a bit longer."

Young Senegalese men from fishing communities in coastal towns and cities were the main candidates for sea migration between 2005 and 2010. Women were rarely allowed on these trips, usually organized locally through networks of relatives and neighbours. So many young men from Thiaroye-sur-mer left during this time that in 2009 the village had to cancel its popular soccer tournaments: they simply could not find enough players. By then Modou had already retired, but it dawned on him that there was a business opportunity in this European Dream. As an old man, he had no interest in migrating himself: his place was in Thiaroye-sur-mer with his family. But he could take others to Europe safely and make some money on the side. He let his neighbours and relatives know he was available to take people to Spain. Soon enough, he had enough young men for one trip on his trusty wooden fishing boat. He took the men to the islands, disembarked them on a beach, and turned around to return to Senegal. He did the trip several times before the Senegalese government started enforcing the 2005 anti-smuggling law, and Modou saw some of his neighbours face fines impossible for someone like him to pay. He heard others were sent to prison. That is when Modou decided that smuggling was too risky.

In Spain and in Senegal, I met many young men like the ones Modou took to the Canary Islands, men who embarked on the trip with their relatives and neighbours. One of them was Mayecor, a Serer from Kaolak, an inland city eighty kilometres north of the border with The Gambia. He was determined to go to Europe. His brother and his sister (who lived in Spain) encouraged him to get a visa and travel as a tourist. But getting a tourist visa was almost impossible, and it required finding and bribing at least one government worker.

This was a widespread practice across all migration programs at the time. For example, all the women I interviewed who had gone to Spain as part of the rushed 2006 temporary agricultural worker program had paid bribes or provided sexual favours to Senegalese government recruiters in exchange for their visa. Men usually had to pay. As Mayecor was considering his options, he found that a relative was planning a trip a few weeks later. He left with his relative after paying the captain (himself a migrant) one thousand euros. But Mayecor's trip was not easy. The GPS ran out of batteries and the captain, an experienced fisherman, had to navigate using the stars. Fights broke out among the increasingly anxious passengers. Two people died. Mayecor was scared himself. At some point, it occurred to him he might not live to see another day. Yet he knew that it was in his smuggler's best interest to get them to port safely — they were, literally, in the same boat. Eventually, they managed to return to the Senegalese coast. Mayecor was partially reimbursed for the failed trip.

Another one of the thousands of young Senegalese men leaving for Spain in 2006 was Djibril, whom I met in Madrid in 2010. The second son of his father's second wife, Djibril was one of fourteen siblings living in a large family household. Djibril had been a fisherman in Senegal where, together with his older brother and a maternal uncle, he had worked the coast from the border with Guinea Bissau to the border with Mauritania. Just like Modou, the Lebou fisherman from Thiaroye-sur-mer, Djibril's family struggled to cover their bare necessities on the meagre income of the men in the family, all of whom lived off the sea. Other young men in the village had left and were already sending remittances to their relatives; they appeared to be living quite comfortably in Europe. Tired of the situation, Djibril found a reliable fisherman-turned-smuggler to take him and his brother to Spain.

Excited, Djibril brought a digital camera to document the trip. In the pictures he took during the first hours at sea he appears relaxed, smiling with his arms over his brother's shoulders, his clothes windswept. Things changed quickly, however. The weather turned, bringing strong winds and heavy rain. Once the storm was over, they continued north, only to realize that the last of their fuel containers was pierced and there was no more fuel left. At this point, he stopped taking pictures: "We were too far from Spain and too far from Senegal. What were we going to do?!" They came across a Moroccan fishing boat and, after much bargaining, bought some overpriced fuel. With that, they returned to Dakar and went straight to the smuggler's house. Djibril told me that "Someone from our boat had died. I do not know what happened to the body, but the man [who had organized the trip] was scared, and he paid for all of us to get back home by bus and gave us back our money. Most of it, anyways."

After the close call of their first attempt, Djibril and his brother decided to organize the journey themselves. They returned to their hometown of Gandiol, where they talked to other young fishermen and collected the money to buy the necessary equipment for the trip. Their boat left a few months later. This time they were intercepted by Frontex when they were close to the Spanish shore and assisted by one of SASEMAR's rescue boats. Afterward, the migrants were taken to detention in Madrid (presumably because the centres in the Canary Islands were full at the time) and released a few days later.

What Mayecor and Djibril's stories have in common is their personal connections with their smugglers, which gave them some degree of protection during the trip. Mayecor was the *cayuco*'s owner's relative, and Djibril was loosely connected to his first smuggler and then became one himself. Their migration was arranged within the known and relatively safe spaces of the household and the neighbourhood. Their stories are personal: these are no criminal networks but small migrant entrepreneurs who take on smuggling to make some money and, in some cases, secure their own migration. This did not make their journeys safe, but relatively safer than they would have been had they hired smugglers with nothing to lose if the travellers did not make it to their destination.

Most organizations that worked on the ground at the time agreed that, in 2006, roughly one out of three *cayucos* capsized on its way to the Canary Islands. This would bring the number of deaths along this route close to seven thousand that year (APDHA 2007). Anecdotal evidence suggests that the criminalization of human smuggling in Senegal (a process that began in the spring of 2005 and was triggered by Spanish pressures on the Senegalese government) encouraged many local fishermen/smugglers like Modou or Djibril to give up their side hustle. In this sense, the strategy worked. But since there was still demand for smuggling to the Canary Islands, as fishermen like Modou stepped out, organized criminal networks stepped in.

Organized crime is exactly what another Senegalese man, Alioune, encountered on his (aborted) Atlantic journey. Alioune was from the interior. He was not a fisherman and knew nothing about the sea, but he too struggled to feed his family in Senegal. Unable to secure a visa, in early 2009 he decided to reach Spain via the Canary Islands. By then there was too much surveillance in the Atlantic zone, and the fishermen he knew feared being caught and sent to prison. He heard that there was somebody in Mauritania who could sell him a spot on a boat. Alioune went to Mauritania to meet the smugglers and pay half of his passage. He was told to meet them at a beach near the border a few weeks later with the other half to board the *cayuco* that would take him to Spain. However, when he got there, he only found a group of other would-be migrants shivering on a desert beach in the middle of the night, waiting with the other half of the money to pay the smugglers. The migrants did not know each other, and they had only met the smugglers once. The group stayed there for that night and the following day, then went to the building where they had arranged the trip weeks before: it was empty. Some neighbours said the smugglers had been detained by the police, but Alioune suspected they had simply run away with the money.

It was around that time (2008–2009) that migration by sea from Senegal to the Canary Islands diminished, almost coming to a full stop. Politicians were quick to declare the triumph of the restrictive approach with its combination of externalization, militarization, and sped-up deportations — the approach that would eventually become mainstream throughout the European Union. Others, including Frontex, were more moderate, attributing this change to other factors (Frontex 2009). Indeed, a profound economic crisis was ravaging southern European economies. The PIGS, as these countries were collectively and pejoratively called (Portugal, Italy, Greece, and Spain) had no jobs to offer locals, let alone foreigners. The economic downturn meant less demand for cheap labour, which was perhaps the main deterrent to migration. As migration scholar Hein de Haas (2023) argued, "[e]scaping poverty, violence and the climate crisis are factors [explaining human mobility], but the main driver is rich societies demanding cheap labour." Weakened work prospects, combined with the risks of the journey and of being caught, meant that, for many, migrating just was not worth the risk.

Over time, restrictive border policies (including the 2005 anti-smuggling law) led to the emergence of a criminal business alongside pre-existing local informal smuggling networks. Increased surveillance technology and co-operation agreements made the border harder to cross. Meanwhile, European governments never bothered to create the safe and legal pathways they had promised for economic migrants or even refugees to get to Europe.

In practical terms, this meant that migration would continue to be treated as a passing situation (a "crisis") instead of what it had already become: a permanent and core aspect of contemporary Europe. But, at the time, the temporary lull in the number of arrivals at the Canary Islands seemed to feed into the illusion that it was feasible to seal the maritime border against illegalized human mobility.

SASEMAR DURING THE FIRST "*CAYUCO* CRISIS"

The sudden spike in the number of arrivals in the Canary Islands in 2006 took many by surprise. Perhaps it should not have. It followed on the heels of the first crackdown along the land borders between Morocco and Spain the previous year. Both countries joined forces to stop groups of migrants, Moroccan and Black Africans alike, from jumping over the fences of Melilla and Ceuta. Not missing a beat, the Atlantic routes (longer and more dangerous) appeared as alternatives (Blanco 2014). This is a constant in the history of migration: when governments crack down on one route, people do not stay in place — they find another way in. In other words, the adaptation of migration dynamics in the Western Mediterranean and the Atlantic followed the logics of a hydraulic system: when one route closes, other routes open up.

Policymakers seemed reluctant to admit this fact. This reluctance may explain why there was no response in place when boats started arriving in the Canary Islands. SASEMAR was particularly unprepared. An official publication that recounts the history of the agency acknowledges that rescue demands related to the spike in sea migration "became simply unmanageable on the days of greatest traffic," adding that, throughout the Spanish coast "the actions of the rescue teams increased from 204 assistance interventions and 6,801 rescues in 2005 to 605 assistance interventions and 30,519 rescues in 2006" (SASEMAR 2016, 90). At the time, there was only one coordination centre in the archipelago (in Gran Canaria). Rescue workers had access to one helicopter, but no planes to do reconnaissance and evacuate medical emergencies. There were nine Salvamares but no Guardamares. The government only acquired additional rescue assets later, once the pressure had somewhat diminished (SASEMAR 2016). For comparison, in 2023, a year when forty thousand people arrived by sea to the islands, there were two regional coordination centres, two helicopters, one plane, ten Salvamares, and three Guardamares in the archipelago. Even then, demand still vastly outweighed available assets on some of the islands.

SASEMAR was at the frontline in 2006, struggling to keep up despite the insufficient assets and crews' lack of experience with migrant rescues in the area. Rescue crews deployed in the Canary Islands at the time recalled gruellingly long journeys that merged into a blur of shifts and time off recovering from the shifts. Some also had vivid memories of the Senegalese seamen they encountered during that time and praised the navigating skills of some of the skippers, experienced fishermen with an intimate, bodily knowledge of the sea and its mysteries.

The captain of one of the first Guardamares deployed on the islands recalled, in awe, his conversations with those early Senegalese skippers in a mix of French, English, Spanish, and gestures: "They moved in the deep sea like it was the house where they were born: they were the Ulysses of our era, those men!" This rescuer was certain he had met some of them more than once: "These skippers were amazing: they would disembark a bunch of passengers who were absolutely exhausted after the journey, and as soon as they could they would turn around and do fifteen more days of solo navigation and start all over again. I have never seen anything like it."

For a time, rescue and migration control remained separate. Already the Guardia Civil had started to hold regular meetings in Gran Canaria with actors involved in the rescue and first reception of people arriving by sea in the islands, but this did not translate into a denial of rescue services to migrant boats. Other embryonic efforts to merge rescue and control had dubious results. One idea, for example, was to use rescue boats to patrol the perimeter of the islands, hoping that their presence would act both as a deterrent for migrants and as a way to buff up surveillance. One of the rescuers joked about the futility of the routine surveillance the regional coordination centres ordered them to do.

> We called it the dick patrol [*la patrulla capulla*], because it was just ridiculous. We always talked about "the line." And this line was: you go up the archipelago all the way up to La Graciosa. And then we went down, Lanzarote, Fuerteventura, we spent a day or two there, maybe went into one or two ports, then to Las Palmas, two or three ports, then Tenerife, and we kept going to El Hierro, spent the night in La Restinga and kept going up to La Palma, started all over again. And again. And again. And again. It was a waste of fuel.

Pointless as these rounds were, during this time nobody questioned SASEMAR's activities or interfered with their operations. Nobody publicly accused the agency of facilitating illegal border crossings or of collaborating with criminal gangs. Frontex, who launched its first-ever operation in the islands in 2005 (Operation HERA), had few personnel and a very small operating budget when it was first established: its mission was simply to coordinate operations using the resources put at its disposal by EU member states who chose to participate. At port, Frontex's agents, dressed in blue, would wait for the rescue boats to dock after an operation; they would take pictures and notes, not interacting with the rescuers much. It was unclear why they were even there. Years later, when I asked rescue crews what Frontex's agents did at the port, they would shrug their shoulders and say, flatly: "they took notes." Whatever else the agents did, they did not interfere with SASEMAR's rescue mandate.

The Guardia Civil also had a light hand at the time: the rescuers joked that the agents were there just for the photo opportunity. Indeed, Guardia Civil agents (dressed in olive green) would often get on the orange rescue boats and stand by as migrants walked off the platform. The images in newspaper articles and on the TV news made it look as if they were the ones doing the rescues.

Away from the cameras, the Guardia Civil had more important fish to fry. A couple of years earlier, the force had undergone a major internal overhaul to adapt to the dramatic expansion of responsibilities at sea. This overhaul was partially a response to the creation of the SIVE (Sistema Integrado de Vigilancia Exterior; Integrated System for the Surveillance of the External Border), created in 2001 and which was directly managed by the Guardia Civil. In 2006, the force was focused on the scaling up of the SIVE to the Canary Islands. They also had to address a much-expanded maritime unit which was, among other things, in charge of coordinating collaboration with EU and non-EU actors in security initiatives ranging from Operation Seahorse in North and West Africa to EUROSUR (an expansion of the approach pioneered by the SIVE to the entire southern EU border). The agents were busy, and not particularly interested in rescue.

New actors also appeared in the Atlantic zone. Caminando Fronteras had up until that point been mostly active in the Western Mediterranean. The organization has been a key critic of Spanish border policy from its early days and played a crucial role mediating and advocating for migrants and their families at the border. Following the events of 2006, they started keeping a pulse on the Atlantic zone as well.

Alarm Phone, a pan-European network of activists created in 2014 (after the deadly Lampedusa wreckages), joined them in the Atlantic some years later. Its mandate partially overlaps with that of Caminando Fronteras, but it has a narrower focus: to respond to distress calls at sea and put pressure on EU governments to launch rescue operations. They also follow up on those calls to verify that a rescue did in fact take place, and they organize commemorations ("CommemorActions") in honour of those who died or disappeared at sea and their families. SASEMAR often works with information provided by these organizations, which has proven crucial to locate some of the vessels in distress.

The Red Cross is no longer at sea, although it has an important presence at the ports and reception centres where migrants are transferred upon their arrival. Since migrants started arriving by boat, Red Cross volunteers have been carrying out the initial triage to identify people at risk, such as unaccompanied minors and human trafficking victims, and they hand out blankets, clothes, and food. Red Cross employees and volunteers are also the bulk of the staff at open and closed centres for people on the move on the islands.

In the midst of this increasingly crowded and rapidly evolving environment, rescue crews kept focus on their mandate: to protect human lives at sea. Demand for rescue services certainly overwhelmed SASEMAR at the time, but this did not cause a split of the services, which remained the same for tourists, fisherfolk, and people on the move.

THE RETURN OF THE CAYUCOS

The numbers of migrant arrivals dipped after 2006, and by 2010 the *cayucos* largely disappeared from the waters around the Canary Islands. Seen from the perspective of Spanish policymakers, the delegation of responsibilities onto West African partners had yielded satisfactory results. For a while, it seemed that the "*cayuco* crisis" had really been an exceptional moment that had come to an end. But for migrants who kept taking to the sea, increased surveillance meant that to avoid being caught they had to turn to more dangerous routes. Restrictive policies created a situation where human smuggling became professionalized and put in the hands of, for the most part, criminal networks.

All the while, between 2006 and 2019, SASEMAR acquired new assets. The first Guardamares joined the fleet in 2008. The boats filled an important gap between the faster but smaller Salvamares and the clunkier towboats and polyvalent units. At thirty to forty metres long, they had more autonomy and carrying capacity than the Salvamares, and they boasted a crew of up to eight seamen. These boats were ideal for rescues involving larger dinghies in the huge zone under Spain's rescue responsibility around the Canary Islands.

The uptick in arrivals that started again in 2019 was gradual at first. Then the COVID-19 global pandemic hit. Most countries, including Spain, closed their international borders to try to contain the virus's spread. With all non-essential travel coming to a sudden halt that spring, including tourism, local economies in North and West Africa suffered, which meant that people had less to feed themselves and their families. On top of that, any legal ways that may have existed to cross the border to the European Union closed. But people needed to work, and if jobs were not available at home, they were ready to get on a boat. And so, boats began to arrive again in earnest in 2020.

Journalist Txema Santana had been keeping the pulse of sea migration to his native Canary Islands for a decade and a half by then. He was one of the first to notice that the winds were changing. While mainstream media once again described the rise in migration between 2020 and 2024 as a "crisis," he and others urged people to pay attention to the different currents within the newfound route. One of his colleagues, José María Rodríguez, also a journalist who has been reporting for EFE on migration to the islands since 2011, pointed to at least three stages during this period.

The first stage began shortly after the borders shut down as a result of the pandemic. According to Rodríguez, "the first boats that arrived were *pateras* that left from Dakhla in the Western Sahara and arrived at the island of Gran Canaria." A second stage began in 2021 and continued throughout 2022. At this stage, migrants left from Laayoune and Tarfaya using *pateras* and rigid-hull inflatable boats to reach the easternmost islands of Fuerteventura and Lanzarote. The first routes to be reactivated were thus the "short routes" taking about twenty-four hours to complete. The people using these routes were mainly from Morocco and the Western Sahara. They were fleeing a mix of poverty and political repression.

According to Rodríguez, a third stage began in the summer and fall of 2023: "In 2023, migrants were primarily people from Senegal arriving in *cayucos*, and then, starting in 2024, we saw people from Mauritania as well. The latter came in *pateras* and sometimes in rigid-hull inflatable boats, but mainly they used *cayucos*." Senegalese migrants were fleeing poverty and a lack of opportunities at home, but also an unprecedented democratic crisis and a government targeting discontented and politically active youth. At first, these *cayucos* arrived on the bigger islands: Tenerife and Gran Canaria, in the south of the archipelago. "And then," Rodríguez added, "we started seeing more and more *cayucos* arriving to El Hierro, this little island that is really the last island before there is nothing else," just the open ocean.

Almost forty thousand migrants arrived in the Canary Islands by sea in 2023: 154.5 percent more than the previous year (15,682). As Rodríguez noted, many of those arrived directly at El Hierro, a small island that soon turned into a regular *cayuco* destination. At the beginning, observers thought that migrants were getting there by mistake, and that they were found and rescued before their boats were swept out toward the Americas was a small wonder. Soon, it became clear that migrants were making a calculated, if dangerous, bet. During the 2006–10 period, *cayucos* arrived at the islands using routes that hugged the coast, but, as surveillance in the waters close to the African coast tightened in 2023, boats started venturing deeper into the ocean and heading straight to El Hierro to increase their chances of reaching the islands undetected.

Sometimes a merchant boat would see a dinghy and alert the authorities, and when the rescue services would get there, they would encounter frightful scenes. The number of passengers per *cayuco* also increased exponentially at this time, resulting in worse conditions for those on board. For example, in October 2023, a *cayuco* arrived in El Hierro after a week at sea with 320 people on board. The boat (which came to be known as the *supercayuco*) entered the La Restinga harbour escorted by Salvamar *Adhara*. Both boats were closely followed by another *cayuco* that made it to port on unassisted carrying 211 people. They were lucky. The *Adhara* had a four-man crew and was a metre shorter than the bigger *cayuco*: had any of the *cayucos* capsized, the rescuers would have lacked the resources and carrying capacity to save even half of the passengers.

In fact, the crews of the Salvamar *Adhara*, moored in the port of La Restinga in El Hierro, responded to many of the emergency calls approaching the island. They dealt with some extreme situations. For example, in 2023 they received a call from the regional coordination centre in Tenerife asking them to get ready: a two-hundred-metre-long merchant boat had seen a raft some hundred nautical miles south of El Hierro. Four men appeared to be rowing with what seemed to be pieces of salvaged wood. The rescuers were in disbelief: "A raft? In the middle of the ocean?", one of the rescuers told me he thought upon hearing the news. This seemed quite unusual. The Tenerife coordination centre sent a helicopter first, and they confirmed that there was, indeed, a raft with four Black men in the open ocean. When the *Adhara* approached the raft, the four men insisted that the captain continue navigating southward. Three miles away, a rescue helicopter found the *cayuco* the men had left in their final attempt to find help. The crew of the *Adhara* learned later that the *cayuco* had been drifting at sea for many days. At some point, the passengers had run out of food and water, and people began dying one by one. "Luckily, they had kept the empty fuel cans, which were huge, and they had some fishing nets and some ropes. So, they tied the containers together, wrapped them up in the net, and broke off some pieces of wood from the *cayuco* that they then used as oars," explained a person involved in the rescue. The four men had been rowing toward where they thought the islands were when they happened upon the merchant boat. "Their story could have easily ended very differently," the rescuer concluded.

Rescues *in extremis* became more frequent during the ensuing months. There are different reasons for this. One probable cause was that the militarization of the West African coast to prevent the departure of boats made human smuggling a profitable business. Professional criminal networks that may have been trafficking drugs or other illegal goods simply branched out into human smuggling, with little concern about passenger safety. Additionally, as a consequence of repression along the coast, boats were venturing much deeper into the ocean to avoid surveillance, which meant their trips were longer and more dangerous.

With longer trips in more crowded boats, the condition in which people arrived in the Canary Islands declined sharply. I spoke to a volunteer providing translation services in El Hierro who mentioned, for example, that there was no longer food left in the bottom of the *cayucos* coming from farther south. "Before," she said, "migrants would always leave an extra bag of rice or some cookies behind." More recently, there was nothing left. Cases of *pies de patera* (literally, "*patera* foot"), a rare occurrence before, had also become commonplace. The same volunteer explained that *pie de patera* happens to "people who have spent days with their lower legs submerged in a mix of salt water, urine, feces, and fuel without being able to move, so that even the smallest scratch gets infected. In many cases, by the time they arrive, the infection is so advanced that doctors have to scrape the muscle all the way to the bone or amputate the foot."

As we were having this conversation, there were two people at the hospital in Valverde (El Hierro) who had just had a foot amputated for this reason.

SASEMAR rescue crews, too, cringed when they described the situations that they were now finding in their work on a daily basis. One rescuer told me that "frankly, nowadays when we get onto the *cayuco* to get the last migrants out, half of the time at the bottom there are people who I cannot tell if they are barely alive or altogether dead. This was rare before, but it has become normal." This adds an extra layer of emotional and physical stress to their work. In fact, several of the rescuers deployed in the Canary Islands in 2023 were struggling with crippling anxiety. These were not new crew members discovering the difficulty of rescue work for the first time, but men in their late forties and early fifties with two or three decades of sea rescue experience under their belts.

AN EXHAUSTED RESCUE FLEET

The demands of rescue work have increased dramatically in recent years — not just in terms of the number of hours worked, but also on the toll that changing conditions are taking on workers' physical and psychological health. After two decades of managing emergencies in the Canary Islands, the government has adjusted its response to sea migration. Similarly, rescue crews have developed methods to streamline their operations and make them safer for rescuers and the people they rescue. For example, when I mention to a SASEMAR captain that I am surprised to see more and more images of rescue boats towing dinghies into port, he nods. "We have been learning as we go," he tells me. "Before, we did the transfer from the dinghies onto the rescue boats at sea every single time. But we realized that sometimes the manoeuvre was more dangerous than simply escorting the *cayuco* to port, or just towing it." Transferring people to the rescue boat at sea can be more dangerous for the migrants, because the boat might capsize or they may fall during the manoeuvre, but also for the rescuers — I am told that one of the workers lost a finger a few weeks earlier during a transfer when his hand got caught between the two boats. It was not the only accident.

"We are on the verge of collapse," another rescuer who had been working in the islands for decades told me. Several members of his crew were going on leave due to mental and physical exhaustion. During several interviews, I am struck by the contrast between the appearance of the men sitting in front of me and their level of distress and frustration. The boat crews I meet are for the most part burly seamen in their fifties, and the air crews are experienced and athletic men in their thirties and forties; they have seen a lot during the course of their work. But the message is clear: they feel left alone on the frontline.

In fact, rescuers are not allowed to talk to me. The air personnel in particular are explicitly forbidden from sharing information with outsiders. But they need to talk: they are troubled by what they see at work. A helicopter rescuer tells me he is tired of leaving for a rescue operation with no information and little equipment to deal with the medical emergencies he finds once he arrives at the site. "More than once I have found myself in the water without the proper equipment," he tells me, "and I thought I wouldn't live to tell the tale."

A Salvamar captain grapples with the weight of responsibility for his crew's safety. He fears he is not always in the right state of mind to make good judgements, "but how can I make decisions with a clear head when we have all been working twenty-hour days for one or two weeks straight?" At sea and in the air, rescuers in the Canary Islands feel that they are being pulled in two different directions: what they are supposed to do as rescuers, and what they are told to do (and not to do) when an operation is launched. In this situation, rescue crews pay for the tension and the overwork with their health.

A Shifting Boundary, Externalization, and the Military

Externalization of border controls around the Canary Islands has created rapid changes in sea migration and moved the goalposts for rescuers in the Atlantic zone. One illustrative example happened on a sunny day in the summer of 2023. The NGO Caminando Fronteras had received a call from the relative of a person who had left on a boat from Cabo Bojador in the Western Sahara a few days earlier. The rigid-hull inflatable boat was headed for Gran Canaria. It carried sixty-three people, including several children. They were having difficulty at sea and needed help. Caminando Fronteras called the emergency services, which called the Las Palmas Regional Coordination Centre (MRCC).

The coordination centre sent the SASEMAR 101 (a small reconnaissance plane) from Gran Canaria to locate the boat. The conversation between the control tower and the pilot of the SASEMAR 101 was leaked a few days later to journalist Nicolás Castellano, who shared it on national radio (Castellano 2023).

> Tower: I am going to give you a position. We would like you to check it out without entering the Moroccan SAR zone. [gives position]
>
> Pilot: Can you please confirm that it is about fourteen miles southbound from my position?
>
> Tower: Affirmative, that is correct. It's in the overlapping zone, about four or five miles. I don't know if you could stay on our side of the line, can you check from there?
>
> Pilot: I understand. The position is inside our SAR zone. No, it shouldn't matter.

The pilot sounded surprised. He was certain he would not have to enter the Moroccan SAR zone, because the maps SASEMAR used *up until that day* did not show a Moroccan zone of responsibility in this part of the Atlantic.

Hours later, the pilot communicated that he had located the boat.

> Tower: Ok, let me know when you have an approximate number of people to confirm, because we are calling Morocco. Laayoune [the capital of the disputed territories of the Western Sahara] is close, thirty-something miles away ....
>
> Pilot: Look, about the inflatable [boat], we were looking at the pictures and there are about fifty people on board. They are from North Africa [*magrebís,* meaning not Black]. They seem to be in good health ....

The data about the number and presumed origin of the migrants on the boat were important because it would be used by the personnel at the Las Palmas MRCC to decide if that was the boat Caminando Fronteras had alerted them about, or a different one. The information about its occupants' well-being was also relevant, because the state of the boat and the people within it would dictate the course of action — whether the tower had to launch an emergency rescue operation immediately or not. How passengers' race and state of health could be determined from a blurry black and white picture taken from above is a different matter. Meanwhile, Caminando Fronteras continued posting updates on their social media accounts and calling for an intervention.

Once the pilot confirmed that the boat was not sinking and there was no one in the water, the controller instructed him to return to base. SASEMAR then asked a container ship that was in the area, the 260-metre long *Navio Azure*, to approach and keep a close eye on the migrant boat in case the dinghy capsized, which would have triggered a rescue immediately. Meanwhile, having transferred the information to Morocco, Spain stepped back. The Guardamar *Calíope* (based in Fuerteventura at the time) was less than an hour away, on its way to port after another rescue operation involving a different migrant boat. It could have changed its trajectory to assist on the rescue, but it was not called.

At sea, the migrants waited. And waited. By the time the Royal Moroccan Navy showed up ten to twelve hours after the initial distress call, thirty-nine people had died. A helicopter from the Spanish rescue services was eventually mobilized to retrieve a dead child's body from the sea. We do not know, and will never know, what happened to those who were taken back to Morocco. Were they deported? If so, where? Were they detained? Left on the streets? Given access to medical services for dehydration, exposure, chemical burns? Given access to psychological care for the trauma of spending days at sea, being deemed unworthy of a timely rescue, surviving a wreckage?

In this case, the militarization of rescue was both domestic (it seemed obvious the Spanish military had intervened) and foreign (as the main agency responsible for rescues in Morocco was the Royal Navy). And while there is nothing wrong with rescues done by military forces, the opacity of these operations means that there is no evidence rescues were actually carried out, or what happened to the people on the move once they reached Moroccan shores.

A rescuer I talked to shook his head when he remembered other cases where he had witnessed the Royal Moroccan Navy transferring migrants onto their patrol boats: "they just lift people by their clothes and throw them around as if they were a sack of potatoes. People hit their bodies and their heads on the metal of the boats … it's horrible to watch. And, sometimes, we have gone back to the site of the rescue to pick up debris from the boats and there were still people in the water!" And herein lies one of the most insidious issues with the externalization of rescue responsibilities to countries like Morocco, Mauritania, or Senegal: we do not know when, where, how, or if rescues actually happen. Morocco only releases gross numbers of rescues in the weeks preceding negotiations with Spanish or European authorities, and there is no background data to back up those numbers. Senegal and Mauritania do not share any data on their rescue activities. And so, the black box of maritime rescue along the southern EU border grows. As Canadian scholar Alison Mountz argues, those who drown at sea do not just lose their lives, they also experience a political death (Mountz 2020). In other words, they no longer matter.

There is resistance to this vanishing of migrant deaths from public view. A day after the wreckage, the Defensor del Pueblo opened an investigation to clarify responsibilities. The NGO Caminando Fronteras made a separate request a couple of weeks later, asking the Public Prosecutor's Office to launch a criminal investigation into the Spanish government's failure to render assistance. They also submitted the information to the United Nation's High Commissioner for Refugees (UNHCR), since they argued that several people on the boat were eligible for international protection; and to the United Nations Children's Fund (UNICEF), since three children died as a consequence of Spain's failure to intervene (EFE 2023).

For the rescuers, though, a key issue was that a new boundary had suddenly appeared — a boundary that could potentially have important implications in their everyday work. Which map should they use: the one with or the one without the Moroccan zone of responsibility? Worse yet, they had no one to turn to for answers. Rumours started circulating. On their social media accounts, the rescuers' main union denounced what they saw as a sudden change to Spain's rescue policy that interfered with their work. In fact, Morocco had long claimed this zone as its zone of responsibility in a move that some interpreted as a first step toward broader claims for jurisdiction and ownership of the natural resources off the coast of the Western Sahara. But until that very day, the Spanish government had never officially recognized a Moroccan zone of responsibility in this part of the Atlantic.

GEOPOLITICS AND RESCUE RESPONSIBILITIES IN THE ATLANTIC

In the previous chapter, we saw that conflicting geopolitical goals involving territorial claims on the part of Morocco were central to the renegotiation of rescue responsibilities in the Western Mediterranean. Migration (more specifically, people on the move) had become simple currency in this exchange. Morocco used these men, women, and children as a threat to increase its bargaining power with Spain and the European Union. The situation was similar in the Atlantic, but here there was much more at play. For one, there was the political situation of the Western Sahara, which Morocco had long claimed as part of its territory. Also related to the colonial history in the region is the old and ongoing dispute over the limits of both countries' Exclusive Economic Zones in the waters between the African coast and the Canary Islands. The area is rich in fish but also in rare minerals — especially tellurium, one of the least common elements on Earth, used to make electric car batteries and solar panels. For Morocco, the geopolitical and economic importance of the area far outweighs migration as a domestic concern. But the control of human mobility is a useful asset in Morocco's negotiation with Spain and the European Union.

Back in 2012, Morocco had already defined its zone of responsibility to overlap with that of Spain. Even though the country deployed scarce rescue assets to address emergencies in this area, the existence of the Moroccan zone of responsibility seemed to support and legitimize the claims over these waters that came later. A few years later, in 2017, the government announced its intention to revise its legislation to expand its Exclusive Economic Zone, which it did eventually, in 2020. That year, Morocco passed two bills to update the country's maritime law and declare its sovereignty over the waters off the coast of the Western Sahara. There was not so much as a peep from the international community, who had at the time found itself scrambling to come up with a strategy to stop the spread of the COVID-19 pandemic.

There was significant overlap between Morocco's new sovereign area in the Atlantic and the zone of responsibility the Moroccan government had defined years earlier without ever assigning any rescue assets to it. A possible interpretation offered by some of the people I interviewed is that the King of Morocco saw Spain's increased dependency on their role as a border guard as an opportunity for the country to redefine its sovereign claims in the area. In other words, the country asserting rescue responsibilities in the Atlantic region might have been a strategy to strengthen its sovereignty claims in the area and secure access to the ocean's resources.

The diplomatic crisis of 2021 discussed in the previous chapter, which was triggered by Spain providing medical care for the leader of the Polisario Front, put the country in a weak negotiating position. During the months that followed the crisis, and perhaps in an attempt to decrease tensions and ease the negotiations surrounding migration control, Spain reversed its historical position on the need for a referendum for the determination of the administrative status of the Western Sahara. Spain never went as far as the United States, who, under Donald Trump, recognized "Moroccan sovereignty over the entire Western Sahara territory" a year earlier (Trump 2020). In this case, US support for Morocco was part of a broader strategy to normalize relations between this country and Israel. Instead, Spain changed its long-standing demand for a referendum on independence and got behind Morocco's official proposal for a scenario where the Western Sahara would be autonomous under Morocco's "supervision." This was an unexpected U-turn from the previous fifty years, since the territories gained independence from Spain. It was also a major success for the Moroccan government's lobbying efforts to take control of the Western Saharan territories.

Morocco's efforts to enhance its rescue capacity and assume greater responsibility in its Atlantic zone unfolded within this complex geopolitical landscape. The country's co-operation with European migration control allowed Morocco to advance its long-standing strategy to integrate the Western Sahara and surrounding waters into its territory. Morocco did not particularly oppose the theoretical obligation it acquired to conduct sea rescues, as it helped legitimize much more existential geopolitical claims in the region.

Changes in the way rescue operations are carried out (or not) in the Atlantic mirrored those in the Western Mediterranean described in the previous chapter, although the timeline and the consequences for the provision of services to people on the move differed. At the time of writing, any conclusions on how these changes affect the number of people dying at sea are just preliminary: the dust must settle before we can see any long-term trends. Moreover, there are more actors to consider in the development of a new rescue landscape in the Atlantic region. The wreckage in June 2023 and the debate over the boundaries of each country's zone of responsibility were a reminder that, obsessed with the goal of keeping migrants from poor countries out, governments were changing policy at breakneck pace, without necessarily communicating those changes to those on the ground (or, in this case, on the planes and boats).

Much like in the Western Mediterranean, Spain's approach to migration control in the Atlantic hinges on three main strategies (externalization, militarization, and repression), all of which impact maritime rescue and the workers who labour to realize the goals and vision of the SAR Convention. The first strategy is the externalization of rescue responsibilities to non-EU states, with little capacity or motivation to protect migrants' basic rights — including their right to life. This should come as little surprise: externalization has become an article of faith in today's European approach to migration and border control. It is enshrined in bilateral and multilateral treaties with Libya, Türkiye, Egypt, and Tunisia, and in the new European Pact on Migration and Asylum that the European Parliament adopted in 2024.

In the Atlantic, Spain and the EU's main partners in this endeavour are the Moroccan Royal Marine, the Senegalese Gendarmerie, and the Mauritanian Gendarmerie. This highlights the increasing role of militarized actors in the provision of rescue services in the region. But militarization also happens at home. Although there is no equivalent to the military-led MUO (Mando Único Operativo; Single Operative Command) and the CCOE (Centro de Coordinación de Operaciones de Emergencia; Emergency Operation Coordination Centre) in the archipelago, the Guardia Civil has run the CCRC (Centro de Coordinación de Rescates de Canarias; Canary Islands Rescue Coordination Centre) since 2006. The Guardia Civil coordinates monthly CCRC meetings attended by SASEMAR, the police, and civil society groups involved in the provision of services for those rescued at sea such as the Red Cross (Frontex does not participate in these meetings). The CCRC also takes over the coordination of rescue operations involving migrants: in other words, a parallel rescue system for emergencies related to sea migration has emerged in the Canary Islands. While militarization has been less publicized here (unlike in the Western Mediterranean), it has still happened, with consequences for the full and meaningful implementation of SASEMAR's mandate. The Guardia Civil's role coordinating the CCRC means that operations involving people on the move have been transferred to the military, at least partially. Meanwhile, coordination for operations involving everyone else remains in the hands of SASEMAR's civilian personnel. In addition, there are several Guardia Civil patrol boats permanently deployed in the area that conduct a small but steady number of rescues, including the *Río Tajo* and *Río Segura*. Still, the creation of a two-tier rescue system is not as clear in the Atlantic as it is in the Western Mediterranean.

Spain also enlisted countries of origin and transit in the Atlantic region to criminalize people on the move, detain, and deport them, and so prevent migrant people from ever reaching EU territory. All this is made possible through the deployment of extremely costly advanced technologies used to detect irregular movements of people at and near borders and create biometric databases to identify and share their profiles with countries among and beyond EU authorities.

As for rescues, there are signs we are headed into a situation similar to that in the Central Mediterranean, where European drones patrol the waters of co-operating countries to launch rescue operations *before* the boats reach member states' zones of responsibility. The line between a pullback and a rescue is a thin one in these cases. Either way, we have only anecdotal evidence of rescue operations carried out by Spain's partners in the Atlantic. This does not mean these operations do not happen, just that we do not know if and how they happen. Opacity is a major problem: the only information we have regarding rescues in the area comes from NGOs or surfaces in specific circumstances.

In their wish to move away from rescue and stop migration at the source, Spain and the EU have focused their efforts on disarticulating smuggling and human trafficking networks. But lawyers on the islands have denounced police practices such as consistently identifying and punishing two skippers per boat as missing the mark. The people identified as smugglers often are the men who happened to be near the engine when their boat was first sighted, those who made the emergency call, or those in charge of cooking and distributing the food during the journey. Other passengers are promised a more lenient treatment if they name the persons in charge of the boat. The problem is that criminalizing two migrants per boat who happened to be in the wrong place at the wrong time has no impact on the smuggling business model.

It could be argued, then, that Spain and the European Union's three-pronged strategy has not stopped sea migration: it has simply forced people on the move to take more dangerous routes. According to the organization Caminando Fronteras (2023, 4), 6,618 migrant people drowned on their way to Spain in 2023 alone. The vast majority of them (6,007) drowned on their way to the Canary Islands. Their deaths, and the impact their deaths have on the communities they leave behind and those faced with the trauma of witnessing never-ending tragedies, are a testament to the failure of the dominant contemporary approach to both migration control and border policy in Europe. These approaches focus on water-tight border management, zero in on spaces of origin and transit, and are fundamentally repressive.

This repression has given birth to a growing constellation of spaces of grieving and death in communities on both sides of the border. They have also created the conditions for a highly profitable smuggling business. Because self-directed migration is less and less likely to succeed in this context, people on the move must often hire the services of criminal smuggling actors, which results in increased physical, emotional, financial, and sexual violence. Yet, despite mounting evidence attesting to the failure of these strategies, EU member states have doubled down on their repressive approach. Maritime rescue has become a victim of this stubbornness. As Europe's approach to human mobility flounders, the withdrawal and shrinking of rescue services from migration areas seals migrants' fate. But there is resistance to turning rescue missions into another instrument for border control. Perhaps unexpectedly, some of this resistance comes from the rescue crews, who are pushing back.

6

The Rescuers' Union: Resistance from Within

"We don't rescue migrants: we rescue shipwreck victims."

—ISMAEL FURIÓ, General Secretary, CGT,
Mar y Puertos and CGT SASEMAR (2019)

IN LATE SEPTEMBER 2020, the Salvamar *Menkalinan* was sent to rescue a boat carrying forty-one migrants. The dinghy was about twenty-four kilometres (thirteen nautical miles) south of the island of Gran Canaria. Having tied the boats to each other, the rescuers were about to begin transferring people from the dinghy to the *Menkalinan*. "At that point, operators and the tower [the regional coordination centre] understand you are busy, so they will let you get on with the operation," the captain of another rescue boat told me. But not this time: in the middle of the manoeuvre, with the boats tied together and rescuers and migrants getting ready for the transfer, the operator called off the operation and ordered the captain to untie the ropes and leave. A military patrol would complete the rescue.

A worse moment to interrupt a rescue operation does not exist. After days or weeks at sea, people become impatient to get off the boat when they see a rescue is imminent. They often stand up, causing the boat to rock and sometimes capsize. People fall into the water. Some cannot swim and others can barely move after days sitting still. They may drown, right there, in front of the rescue boat. Crew members are forbidden from getting into the water during a rescue, for their own safety and that of the people at risk, and there is little they can do to save people who fall out of the dinghy. "You throw them *anything* that floats, and hope they will make it," a rescuer told me. With this in mind, the captain knew that telling the migrants to sit back and wait for another ship to come and get them could cause things to go terribly wrong very quickly.

In the conversation that journalist Nicolás Castellano leaked to the media, the captain is silent for a few long seconds (Vega and Martín 2020). Incredulous, he reacts: "I am in the middle of the manoeuvre, what do I do?!" Hesitantly, the operator replies, "[The National Coordination Centre] has told me that the *Río Segura* will pick them up." The *Río Segura* is a Guardia Civil patrol boat. That day, when the coordination centre contacted the rescue team, it was miles away from the *Menkalinan*. More importantly, it was not already tied to a barely floating wooden fishing boat filled with physically and emotionally exhausted people scared for their lives and already standing up. A few more seconds of silence follow. When the captain responds, he is yelling: "But I already have [the dinghy] tied to the side of my boat, dude! What am I supposed to do now, let go of the ropes?!" The coordinator answers again, slowly, uncertain: "The *Río Segura* is supposed to go there to take them back to Tenerife. Are you in contact with the *Río Segura*?" Silence. The captain's voice booms through the comms system: "But how can you tell me this now, we are already tied up!"

A tirade of expletive swearing follows. The captain attempts direct communication with the *Río Segura* once, twice, three times. No answer. The clock is ticking and the two boats are still tied to each other, rocking in the waves, the people growing restless. The rescuers are signalling to them to sit down and wait, wait a bit longer. None of the migrants speaks Spanish; the rescuers use the few words they know in French and English, their hands, and their bodies to communicate that it is not yet time to get off the boat.

Eventually, the *Río Segura* responds. The other captain is surprised. He has not received orders to go anywhere or rescue anyone. He needs to check. More silence. Furious, the captain from the *Menkalinan* asks the tower operator for instructions once again. When the operator starts repeating the command to withdraw from the operation, he does not let her finish and gives orders to abort the rescue operation. "Hoist the ropes!" he yells to his crew, leaving the communication line open, perhaps intentionally. Silence. Picking up the conversation with the operator, the captain tries to calm himself down: "Look, you can't do this. I am hoisting the ropes, but you have to make up your mind before you send a rescue boat to the area! [...] I am playing with lives here!"

Shortly afterwards, the captain seems to resign himself to the fact that he has no choice but to follow orders. His breathing is still uneven, shallow. He manages to pin down the details of the rescue operation with the captain of the *Río Segura* patrol boat in a tense conversation marked with silences and half-finished sentences. In the meantime, a boat full of people who had spent ten days at sea and thought they were finally safe was left to drift away. One can only imagine the confusion and despair among those left waiting in the middle of the ocean.

SASEMAR's Comité intercentros de seguridad y salud (Health and Safety Committee) denounced this event and asked the agency for an explanation shortly afterward. Union representatives were furious. They found that these situations were becoming more common as the military gained control over some of SASEMAR's mandate in the Spanish zone of responsibility — specifically, in operations involving people on the move.

Referring to the troubling experience of the *Menkalinan*'s crew, the union denounced that the involvement of the military put the safety and well-being of rescue crews at risk and endangered those in need of rescue at sea. We could add that situations such as this showcase a conflict that has become central to SASEMAR's existence: the agency is trapped between its mandate to rescue and the political impetus to fold it into the border control apparatus. This tension places a significant burden on rescuers, especially when arriving at the scene of a prolonged emergency or when people are already in the water; in these situations, workers must make split-second decisions about who will be saved and who may be left to drown. This is a tremendously difficult position to be in. The captain of the *Menkalinan* (a man with several decades of rescue work experience) went on medical leave due to stress shortly after the incident.

Just a couple of years earlier, none of this would have made it to the media: not the leaked conversation and certainly not the union's opinion of it. Paradoxically, it was in the fallout of a communications gag imposed on SASEMAR workers in 2018 that the primary union representing boat crews became much more visible. The gag order happened at the same time as the creation of the military Single Operative Command in the Western Mediterranean in 2018. The timing was not a coincidence. The government sought to make the rescue of migrant boats less visible, and thus harder to exploit by the extreme right before the 2019 general election. SASEMAR press office suddenly stopped reporting on rescue operations in migration areas. But, by law, union spokespeople cannot be forbidden from speaking with the media about the working conditions of its members. The most vocal of the unions was the CGT SASEMAR, a branch of the larger anarcho-syndicalist Comisión General del Trabajo, the main union representing boat crews.

Using their social media platforms, representatives from this union were able to get their message across directly to the media and to anyone who wanted to listen. As a labour union, they were tireless in their demands to improve the working conditions of their members. But the CGT (the larger union encompassing CGT SASEMAR) is not just another run-of-the-mill labour union: as an anarcho-syndicalist union, they see the solidarity they foster among workers as part of a larger, international movement to dismantle class hierarchies created and reinforced by capitalism.

Because of these principles, the union was adamant that improvements to the working conditions of its members should not infringe on their promotion of class solidarity across borders or the rights of sea migrants who they saw also as losers in the capitalist game. Thus, the CGT SASEMAR spokespeople built a discourse where the fight for better working conditions and cross-border class struggle were two sides of the same conflict. At a time when implementing restrictive border policies at sea seemed an inevitable aspect of the European Union's approach to migration, the union's media presence offered an alternative way of framing maritime rescue in contexts of migration.

But how did SASEMAR rescue crews — a group of government workers, many of whom do not even identify as anarchists — end up electing one of Spain's most radical unions to represent them? And what impact, if any, did the CGT SASEMAR have on the transformation of the Spanish maritime rescue system?

THE ARRIVAL OF THE ANARCHISTS

As we have already seen, through the late 1980s, rescue services in Spain were a fragmented set of rescue assets, some managed by regional governments and some subcontracted through private companies. Nothing resembling a national maritime rescue system was in place at that time, and the fleet existed more as a set of objectives written on paper than a reality. SASEMAR grew from the first towers and boats, integrating air units later on. At sea, rescue operations were done by a motley mix of trawlers, multipurpose boats, and motorboats either donated by the Red Cross or hired (part- or full-time) from large companies. The first four Salvamares were functional in 1991, but they struggled with rescues far from the shore. The first helicopter (a Sikorsky S-61N) arrived that same year. Even with the additional assets from regional rescue services, these resources were insufficient and largely inadequate for the size of the area covered by Spanish search and rescue (three times the country's landmass) and the magnitude of the work at hand. Throughout this evolution, the rescue crews were, as in any other rescue service, the backbone of the system.

The first rescuers employed in the emerging national rescue system in the late 1980s were typically former fishermen and seamen subcontracted through REMOLMAR, a private company that would eventually be absorbed into SASEMAR. Their shifts were long and arduous, without guaranteed time off or vacation. At the time, rescuers worked in cycles of three weeks on/one week off, year-round. Breaks between shifts were not guaranteed, because REMOLMAR relied on what they called "polyvalent personnel": workers who could fill different roles within the crew, serving as a sailor one day and a boat mechanic the next, for example. In practice, this meant that the service was severely short-staffed. Whenever one of the workers was on leave or a position was vacant, the other members of the crew had to fill that position, even if they had just finished their three-week shift or if they were supposed to be on vacation.

Enric Tarrida was a captain in the first cohort of men hired to do rescue work in Spain. He was in his twenties and joined REMOLMAR after years working in the fishing industry. He recalled one time when he was sent about seventy-four kilometres offshore (forty nautical miles) on a flimsy ten-metre fibreglass boat on a man-overboard mission. A force nine gale was raging that day, a storm with winds up to eighty-eight kilometres per hour and waves up to ten metres tall. After twenty hours labouring in these conditions, they ran out of fuel. They were ordered back to port to refuel and then immediately sent out again to respond to two other emergencies with no improvement in the weather. Shifts like this, lasting longer than eighteen hours, were frequent. Thinking about the early days, Enric recalled that, "Even back then, as a sailor used to terrible working conditions, I said to myself, 'How can this be? I mean, this is crazy, isn't it?'" Their contract at the time stated they worked 243 twenty-four-hour days, for a salary barely above minimum wage.

I met Enric Tarrida in person in 2023. After years of conversations with spokespeople from the CGT SASEMAR, I was intrigued by a certain hard-headed man everyone mentioned as key to the union's origin story. Nobody wanted to name this person who, in his own time and with his own money, had criss-crossed the country in the early days of the Spanish maritime rescue system to talk to other rescue crews who did not know each other. He asked them about their labour conditions, what they needed, what they wanted, and organized them from the ground up.

By the time I met Enric, I assumed that this man was either a legend or long gone — or both. It was not until halfway through our first interview that I suddenly realized he was the original anarchist in SASEMAR's rescue crew many others had told me about. He was describing how the first collective agreement in the Spanish search and rescue sector came into being — in secret, to avoid backlash from both the rescuers' employer and the powerful larger unions — when I finally connected the dots.

It is important also to appreciate the context in which Enric first began organizing rescue crews. Spain was emerging from four decades of fascist military rule that had harshly punished political dissent, particularly anarchism. Enric was an anarchist and a fisherman in the 1970s, which meant he was both a political dissident and working class. For those in the fringes, the 1980s ushered in a sense of momentous change. The young democracy signalled an economic and political opening to the world after decades of isolation and brutal repression. Exiled anarchists came back to a country that had changed in their absence. Upon their return, they met those like Enric, who had stayed behind, organizing in secret with little contact with their comrades abroad. However, the years apart had shaped the evolution of their thought and strategies differently. Returned exiles and those who had remained had very different, and sometimes clashing, visions for the future of anarchism in the country. The movement came out of the dictatorship weak and fragmented.

At the time, sea migration was not a pressing concern for Spanish anarchists. Emergencies at sea typically involved fishermen, commercial boats, and the occasional but devastating environmental disaster. The urgency was on land, where the country's political landscape was shifting. The communists had taken a seat at the negotiating table with the government, the socialists were poised to win the first truly free elections since the Second Republic, and fascists still clung to positions of power. In the midst of this upheaval, anarchists sought to find a way to become relevant political actors again.

Meanwhile, emboldened by these tectonic changes, rescuers began organizing to demand better wages and, above all, improved working conditions. They were determined to secure the rights they had long been denied. For a while, workers sought the support of Spain's largest unions. Enric and another colleague, Oriol Estrada, started working with the Unión General de Trabajadores (UGT), a cross-sector labour union traditionally aligned with the Socialist Party. However, after months of negotiations, the rescuers were frustrated and felt that the UGT was not taking their demands seriously. As Oriol, an active CGT SASEMAR member then and now, summarized it, "we [rescue workers] needed a better collective agreement, and [UGT] was only willing to negotiate whether we had to wear high boots or low boots at work and things like that, totally inconsequential issues, instead of the things that really mattered to us. They were useless."

Oriol thought UGT had sold out to their employer (REMOLMAR); Enric agreed. To add insult to injury, Enric added that the two (UGT and REMOLMAR) had signed agreements behind the rescuers' backs that did not reflect the content of the conversations the workers and UGT had been having for months. Enric recalled that "UGT reps said the workers should accept those agreements as they were and fight to have them amended later. Did they think we were born yesterday? That's not how things work."

Enric did know how these negotiations were supposed to go. He had been moving in anarchist circles since he could remember, when those groups were still illegal and actively persecuted by the Francoist regime. Thanks to his work as an active member of the anarchist organization Confederación Nacional del Trabajo (the National Workers' Confederation or CNT, from which the CGT would be born some years later), Enric was well versed on the realities of union work even before joining REMOLMAR, and he arrived at the negotiation table with his head full of ideals and ambitions.

After what they saw as the betrayal by the UGT, the rescue workers started organizing. This was around the turn of the decade, in the late 1980s and early 1990s. Spain already had a National Maritime Rescue Plan in place, but no structure to execute it. Enric began by preparing a statement, "a sort of list with what I thought was the bare minimum to make our labour conditions reasonable." The list was written by hand and sent by fax to trusted fellow rescuers whom Enric had met during his travels to try and mobilize other crews. Together, by fax, phone, or at in-person meetings, they modified the list. All these meetings were semi-clandestine: the workers were afraid other unions or the company might try to hijack the negotiations.

After some months of back and forth, each crew chose a representative and paid for him to go to Madrid for a final meeting — the meeting from which the CGT SASEMAR grew. Halfway through our conversation, Enric stopped and looked through the window wistfully. "Those days were so challenging!" he told me. "I would finish my three weeks on call, get on the sleeper train from Girona to Madrid, spend the day at meetings, back on the sleeper train the next day, straight from the train to the boat. And we had no support from anyone. We just supported each other and ourselves." Organizing the rescue crews in the early days was a titanic effort that demanded significant sacrifice: "We used to joke that we were the idiots working one hundred hours a week to have a forty-hour work week!"

From then on, rescue crews' support for the CGT grew. Previously, the rescuers had been within the CGT section for seafarers and dockworkers, the CGT Mar y Puertos. A new section of the union specifically representing rescue workers was created in the early 1990s — the CGT SASEMAR. The agency's maritime crews went from having just one anarchist in the early 1990s (Enric) to electing a majority of anarchist representatives in every election since. These representatives met at SASEMAR's Work Council, the body that brings together representatives from all unions voted by the workers. In the 2024 elections, eleven of the twenty-three representatives that rescuers elected to defend their interests in this Council were from the CGT.

The historical dominance of the CGT SASEMAR does not necessarily reflect widespread worker support for anarchist ideals. In fact, most workers do not consider themselves anarchists at all. They vote for the CGT because this union has been more vocal, more visible, and more successful advocating for the rescue fleet than UGT and CCOO, which also have representatives in the Work Council. Still, the ideals of class solidarity and internationalism have prevailed over the decades, colouring everything the CGT SASEMAR does, both on behalf of its members and as a defining factor of the fleet's public position regarding migration and borders.

ANARCHO-SYNDICALISM IN SPAIN: A BRIEF HISTORY OF THE CGT

The strength of the CGT among SASEMAR crews is somewhat unusual. Anarchism has a rich history in Spain (particularly before Franco's dictatorship), but the CGT is a small union compared to others in the country. The largest unions are Comisiones Obreras (CCOO) and the UGT. CCOO appeared in the 1960s and was a result of workers' resistance against rigid forms of labour organization imposed by the dictatorship. It is ideologically aligned with the communist left and had 980,000 members across sectors in 2022.

UGT is an older union; it was born in the late nineteenth century. Historically, it sides with the socialist centre-left and is a close second in terms of membership, with 950,000 members across sectors. The third largest labour union in terms of membership is the Unión Sindical Obrera (Workers' Union Coalition, USO), which was created during Spain's transition to democracy and represents about 133,000 members. In 2024, CCOO and the UGT had 5 and 7 representatives respectively in SASEMAR's Work Council and the USO had none. Nationally, the CGT is a much smaller force compared to the other three, with fewer than 80,000 members across sectors in 2022. The CGT is not associated with any specific political party. So, what do they stand for?

It is possible that anarchism is the most poorly understood political ideology of our time. Despite its richness and internal diversity as a theory and a political movement, in everyday conversations anarchism has been reduced to a synonym of chaos and radical individualism. The people that seem to represent it in public discourse today are either tech bros (Elon Musk is a self-proclaimed "utopian anarchist") or Molotov cocktail-throwing, balaclava-wearing, discontent punks.

By contrast, the CGT sits at the collectivist end of the anarchist spectrum. As anarcho-syndicalists, its members advocate for direct collective action, solidarity, and workers' self-management. They believe that the working class must self-organize to gain control of the economy and build a better, fairer society — one where class divisions do not exist and there is no room or need for government institutions (including international borders). This society would be governed through direct democracy, following the assembly model that is not unlike the definition of the anarchist federal model proposed by Peter Kropotkin (1910 [1995], 233) more than a century ago:

> An interwoven network, composed of an infinite variety of groups and federations of all sizes and degrees, local, regional, national and international temporary or more or less permanent — for all possible purposes: production, consumption and exchange, communications, sanitary arrangements, education, mutual protection, defence of the territory, and so on; and, on the other side, for the satisfaction of an ever-increasing number of scientific, artistic, literary and sociable needs.

In Spain, collective anarchism has historically been represented by the CNT. Since its origin in 1910 and to this day, the CNT retains the view that representative institutions are illegitimate. Instead of delegation, they advocate for self-representation. However, there have always been CNT militants who have wished for a more pragmatic and instrumental relationship with government institutions, a relationship they hoped to use to bring certain aspects of the anarchist agenda into public life. These anarchists have been known as the "possibilists" or "reformists" within the movement. For example, during the Second Republic (1931–1939), four ministers were anarchists *and* CNT militants (Marín Silvestre 2005). Juan García Oliver was Minister of Justice, Juan López Sánchez was Minister of Commerce, Federica Montseny (an anarcho-feminist and the first woman in history to serve in the Spanish cabinet) was Minister of Health and Social Assistance, and Joan Peiró was Minister of Industry.

These ministers embraced the paradox of being anarchists in power. Ultimately, their goal was to run the country and help bring back the democratically elected constitutional government. In the meantime, they enacted radical legal and social policies that were far ahead of their time, including the legalization of civil unions, the introduction of a new adoption law, the legalization of occupying vacant residences, the establishment of a system of subsidized rentals, and the creation of public canteens (Marín Silvestre 2005). Though their time in government was brief, their actions expanded the realm of political possibility.

The golden age of anarchism ended suddenly with Franco's victory and the end of the Civil War. When the dictator died almost forty years later, the long-standing conflict between anarchists who wanted to influence state politics from within the system and those who preferred to act from its margins came to a head. The main point of friction was participation in government institutions. More orthodox anarchists in the CNT refused to support union elections, which they saw as a move away from self-representation and a concession to the state. More pragmatic anarchists pointed to the example of the anarchist ministers during the Second Republic and wanted to participate in mainstream politics (including union elections) to change the government from the inside. After years of legal battles between the two camps, the debate was settled in 1989 when the faction supporting an instrumental relationship with the government officially broke from the CNT to form the CGT. Today, these two anarchist organizations coexist uncomfortably.

As for the CGT, the union defines itself as a "class-based, autonomous, member-managed, federalist, internationalist, and libertarian" union, guided primarily by its affiliates' enthusiasm for "an alternative trade union and social project that challenges the exploitation of man by man: a world with neither exploited nor exploiters" (CGT 2022, 7). In short, the

CGT is an anarchist union who believes in collective alliances and wants a seat at the table to change things from the inside. Where the CNT keeps a distance from representative government institutions and refuses to hold internal elections, the CGT elects its delegates every four years. Rescue crews participate in the elections by mail, since at any given time, roughly half of the membership will be deployed at ports throughout Spain. The CGT also negotiates within democratic structures and accepts subsidies from the state (CNT n.d.). That an anarchist organization behaves this way may seem paradoxical and potentially incompatible with the fundamental tenets of the movement. However, the case of CGT SASEMAR demonstrates that this approach can be highly effective in defending its members and challenging official discourses.

The longest-serving General Secretary of the CGT SASEMAR, Ismael Furió Genovés, sees this clearly. When I met him near his home in Valencia in 2023, he readily admitted that the society imagined by anarcho-syndicalists is out of reach, a utopia: "We'll never get there. But if you keep your eye on it, every decision you make will be an improvement. The journey will be worth it, even if you never make it to your destination." This pragmatism explains the paradox of an anarchist union that fully (if critically) embraces government-imposed processes such as internal elections and work councils, while also pursuing its own anti-government agenda. It is from this seemingly contradictory position that the union handles its approach to government-run search and rescue.

CGT SASEMAR: A WORKERS' ORGANIZATION AND AN ACTOR OF CHANGE

Members of the union see their organization as a two-headed creature: one head focuses on the working conditions of its members, the other on setting the stage for a world where the anarchist ideals of class solidarity and internationalism may perhaps reign one day. They see these two missions as not just connected, but dependent on each other and built upon the guiding principles of mutual aid and direct action. Achieving their goals is a tall order, though. Aiming toward and articulating the goals of the CGT as a labour union and as a bringer of political change demands not just a robust structure, but also a strong social action arm and an effective public relations strategy. And the union must do this while operating on a shoestring budget and relying on the dedication of its members, staff, and volunteers.

To add to this challenge, as a good anarchist union, CGT SASEMAR aims to function in a non-hierarchical manner, while at the same time existing within a larger state system defined by and through hierarchies. In contrast to the government and other national labour unions with a similar national super-structure, the CGT is a horizontal organization that brings together smaller sections of the union organized around activity sectors and geographic areas. The relationship between the different sections that form the CGT is functional rather than hierarchical. Put differently, the section of the CGT representing SASEMAR's rescue fleet is, for logistical purposes, placed within the section of the CGT that represents seafarers and dockworkers (CGT Mar y Puertos); both exist within the broader umbrella of the national CGT structure. However, this does not mean there is a hierarchical relationship between them: the national, sectoral, and company-specific unions have the same power and authority. This has important implications for the union's relationship with the government — which is, in the case of SASEMAR workers, also their employer. Government actors and policymakers, who exist in firmly hierarchical and siloized power structures, do not know how to deal with this.

The following anecdote points to the difficulty mainstream institutions sometimes have interacting with the CGT (and, one would assume, other non-hierarchical organizations). The exchange happened during a particularly acrimonious negotiation between the government mediator and Furió, who was, at the time, the secretary for both the seafarers' and SASEMAR's section of the CGT (CGT SASEMAR and CGT Mar y Puertos). Frustrated and angry about what he perceived as Furió's unwillingness to yield, the mediator asked to speak with his "superior" to complain. The mediator assumed that the General Secretary of CGT's national union would be Furió's boss, and asked Furió to call him. "I shrugged my shoulders and said, 'Sure, whatever you want,'" he told me. But the CGT' General Secretary's response was, "Listen, I don't care what your problem is, the person you need to talk to is [Furió]. I don't tell him what to do."

The way Furió sees it, he does not tell anyone else what to do either. Instead, the CGT follows a deliberative assembly model. First, union representatives are democratically elected. These representatives then make proposals based on the information they have, usually concerns or complaints brought to them by individual members. Those proposals are circulated by email and discussed during assemblies, and decisions are made by consensus. Proposals for direct labour action (such as strikes) follow this procedure, too. The exchanges within the union can last a while before a decision is made, depending on the urgency of the situation. This is why, when matters are particularly urgent, union representatives may decide to speed up the process and forego some of the consultation. Internal processes are important because they ensure that union members have actually agreed on positions that the visible heads of the CGT take, such as CGT SASEMAR's position on the role of rescue crews in Spain's border policies.

CGT representatives also meet with elected representatives from the other unions to form the Work Council. The Work Council is a body that meets (at least in theory) every three months to discuss matters that are important to their members, the rescue crews. In practice, and according to the people I met, since the beginning of the COVID-19 pandemic, they have met much less often. Besides these quarterly plenary sessions, members of the Work Council can call for extraordinary sessions to discuss one, and only one, specific and urgent matter. Sea migration has become a focus of many of those meetings. This is hardly surprising; after all, a lot of the crews' work these days relates to migrant boats.

Matters related to the everyday work of rescue crews are handled by the Work Council and its committees (which are smaller groups of workers focused on specific issues), who may decide to bring these issues up with their employer to demand changes. The most important and active of these committees is the Health and Safety Committee (the committee that denounced the military's interference in the September 2020 rescue operation off Gran Canaria, during which the captain of the *Menkalinan* was ordered to abort a rescue already in progress.) In recent years, the Health and Safety Committee has handled complaints regarding the safety of the crews during the pandemic, the handling of the growing number of corpses found at the bottom of migrant boats when SASEMAR failed or refused to provide appropriate equipment to do so safely, and the consequences of having the military increasingly involved in the coordination of rescue operations in areas of migration, among other things. Issues related to overwork, the administrative situation of the crews, and more structural demands are usually handled by the Work Council, which has a broader mandate.

As the union holding the most seats in the Work Council, the CGT drives the negotiations regarding labour disputes. Just as not all (or even most) of the rescue workers identify as anarchists — not even those who vote for the CGT — some of the elected CGT representatives who sit in the Work Council are uncomfortable with this label. If they vote for the CGT and pay their union dues, it is primarily because the union has been incredibly effective at improving the working conditions of the crews — and this, despite increased hostility from SASEMAR'S management and a certain segment of the political class, who perceive sea migration (and, by extension, the nonmilitarized rescue system that SASEMAR represents) as an easy target in their quest for votes. In this context, the CGT SASEMAR has become even more of a target due to its public stance on sea migration. This is the case because, while the union has fought tooth and nail for its members, its social action arm has also promoted a distinctly pro-migrant and border abolitionist stance. For that, they have used a multi-pronged communication approach directed both toward its members and toward the rest of Spanish society.

THE UNION'S NEWSLETTER

The union uses several tools to get their message out. The one they have the most control over is their monthly newsletter, *Noticias Marítimas*, distributed to CGT Mar y Puertos membership (which includes, but is not limited to, the SASEMAR rescue fleet). According to Juan Miguel Font, the volunteer and militant with the CGT Mar y Puertos responsible for putting the newsletter together, *Noticias Marítimas* is primarily a tool through which members articulate and share the union's demands. The union uses the newsletter to keep other members informed of what they think are some of the important issues that deserve collective attention and possibly direct action. Individual members are encouraged to submit articles on issues they find interesting or relevant, either about problems they are finding at work or in general, to "amplify the [labour] conflict and hopefully have other sectors of the CGT engage with it," according to Font. In other words, it is a tool to educate union members, nourish the sense of collectivity among them, and fuel their labour actions.

The newsletter is not limited to the issues that impact its members directly. Each of the more than one hundred issues of the newsletter published between 2015 and 2024 spill over from strict labour issues to the promotion of the union's aspiration for broader social change. It is true that many of the articles cover seafarers' working conditions, struggles, and potential collective action. But the newsletter also publishes articles filled with technical information (for example, about the corrosion of materials exposed to salt water) and spreads the word on social action initiatives by union members and others. Most notably, virtually all of the issues engage with sea migration in Spain and other sections of the European Union's southern maritime border. This engagement takes different shapes: there are reports on the situation of sea migration in the Mediterranean, articles from the field from members who have volunteered at rescue NGOs or have helped launch them, and op-eds denouncing Spain and the European Union's border policy. Often, mention of sea migration starts on the first page.

For example, the March 2016 edition of *Noticias Marítimas* opens with a three-page article by Enric Tarrida, then General Secretary for the CGT Mar y Puertos. In this text, Enric delivered a passionate call for members to reconnect with the core ideals of anarcho-syndicalism by showing empathy for people on the move — individuals who are turned into "illegal" migrants by restrictive policies:

> It is delusional to think that we can build a wall around ourselves that will protect us from "those outside," because those [people] outside are also us, they are our brothers, our equals. And because there is no wall or fence that can stop the yearning of people for a future. [We must demand] a tomorrow for them and theirs. [...] We must focus on who we should be really worried about, [...] those who encourage Europeans to see refugees as a danger, those who encourage the poor to fear the poorer, while [the wealthy] look at everything from behind a barrier, satisfied, convinced that they will not be splashed with the blood [from these fights among the working class].

This sort of border abolitionist discourse is a constant in the publication. Three years later, in 2019, the cover of the newsletter read: "How much is a life worth?" In the picture, a Black man struggles to reach a ring buoy. According to Font, the image was part of a broader campaign to demand that more resources be deployed in migration areas. The implicit message is a criticism of the willingness to save some lives and leave others to die, depending on their origin and skin colour, something the crews saw reflected in the distribution of rescue assets throughout the Spanish zone of responsibility at the time.

A year later, in 2020, the cover of the newsletter showed one of the most famous works by Spanish impressionist painter Joaquín Sorolla (*Niños en el Mar*, Boys at Sea). But the painting had been modified by artist Fermín Alegre. In the altered image the CGT Mar y Puertos used, the empty spaces among children playing at the beach are filled with the shrouded corpses of migrants who drowned at sea. The direct gaze of a naked boy hooks the viewer to the contrast between the luminous, playful, care-free white youth and the stillness of the brown bodies that lay, covered and stiff, by the shore. Font told me that they chose this image "to denounce the lack of empathy for the drama that many people experience."

Other cover images and articles in the union's newsletter show their support for search and rescue NGOs saving the lives of migrants in the Eastern and Central Mediterranean. Some of these organizations originated in Spain, and there are many overlaps between SASEMAR and volunteer rescue crews. This is the case of Salvamento Marítimo Humanitario, sometimes referred to as *Aita Mari* for the name of their rescue boat, which has operated in the Central Mediterranean since 2018. Another NGO active in the same region, Proactiva Open Arms, headed by rescuer and entrepreneur Óscar Camps, provides emergency services both at sea and on land and has been the subject of several articles published in *Noticias Marítimas* since 2015. One of their two boats (the *Open Arms*) is a thirty-seven-metre tugboat formerly employed by SASEMAR. A lesser-known organization is Proem-Aid (from Professional Emergency Aid), created in 2015 by a group of volunteer emergency service workers including firefighters, health professionals, divers, and rescue swimmers, some of them current and former SASEMAR employees. Like the other two NGOs, Proem-Aid was created by citizens who were concerned about the situation in the Eastern Mediterranean in 2015, when hundreds of thousands of people from Syria and other countries in the Middle East and central Asia risked their lives crossing the waters between Türkiye and Greece. When volunteer organizations were forced to leave the area, the three organizations moved their operations to the Central Mediterranean (where the deadliest sea routes to Europe are found). They remain there to this day.

In the Central Mediterranean, Spanish rescue NGOs encountered other organizations from across Europe that earned both attention and public support from the CGT Mar y Puertos. The cover of *Noticias Marítimas*' June 2019 issue featured the text "Free Carola Rackete" along with a full-page image of the German sailor and activist. Rackete, then captain in charge of the *Sea-Watch 3*, had been waiting for an authorization to dock in the port of Lampedusa for seventeen days after rescuing fifty-three migrants in international waters not far from the Libyan coast. The crew and the rescued passengers waited and waited for an authorization that never came. Eventually, Rackete decided to disobey orders from the Italian government and dock regardless. She was arrested by Italian authorities, and only acquitted of all charges two years later, in May 2021. The message on the cover of the newsletter was unequivocal on its support for Rackete, *Sea-Watch*, and the universal right to rescue (Figure 9). Other cover images had the same message.

As strong as the CGT's commitment to rescue and class solidarity is in the context of *Noticias Marítimas*, here the union is preaching to the choir. The newsletter is an internal tool that the union uses to inform, organize, and educate its own members. To communicate more broadly, union representatives have embraced a close relationship with the mainstream media through the union's social media platforms. A shrewd use of Twitter in particular made it possible for union representatives armed with cheap cellphones to compete with SASEMAR's press office. Great media exposure has allowed the union to spread its labour demands while, once again, sneaking in their own vision for the border. But how did that happen?

FIGURE 9: Cover of the June 2019 issue of *Noticias Marítimas* with the message "Free Carola Rackete" and a picture of the captain. Reproduced with permission.

"THE TWO HUAWEI DUDES"

In a way, the government itself was to blame for stoking the fire of the CGT SASEMAR's media platform. The union had virtually no relationship with the media before 2018. That year, suddenly and without notice, the company's press office stopped informing the public about rescue operations in border areas (Vargas 2019). Instead, its Twitter account began posting only pictures of dolphins and sunsets; every now and then, there would also be announcements related to maritime safety awareness. On top of that, rescue crews were told not to talk to the media or to researchers. This happened at the same time that the number of arrivals in the Alboran Sea reached unprecedented numbers and the militarized infrastructure in this section of the Spanish zone of responsibility became functional. Things were happening, the media wanted information, and SASEMAR workers were under a gag order.

This proved to be a strategic mistake on the government's part. Also in the summer of 2018, the union had launched the campaign "Más manos para salvar más vidas" (More hands to save more lives) to demand a fourth crew member for the Salvamares deployed along the southern border where the workload was greatest (Vargas 2018). Ismael Furió (then General Secretary of the CGT Mar y Puertos and the CGT SASEMAR) and Manuel Capa (spokesperson for the CGT SASEMAR) spearheaded this campaign. They were part of a team travelling the country to raise awareness about working conditions on rescue boats, calling for more and better training for the crews, asking for more boats and helicopters, and demanding the hiring of long-term temporary crews as permanent SASEMAR workers. The silence of SASEMAR's press office on social media and the communications gag imposed on workers were detrimental to their efforts.

One day, on their way back from a union meeting, Furió and Capa were joking about taking over SASEMAR's press office. "We both made the same joke at the same time," Capa told me, "that we should report on rescue operations ourselves to fill in the silence and shed light on the work we were doing. And so we started doing it." It sounded simple when they thought of it. But they had no media contacts at first, so they started calling captains they knew who were working on the rescue boats in Andalusia, gathering information about rescue operations involving migrants, and using the union's Twitter account to spread the information. At port, they also approached people they thought were journalists to talk to them. "If I saw people with cameras and microphones, I would approach them and ask, 'Are you a journalist?' and if they were journalists, I would say, 'We have information you may find interesting.' We would talk to anyone, any journalist, from any media outlet."

The response was phenomenal. Soon, captains and journalists started calling Capa without him asking. "The media realized that they could get from us the information they were not getting from the government." It is easy to imagine Capa talking to everyone, or everyone talking to Capa: he is a jovial, chatty man in his early fifties, a friendly and curious extrovert. Like the other union spokespeople, he is a seaman through and through. Capa's father was a clearance diver (a profession where divers use explosives underwater to help build harbours and shipping channels), and he has spent his entire life at sea, working as a rescuer for over a decade. He has seen it all and he has plenty of stories to tell. It did not take long before the media saw him and the CGT SASEMAR as valuable sources.

The overwhelming media attention caught them unprepared: they needed help. A journalist employed at the union helped them develop a strategy to set boundaries, talk to the right people, and release the information at just the right time. Eventually, union representatives became the default interlocutors when the media was interested in a story about rescues at sea. "Today I have a media roster on my phone. There are at least fifty journalists I can write to at any given point if we need to bring attention to specific issues." But thinking back to the fact that "two dudes with cheap Huawei cellphones" started competing with the company's press office from a rental car between meetings, Capa laughs at the irony: "if SASEMAR hadn't stopped sharing information about rescue operations back in 2019, this would have never happened!"

Their sudden popularity was also largely due to Ismael Furió's savvy and aggressive communication style — always a trove of perfectly crafted soundbites. It was the same for our interviews, which always happened near a port anywhere along the Spanish coast with the squawking of seagulls as a nonstop background noise. Efficient and with a no-nonsense attitude about him, the man exuded charisma. Like Capa, Furió has been at sea since his early youth, first as a volunteer with the Red Cross, then as a sailing instructor, later as a captain for recreational boats and, since 2008, as a captain for SASEMAR's fleet of Guardamares. He defines himself as a man obsessed with anything that has to do with the sea. And he is also passionate about anarcho-syndicalism. Furió began his mandate as secretary for both the CGT Mar y Puertos and SASEMAR in 2017 (the latter ended in 2024). He talks fast, linking different moments of his work with the CGT, current events, and the successes and aspirations of the union, so that once I tell him what I am looking for I barely need to intervene to direct the conversation. There is a sense of purpose, of urgency in each and every one of his words.

Put Capa and Furió together, and it is easy to understand why the media were taken by these two anarchists. They are unapologetically critical of SASEMAR's management, people often freely appointed by the government with little or no maritime experience. But beyond their message, there is the way they deliver it. Over the years, a pattern has emerged. First comes Furió to play the role of the bad cop: as the general secretary of the section of the union representing rescuers, he uses lots of data to engage with high-level arguments and demands more resources to fulfill Spain's international commitments. He finds holes in the arguments put forward by politicians and the decision-makers and exploits them. If the company boasts about the size and quality of the rescue fleet, Furió shows they have been placed too far from where they are needed. If the company praises its workers, he asks, "Why, then, are you imposing twenty-hour-long shifts on the people at the frontlines, denying them a backup?" Gloves off is Furió's default attitude in his media interviews.

And then, soon afterwards, we see Capa: he is often on the dock, orange boat in the background, fresh from a mission, explaining the challenges the rescue fleet encounters daily. More often than not, he is wearing a shirt with the union's logo: two hands holding each other against a red and black background. Capa puts rescuers' physical and emotional exhaustion into words — the need to create a "shell" to preserve their mental health; the need to forget the smell of the corpses they have to remove from the bottom of the *cayucos,* rotting in a putrid liquid; the joint pain, the back pain, the knee pain; the lack of bathrooms on the docks so that they have to ask restaurant owners to use their facilities; the relentless physical labour that erodes their bodies and their dignity. Where Furió engages with decision-makers, Capa forces viewers to engage with the everyday realities of rescue work at an emotional level, using stories that demand their empathy toward both rescuers and migrants. The combined message is powerful.

Noticias Marítimas and media coverage offered the CGT two ways to get their message out to their members and to a broader public. Yet, the message was always the same and revolved around two main arguments. First, working conditions for the rescue fleet need to improve. Here, the union related to the government as the employer who, in a neoliberal system, aligned with private interests and sought to keep workers in a position of exploitation and submission. Second, these improvements must be done while respecting the principles of class solidarity and internationalism at the core of the CGT's philosophy. Here, the CGT SASEMAR saw the Spanish government (and, by extension, the European Union) as a maker of worlds with a vision diametrically opposed to the union's: a borderless global society where radical equality must be paramount, and where the working class is in a position to face down the forces that oppress it.

LABOUR STRUGGLES: THE GOVERNMENT AS AN EMPLOYER

At sea, the first representatives of the Spanish state that sea migrants encounter are often the rescuers. Dressed in their protective gear aboard an orange boat, they have become an institution in border areas such as the Canary Islands. Everybody knows them. In October 2023, SASEMAR rescued an average of 498 people *a day* in the Canary Islands; this amounted to half of all the monthly arrivals in a typical year. Rescues in January 2024 (typically a "slow" month because of poor conditions at sea) increased fourteenfold from the previous year, from five hundred to more than seven thousand (O'Carroll 2024).

This work was not evenly distributed among the crews, however. Of the seventeen rescue boats deployed in the archipelago in February 2024 (one giant multipurpose ship, five medium-sized Guardamares, and ten smaller Salvamares), roughly half were on the frontlines. The other boats were in areas too far from arrival points to be deployed regularly. In other words, as the majority of the arrivals came from the south, the units that responded to emergencies involving boats carrying migrant people were mainly the Salvamares moored on the islands of El Hierro, Gran Canaria, and Tenerife — and, to a lesser extent at that particular point in time, Fuerteventura and Lanzarote.

Salvamares are fast fifteen- to twenty-metre boats that can reach speeds of up to thirty knots and run on three- to four-person crews. Two people (the captain and the mechanic) are in charge of the boat, while the two rescuers handle the transfer of passengers from boats in distress to the Salvamar or manage the towing or escorting of the dinghies to port, depending on the circumstances. In months like October 2023, the two rescuers on the Salvamar *Adhara* (moored in El Hierro at the time) could rescue almost two hundred people in one day. Their working days were up to twenty hours long, and they worked on two weeks on, two weeks off shifts (as opposed to the one week on, one week off shifts more common in other ports). During their shifts, rescuers had to remain within ten minutes of the boat in case of emergency. In the case of the Salvamares, crews often live near the port for this reason. But, at times, this restriction could be irrelevant; for example, in El Hierro in late 2023 and 2024, emergencies were so frequent that rescuers spent their entire shifts on the boat or on the dock next to it. These boats are not designed to function as living quarters. They lack enclosed cabins, have only one bathroom, and the one common area is usually so crowded with rescue equipment that workers often prefer to stay on deck.

On the other hand, crews on the Guardamares (twenty-five to thirty metres long and with a maximum actual speed of twenty-two to thirty knots during emergency operations) are eight-men strong. Their shifts are longer: one month on, one month off. While deployed, staff live on the boat and must also remain within a ten-minute radius of the port for the entire month of duty. Crews have described these boats to me as "the closest thing to a submarine from the Second World War: noisy and uncomfortable and oppressive. You don't sleep well with all the constant clanking and creaking. You hear everything on the boat, you don't have privacy. By the time the shift is almost over, you feel you are losing your mind."

A month living in close quarters with the same seven men around the clock without even the possibility of going on a proper walk stretches out forever. The men are not always on active duty during that time, though. Shifts in the Guardamares were, in theory, eight hours long. But since they live on the boat, they are physically present any time there is a rescue operation, even if they are technically off duty. After a couple of weeks, the men are tired, restless, irritable. Rescuers on both Salvamares and Guardamares have gone on medical leave for psychological distress and physical injuries suffered while at work. Others have asked to be relocated away from migration areas, hoping to catch a break.

Rescuers' working conditions are nothing like those Enric and Oriol knew when they first embarked in the late 1980s. Rescue crews' salaries are now higher, they have guaranteed time off, and they enjoy most of the protections other public workers do. Instead of 243 days, they work 182.5 days (exactly half the year).

They have made other, smaller gains that improve their everyday lives. For example, crews today have a discretionary allowance. Some crews have bought electric scooters that allow them to go a bit further when their boats are docked, perhaps to a coffee shop nearby, as some ports on the Canary Islands can be quite far from commercial areas. Other crews have used that allowance to buy bikes for the same reason. When not on a mission, the workers need time and solitude to process their experiences. "Walking on the putrid water, and collecting corpses from the bottom of a *cayuco*, picking up bodies with a net ... those are not things we have been trained to do," says Capa. "After one of those missions, your head is not in the right space; you need time to recover, and you need to be alone for a bit."

Still, as of late 2023, the ports of La Restinga in El Hierro, Arguineguín in Gran Canaria, and San Juan in Tenerife did not have a space at port with a bathroom for the crews, or, in some cases, even a place to change and rest in between operations (Delgado Sanz 2023). At most, a refurbished shipping container served as an office. These were also some of the ports that had the highest workload in the archipelago throughout 2023 and early 2024.

In addition to demanding improvements to rescuers' working conditions, the CGT SASEMAR spent a decade fighting to regularize rescue crews in the maritime units. From 2012 onwards, these crews had been hired on temporary six-month contracts. For instance, between 2012 and 2023 Manuel Capa, rescuer and union spokesperson, was hired on a series of consecutive six-month contracts. Many of the other members of the boat crews were in a similar situation. "You didn't have to be very clever to realize that if all newly hired personnel at SASEMAR were temporary, and all rescue crew positions were terminal [*a extinguir*], in ten years the agency would go the way of the dodo," Furió told me. As the general secretary for the main union representing rescue crews, fixing this situation was a priority. Furió kept knocking on doors with no results to show for his efforts. No politician was willing to support the demands of the rescue fleet.

SASEMAR's hiring practices were symptomatic of a broader trend in the Spanish public administration, which had one of the highest rates of public workers on temporary contracts in the European Union: 28.2 percent of all public employees and 45.7 percent of public employees between the ages of 30 and 39 had temporary contracts in 2019 (Gómez 2019). Eventually, a mandate from the EU forced the government to move away from temporary contracts in, among other sectors of public work, maritime search and rescue. The "regularization" of temporary crew members (who became public workers with permanent contracts) was largely completed by the end of 2024.

These demands and successes happened in the context of the larger realities of the maritime sector. The CGT Mar y Puertos (within which CGT SASEMAR exists) is one of the unions representing seafarers and dockworkers employed in Spain. The union is engaged in fights for better legislation at port and on boats, improved regulation of seafaring professions, enhanced availability of specific trainings, and, in general, fights for the improvement of the working conditions of its members. Although rescuers are a fraction of the workers represented by the union, the CGT Mar y Puertos also stands behind demands for reduced shift lengths on the bigger rescue boats and increased minimal crew requirements on rescue boats. Many of the rescue workers' struggles coincide with those of other seafarers. Others do not, although there are still common interests at play.

For example, the modern fishing industry has always depended on foreign work, be it free, indentured, or enslaved. Even today, the exploitation of seafarers (often racialized crews from poor countries) is widespread in the sector. Boats and ports are spaces where different worlds mix and where the labour struggle takes place. This was true in the eighteenth century and remains true today.

At times, exploitation of seafarers and migration overlap. Another example: in 2021, not far from where SASEMAR's Salvamar was moored in the port of Arrecife (Lanzarote), the Spanish captain of a fishing boat abandoned his thirteen-men crew, all Senegalese men, who had been working for eight months without receiving a salary. They were discovered by Laetitia Marthe (co-founder of Lanzarote's Network of Solidarity with Migrant People) and other activists, who had been bringing meals to a group of five teenagers hiding in some nearby ruins. They realized the boys were consuming way more food than seemed reasonable. It turned out they were sharing the food with the stranded fishermen, who had been told by the police to stay on the boat or they would be deported. Eventually, a labour inspection was called and the fishermen's situation was sorted. Following this incident, some of the fishermen remained on the island, while others were flown to mainland Spain and a smaller group chose to return to Senegal.

Another way in which migration and the sea sector overlap is through the well-established practice of hiring an immigrant force for a lower fee. As we saw in Chapter 2, this is far from new. One of CGT Mar y Puertos' long-standing fights is to remove seafaring occupations from the *Catálogo de ocupaciones de difícil cobertura* (Catalogue of Hard-to-Fill Occupations), published every three months by the Servicio Público de Empleo Estatal (the Ministry of Labour's Public Employment Bureau). These are occupations Spanish employers struggle to fill with local workers. Having a profession listed in this catalogue means that employers are legally allowed to hire foreign workers with minimal paperwork. The CGT Mar y Puertos argues that there are many unemployed seafarers who could fill those positions and that, since 2015, the catalogue has been used by employers to circumvent more stringent domestic regulations and hire foreign workers at lower salaries and with worse working conditions. So far, the union has been unsuccessful. However, while this is an issue in other areas of the maritime industry, it is not a problem that rescuers have to worry about. At least, not yet.

In other words, since the creation of the rescue agency, the CGT Mar y Puertos and the CGT SASEMAR have worked — sometimes successfully — to improve the working conditions and job stability of the general seafaring workforce. So far, the union has also managed to keep non-governmental rescue actors out of the Spanish zone of responsibility.

Why Are There No Rescue NGOs in the Spanish Zone of Responsibility?

To recap, then, many of the NGOs who have provided life-saving services in the Eastern and Central Mediterranean over the last decade were Spanish, and several have significant links with SASEMAR. On the other hand, the main union representing SASEMAR rescue crews, the CGT SASEMAR, has repeatedly shown its support for migrant rights, for universal rescue services, and for NGO rescue workers elsewhere along the European Union's southern maritime border. Given this context, the fact that has activists scratching their heads throughout Europe is this: why has the union repeatedly and categorically refused to collaborate with NGOs to make sure more lives are saved in the Spanish zone of responsibility?

I asked Capa this question in early 2024. We were sitting in his kitchen, sharing a delicious bean stew with his mother and children. This is a question he has been asked often, and one we have discussed more than once. "That's an easy one," he answers with a smile, "the are no NGOs because maritime search and rescue is the responsibility of the state."

Over the last few years, different Spanish and international NGOs, recognizing SASEMAR as the main rescue actor in the country but not fully understanding how the agency works, have approached the union asking to collaborate with them. Some, like Pilotes Volontaires (a French charity created in 2018 that flies reconnaissance aircraft in search of boats in distress in the Central Mediterranean) want to assist with the location of vessels in distress. Others, like Médecins Sans Frontières (MSF, originally from France) and Salvamento Marítimo Humanitario (Spanish) have tried to deploy their own rescue boats in the Spanish zone of responsibility. In late 2024, MSF launched their own rescue operation in the Atlantic, off the coast of Senegal. The focus of this operation was to train Senegalese security forces on the principles and obligations of maritime rescue.

The union does not oppose rescue NGOs as long as they stay out of the Spanish zone of responsibility: if MSF wants to deploy boats in the Senegalese, Mauritanian, or Moroccan rescue zones, they have no problem with it. But union leadership has categorically refused to collaborate with these organizations if they enter Spain's search and rescue area. They have been harshly criticized for this. In conversations with rescue NGOs who wanted to expand their operations to the Western Mediterranean and the Atlantic, I have often been asked why the rescuers are not willing to put politics aside to prevent deaths in the Atlantic, the deadliest maritime route in Europe. Furió and Capa (who represent rescue crews) argue that it is a matter of weighing the short and long-term consequences of such a decision. True, letting rescue NGOs act in the Spanish zone of responsibility could lead to fewer lives lost in the short term. But these short-term gains would mean unacceptable long-term losses, both for their membership and for the survival of the Spanish approach to maritime rescue. "Can you imagine inviting volunteer doctors working for free to perform surgeries at a public hospital?" asked Capa. "How long before the government realizes that they can save money on contracts by replacing hospital workers with free labour under conditions that do not need to respect a collective agreement?"

Moreover, outsourcing maritime rescue could potentially lead to its disappearance altogether. Maritime search and rescue has become a highly politicized issue in Europe. A rescue service largely run by volunteers on private and public donations could easily have its funding cut and its staff criminalized. This happened in Greece after the 2015 "Long Summer of Migration" and in Italy after Matteo Salvini became Minister of the Interior in 2017. At first, following the Lampedusa shipwrecks in late 2013, the Italian government invited rescue NGOs to its zone of responsibility to help with emergencies at sea. Two years later, when their presence became politically inconvenient, the government imposed draconian conditions on the civil fleet. As a result, rescue NGOs have all but disappeared from the Eastern Mediterranean, while those in the Central Mediterranean face growing obstacles to their work amid the criminalization of their activities. Having NGO rescue boats replace SASEMAR's government-owned ones only to be removed from the area when their presence becomes politically inconvenient is not a happy prospect for union members, for the Spanish rescue system, or for people about to drown at sea.

Instead of bringing NGOs to the Spanish zone of responsibility, union spokespeople argue that what is needed is for the agency to keep doing its work and retain their independence from the military as much and for as long as it is possible. They need more boats that are better maintained, more helicopters and planes equipped with technology to locate vessels in distress, more personnel with more time to rest between shifts, more opportunities to obtain and update specialized training, more people in positions of authority within the agency that have extensive experience at sea, and, if possible, air crews that are integrated into the regular crews and benefit from better working conditions. What they need, in other words, is to strengthen SASEMAR's mandate and capacity and make the Spanish approach a model for the rest of the European Union. What is needed, they argue, is for Spain and the European Union to stand firmly by the principles of the SAR Convention, so that all emergencies are addressed equally regardless of the nationality, skin colour, and legal status of those whose lives are at risk at sea. This is not something that can be achieved by letting NGOs come into the area, each with their own approach, assets, and stance on Europe's migration policy. The state has willingly acquired the legal obligation to keep the waters safe for everyone, regardless of where they come from, and it is the job of state agencies with a stable budget and a long-term vision to do so. This may be a hard sell in the current political climate, although anarchists are used to fighting uphill battles. The union is also used to navigating contradictions. In this case, they (a group of anarchists employed by the state) find themselves demanding that the government uphold its own laws. The irony is not lost on anyone.

LOOKING INTO THE FUTURE

We are back in Valencia, sitting at the coffee shop right by Furió's family home, talking about the captain of the Salvamar *Menkalinan*, who had to untie the ropes in the middle of a manoeuvre to let a military boat carry out the rescue. The port is just steps away. The seagulls are cawing. We have been talking about the CGT SASEMAR's work for a couple of hours now. Furió will soon step down from his position as General Secretary of the union, but he will stay around "to play the bad cop when we negotiate with the government and help the new secretary, give him some hints — do the same for him as Enric did for me." Capa will also stay on as union spokesperson.

In the background, the union will keep building bridges between the CGT's labour union mission and their social action arm. Enric Tarrida, the original anarchist in the rescue fleet, is now more focused on the union's social action initiatives than in the labour struggles. Font has no plans to go anywhere. And so, they will continue spreading the anarchist gospel through their newsletter and through the media, defending the interests of the working class across borders and building alliances (however ephemeral) with like-minded people. They will keep walking a tight rope of strategically collaborating with other pro-migrant organizations without compromising their independence. The will continue because their cause goes far beyond sitting on SASEMAR's Work Council to fight against long working hours. They will go on. In this regard, the CGT SASEMAR is part of a broader constellation of actors resisting the European Union's border policy — and they see themselves as such.

7

Death, Resistance, Hope

Where are your monuments, your battles, your martyrs?
Where is your tribal memory? Sirs,
In that gray vault. The Sea. The sea
Has locked them up. The sea is History.

—Derek Walcott, *Poems* (1965–1980)

THE WORDS OF NOBEL PRIZE-WINNING POET Sir Derek Alton Walcott, a native of St. Lucia, convey the deep sorrow and shock over the loss of culture, history, and life caused by the European trade of an estimated fifteen million enslaved African people between 1500 and 1866. More than a century later, the most conservative estimates suggest that at least thirty thousand people on the move (from Africa and other parts of the world) have died or disappeared along the European Union's external maritime borders since 2014 (IOM n.d.). These figures highlight the unbroken link between the old colonial order built on enslavement and today's European neocolonial reality, which continues to feed on cheap, mobile labour — forced or otherwise.

Much like in Walcott's poem, the sea plays a role in this new, yet familiar and highly unequal, mobility regime. Death is what happens when rescue boats, helicopters, and planes disappear from sight in the areas where dinghies are going under and the sea becomes, once again, the "grey vault" where the memory and the history of the poor, racialized people of the world are laid to rest.

The story does not end there, though. Throughout this book, we have seen how the Spanish government has tried to reclaim rescue services to control access to its territory. In doing so, the government has triggered resistance from civil society and encountered an unexpected obstacle: the workers of SASEMAR, the government's own rescue agency. The origins and evolution of SASEMAR make it an exception in Europe. The agency has spent decades focused more on the prevention of environmental disasters than migrant rescue. Until 2006 in the Canary Islands and 2018 in the Western Mediterranean, SASEMAR operated independently from the Spanish military. However, as maritime rescue has become increasingly militarized across the European Union, the main union representing sea crews has emerged as a significant obstacle to the agency's transformation into another instrument in the border enforcement toolbox.

The tension between saving lives and stopping sea migration exists for the simple reason that the principles underlying border control and maritime search and rescue are fundamentally incompatible: while rescue policy is meant to be universal, border policy is, by definition, exclusionary. The government created SASEMAR specifically to uphold the objectives and values of the SAR Convention, which means that the agency is inherently incapable of functioning as a border control force. Its boats, helicopters, and planes are there to minimize the loss of life, not to prevent the movement of people.

To reconcile the conflicting logics of care and control, EU policymakers have developed what scholars have called the "humanitarian border." Within this framework, undocumented border crossers are simultaneously framed as both being *at risk* and as *a risk* to national security (Pallister-Wilkins 2018). Paradoxically, this means that people who migrate are viewed both as victims that need protection and as criminals that must be punished. Only through this discourse can the withdrawal of rescue services be framed as a form of humanitarianism, based on the false claim that removing life-saving assets from the sea will deter human smuggling and ultimately make people on the move safer.

In Spain, this tension between the logics of care and control, combined with SASEMAR's inability to function as a border enforcement agency, has led to the fragmentation of the national rescue system into two tiers: one for migrants, overseen by the military chain of command, and another for all other individuals and vessels in distress at sea, managed by civilian personnel. This bifurcated system undermines the universal rescue mandate of the SAR Convention, effectively making the rescue of poor, overwhelmingly racialized people on the move a matter of discretion rather than duty. This policy of organized abandonment at sea is an example of racist necropolitics at work.

It is important to emphasize that, when governments justify the removal of rescue assets from areas of migration by claiming that their presence encourages undocumented crossings by sea, they are not just lying: they are directly causing more violence and more death. When they attempt to seal borders with ever more advanced and costly technology, they are making smuggling and trafficking more profitable while wasting taxpayer money on a pipedream of control, causing more violence and more death. And when they create policies that push migrant people into illegality and precarity upon arrival in Europe, they are feeding them into a system that exploits their cheap labour and treats their lives as disposable — once again, causing more violence and more death. But also, when governments do these things, they are planting the seeds of resistance and hope. Nowhere is this more evident than in the Canary Islands.

DEATH

On February 15, 2009, a boat sank twenty metres off Cocoteros Beach in Lanzarote, the northern-most of the Canary Islands (Europa Press 2015). There were thirty-two people on it, including adults and children from Morocco, the Western Sahara, and Mauritania. They had departed the day before from somewhere near the city of Guelmim along Morocco's southern coast. The five-metre boat approached the island undetected by the radars and patrol boats. SASEMAR was never called. The boat got closer and closer to the coast. Despite its name, however, there is no beach in Cocoteros, just jagged volcanic rocks that become cliffs in some areas. At around 6:30 p.m., the waves slammed the boat against the rocks. The prow got stuck, a wave went over the stern, and the boat capsized, tossing those on board into the water. Some surfers and tourists who witnessed the accident were able to save six people. Over the next few days, twenty-five corpses were recovered by SASEMAR, the underwater unit of the Guardia Civil (GEAS), and the Lanzarote emergency service (EMERLAN). Seventeen of the victims were minors.

A decade and a half later, I stand in front of the small memorial set near the site of the wreckage. It is a humble homage to the people who drowned there: a small block of cement with a weather-worn plaque that reads, "In memory of the 25 people who died in this place on February 15, 2009, when they tried to reach a better future." The text ends with a quote by Nicaraguan writer Gioconda Belli: "Solidarity is the tenderness of peoples" ("La solidaridad es la ternura de los pueblos"). The memorial stands at the northern end of a small clump of white houses, in a sort of no-man's land where locals walk their dogs. The artificial flowers at the base of the memorial have been there for quite some time and someone has scratched their name on the plaque. It is not an inspiring place: the contrast between the written words and the context is jarring. I walk to the edge of the path and toward the sharp volcanic black rocks by the water.

I make my way over the plateau that forms a sort of balcony some three metres above the crashing waves. It is a cloudless, windy day and the sea is choppy, but not terribly rough. I try to imagine what this place must have looked like as the crowded boat approached from the sea. In the legal decision condemning the smugglers, the journey is said to have happened under "inhuman conditions": only one of the passengers wore a safety vest and the boat was wholly inappropriate for open ocean navigation. Here, at the site where it capsized, there is not much except for a cluster of white-washed houses and a natural pool where tourists come to sunbathe. After a night and a day at sea, it was probably windy when the boat came near (it is always windy in Lanzarote). I look down: the sea is pulsating, heaving, crashing against the rocks and finding its way into a few barely visible shallow caves, then the water comes back out, pushing against the incoming currents. A few minutes later, I am covered in sea spray and nauseous. I need to sit down, but am surrounded by sharp rocks.

What would it have taken for the people who were on that *cayuco* in February 2009 to be alive today? Had SASEMAR been called earlier, the agency would have sent helicopters and rescue boats to handle the emergency, just as they did the next day when rescuing a German tourist entangled in his kitesurfing gear in the same area.

This is the key difference between SASEMAR and other government rescue agencies elsewhere in Europe. In Malta, the government has long refused to address emergencies involving people on the move at sea. In Italy, the official stance alternates between intervention, non-intervention, and a reluctant collaboration with NGOs deployed in the Central Mediterranean, who find ever-growing obstacles to fill the gap left by government agencies. In Greece, the Hellenic Coast Guard has pushed migrant boats back to Türkiye, left families floating in the water in rafts without engines, and intervened in operations that have caused deaths, as we saw with the *Adriana*. By contrast, in Spain, the public rescue agency (SASEMAR) remains committed to its mandate, although the tenet of universal rescue it has upheld for the last thirty years is currently cracking due to a partial dismantling of the rescue system being achieved through a combination of underfunding, the militarization of rescue operations, and the externalization of rescue responsibilities to countries like Morocco, Mauritania, and Senegal.

As the principle of universal rescue is eroded, the Western Mediterranean and the Atlantic have become vast graveyards where people on the move — and their dreams and potential — sink into a "grey vault" of oblivion. We often think of these deaths mainly as a loss for their countries and a tragedy for their families. This is most definitely true. But the weight of the death also falls heavily on the strangers unexpectedly tasked with caring for them, compelling them to action.

During a visit in late 2023, Laetitia Marthe, activist and co-founder of Lanzarote's Network of Solidarity with Migrant People, took me to baby Alhassane Bangoura's tiny grave in the Teguise municipal cemetery. There are not many places for Muslim burials in the islands, and public resources are scarce and stretched to the limit. In the midst of an open conflict between the central, regional, and municipal governments, some towns in the archipelago have refused to cover the costs of burying those who drown at sea (*Canarias7* 2023).

At the time of writing, Teguise is still footing the bill. There, civil servants print whatever information they have about the deceased with an electric labelling machine and tape the label onto white tiles that resemble something one would use in a cheap bathroom renovation project. In some cases, civil servants have no information whatsoever about the person. Those tiles simply read "unidentified migrant" (in Spanish, always in the masculine: another post-mortem affront) followed by the court proceeding number. But the quality of the tiles is poor, and the sun quickly bleaches out the tape. Most of the graves end up with just a white tile on top, often cracked, sometimes gone altogether: an unidentified migrant in an unidentified grave. Some of the graves are caved in.

I am told that the technicians follow procedures defined by the Interpol: personal belongings and DNA information are stored under the court proceeding number, and somewhere there is a list collating the person's file with the location of the grave.

Laetitia Marthe and Julie Campagne (both co-founders of Lanzarote's Network of Solidarity with Migrant People) are not so sure, and neither are some public workers employed at municipal funeral homes on other islands of the archipelago. Julie is a physical anthropologist with extensive experience in archaeology and human remains excavation. She was alarmed when she learned how the remains of those who die at sea are put to rest. Just in case, she keeps a log with all the information they can gather about the graves. She has reasons to be concerned: only one of the approximately twenty-five graves in the small Muslim area of the Teguise cemetery has a proper tombstone. On a slab of grey marble, under the name and date of the person buried there, it reads: "Illegitimi non carborundum" (Don't let the bastards grind you down). Not too far away, on a tiny grave marked by stones, there are some flowers and a bowl with a name. The name on the bowl is the only way to identify the place where Alhassane Bangoura lies, one of the youngest victims of the European Union's border policy (Kassam 2023).

At the opposite end of the archipelago, on the island of El Hierro, Haridian Marichal Niebla (journalist) and Dácil Trujillo Hernández (municipal social worker and volunteer) do their best to make sure that unidentified people who died at sea are treated with dignity. Much like Julie and Laetitia in Lanzarote, they keep a record of each one of the deceased, in case their families are found. They also attend the funerals, make sure the graves are well maintained, and occasionally bring fresh flowers. On the island of La Gomera, the tombstones of graves where unidentified people on the move rest bear the inscription "citizen of the world": a small gesture to honour the humanity of those buried there.

The graves that Dácil and Haridian take care of are just some among thousands of others in hundreds of cemeteries in villages and towns along Europe's southern border: Kato Tritos in Lesbos, Teguise in Lanzarote, Catania in Sicily, Motril in southern Spain, Adolorata in Malta. These cemeteries and graves are sorrow stars in a constellation of pain and shame for the families of the people buried there and for many sea-facing communities across Europe. At least one thousand other people on the move rest in unmarked graves along the external borders of Europe, while bodies are "piling up in morgues across the continent" in frontier regions (Lawrence et al. 2023). There is also the vast cemetery we cannot see, the one under water that takes in the bodies of those listed as "disappeared" in official statistics. It is a massacre.

The stories of those we lost are each unique, yet nearly all who drowned at sea came from poor, Muslim-majority countries and were racialized individuals. Seeking safety and a better future for themselves and their families, and with no safe or legal pathways to reach Europe, they braved the sea. In waters with few rescue services, they drowned. Because of these deaths, people on both sides of the border are coming together to confront official narratives and demand change, so that similar tragedies never happen again.

RESISTANCE

In the midst of all this death, there is a growing resistance against the relentless advance of increasingly violent borders, the rise of anti-immigrant far-right movements, and the promotion of the three pillars of hate (externalization, militarization, and repression) at the core of European border policies. The anti-immigration far-right is making electoral gains in the continent, and the European Union's 2024 Pact on Migration and Asylum entrenches these brutal tools. Yet across Europe, citizens and activists are standing up and refusing to accept these strategies as the new politics as usual.

The fires of resistance are spreading. In Spain, they burn in the work of social worker Dácil Trujillo Hernández and journalist Haridian Marichal Niebla in El Hierro, the activism of Laetitia and Julie in Lanzarote, the union work of Furió and Capa on the rescue boats, the tireless mission of testimony and denunciation of Helena Maleno (founder and head of the NGO Caminando Fronteras) in Tangier; and through Alarm Phone's many-headed hydra throughout Europe, Africa, and the Middle East. They burn in every volunteer on NGO rescue boats and planes in the Mediterranean, in every journalist working with *El País*, EFE, *The Guardian*, *Lighthouse Reports*, and other media platforms that are covering abuses and giving people on the move a voice. We witness resistance in the forensic doctors and undertakers demanding authorities respect official protocols and preserve the dignity of those who died at sea and still do not have a name. We witness it in the organizers and demonstrators at pro-migrant rights rallies across the continent, chanting slogans like "Nobody is illegal," "Borders are violent," and "Peace is not eighteen people drowned each day." We witness the resistance of racialized people taking to the streets throughout Spain to demand that their right to seek international protection be respected, and we see it in the white Spaniards bearing witness and acting as human shields standing between them and the police. We witness the resistance in Africans and Afrodescendants in Spain who tirelessly claim their rightful place in society. We witness the individual acts of resistance that stand out within larger movements, such as the campaign for a massive regularization led by Augustín Ndour, the first Black candidate for Spain's presidency — a campaign that could secure the same protections for hundreds of thousands of migrant workers that all other workers in Spain are entitled to.

We also see the many people working behind the scenes and making these acts of resistance possible. They embrace empathy and solidarity with people on the move as antidotes to dehumanizing rhetoric and as powerful weapons of dissent. We see those who organized against the European Union's Pact on Migration and Asylum, the intersectional feminists, the anticolonial activists. We see the resistance of union leaders like Enric Tarrida, who refused to accept the barriers built by those in power to separate the working class based on skin colour and national origin. We see SASEMAR captains who learned to read the stars from Senegalese fishermen they rescued in the Atlantic; rescuers who see their own children in the kids they transport to safety; mothers who see themselves in the women clutching their children in a water-filled dinghy and go to the beach to help; interpreters who volunteer at police stations in migration areas to try and soften the orders of agents desensitized to the suffering of another human; Red Cross volunteers at the San Andrés migrant detention centre in El Hierro, who come up with creative ways to make the minuscule blankets provided by the authorities cover up exhausted people so that they do not get too cold at night; helicopter rescuers who jump into the sea in complete darkness without asking themselves if those who need their help are tourists or immigrants. We see the captain of an NGO boat in the Central Mediterranean who, when making a difficult decision, looks at a sticker on the bridge of her ship that says, "What would a sailor do?" and does not what is convenient, but what is right: she rescues those in distress at sea. We witness the resistance of ordinary people who, in the face of a constellation of death, build a constellation of hope. They forge networks of solidarity from shore to shore, holding on to stubborn optimism about the future, despite evidence to the contrary.

HOPE

Under the light of this growing resistance, there is hope. Hope lives in the continued presence of SASEMAR's orange boats in Spanish ports. Their gentle rocking is a testimony to the power of resistance and collective action: without the work of the CGT SASEMAR and the alliances they have established with actors across the political spectrum throughout the years, those boats might be gone today. But they remain. I see them at every single one of the ports I visit to interview people, and I am reminded of Furió's antidote against helplessness: the strength of utopia is that it gives us a destination, and every step in the right direction is a step forward.

A utopia, after all, is simply a place that does not exist *yet*. The utopia envisioned by many migrant rights activists is a world where people who move across borders choose to do so freely, and where their journeys are facilitated through safe and legal pathways. A world where asylum seekers, refugees, people targeted because of their gender identity and sexual orientation, and those fleeing armed violence, wars, and natural disasters are allowed a safe haven. A world where the plundering of Africa's natural riches finally ends, and people can lead fulfilling lives in their home communities if they so choose. A world where (to borrow from Ruth Wilson Gilmore) all life is precious: where every emergency at sea is treated with the same urgency, where all lives at risk are valued equally, and where the danger of drowning is non-existent because people can migrate safely and legally, without having to gamble with their lives. In this world, there would be no need for NGOs to patrol the waters in search of sinking dinghies. The gates of the sea would be wide open, and yet nobody would cross them out of necessity.

Border abolition is definitely a utopia, but universal search and rescue is written into international regulations. For it to become a reality, EU members states simply need to respect their own laws and policies. The truth, though, is that governments do not want to loosen their grip on the border because migration (in particular, undocumented migration by sea) has proven an endless source of political clout and economic gain. If European governments established safe and open legal routes for migration and honestly confronted the reality that their rapidly aging populations urgently need foreign labour to sustain the welfare state, they would be giving up access to the cheap, easily exploitable workforce that is kept in place by restrictive borders. Because borders are more than a line on a map: they are a double-edged power structure.

One the one hand, borders keep cheap workers in place in countries of origin and transit, where labour legislation is weak, inexistent, or not enforced, and where migrants and potential migrants are compelled to accept jobs that are dirty, dangerous, and demeaning. On the other, when (against all odds) poor people on the move manage to cross the border into Europe, they are forced into illegality, and find themselves in jobs that are also dirty, dangerous, demeaning, and poorly paid. The prosperity of Europe's (and of the West's) privileges hinges on this exploitation. Seen this way, borders are instruments vital to the economic survival of the world we inhabit. And so, Europe digs her heels into its repressive approach at the border.

The new European Pact on Migration and Asylum, adopted in 2024 after years of negotiations, certainly does nothing to move away from it. In fact, the Pact shifts European policy further to the right on matters related to migration, deepening this system of exploitation and potentially laying the groundwork for the systematic criminalization of all migrant rescue at sea. We will have to wait to see what this means for SASEMAR.

Meanwhile, where do we find hope? There is hope in the complete failure of current strategies to stop migration, address its root causes, or respond to the labour needs of both countries of origin and destination of migrants. The European Union has been pumping money at the border to make it more secure, more difficult to cross, more dangerous, deadlier: adding more cameras, more sensors, more satellites, more militarization; paying countries elsewhere to contain migrants and accept deported migrants in increasingly far-fetched schemes. The United States began down this path in the 1950s, with significant escalations in the 1990s under the Clinton administration and then again following the 9/11 terrorist attacks. Yet, despite the staggering resources poured into border enforcement, undocumented migration continues.

Perhaps unsurprisingly, the strategies that have not worked in the past are not working now either. In this sense, paradoxically, past failures are laden with hope. Seen from this perspective, perhaps it is not migrant rights activists who are chasing an unrealistic utopia, but policymakers who persist in promoting border security strategies (such as building higher walls and ramping up sea patrols) that have consistently failed in the past. Perhaps, instead of labelling activists who demand that the state respects its own laws and regulations as radicals, it is time to let go of the current road map and try something new, something bigger, something better: a world where people have the choice to stay put. A world where no one has to risk their life on a flimsy boat just to survive. A world where *all* life is equally protected at sea, and SASEMAR is recognized not as a threat to the new order of things, but as a model to follow.

Endnotes

1. All the names of migrant people in this book have been changed to protect their identity. In this case, I have used the pseudonyms that journalist María Martín gave Daria in the original article.
2. The old men who gather in the main square of my grandfather's small mountain village in southern Spain still recount the sexual exploits of Gerald Brenan, many of which he himself chronicled in his 1957 book, *South of Granada: Seven Years in an Andalusian Village*. More widely known is the work of Ernest Hemingway, who, like Brenan, spent a significant part of his life in Spain. Neither of them was considered an immigrant, but as peculiar foreigners.
3. For an academic exploration of how European governments have deployed the "liquid violence" of the sea to do the dirty work, see, among others, the works of Charles Heller and Lorenzo Pezzani (2020), Laura Lo Presti (2019), Bertille Motte (2024), or Lucinda Newns (2003).
4. See also Blanca Garcés Mascareñas (2022).
5. This sad record would later be surpassed in the sinking of the German hospital ship *Wilhelm Gustloff* in 1945, which resulted in the loss of approximately 9,800 lives; the accident between the Filipino passenger ferry *Doña Paz* and an oil tanker in 1987, causing the death of 4,386; and the sinking of the *Le Joola* passenger ship between Dakar and the southern Senegalese region of Casamance in 2002, which resulted in nearly 1,900 deaths.
6. Defending Portuguese interests, Seraphim de Freitas argued that sovereigns can claim possession of waters adjacent to their land possessions. For Portugal, this meant large swaths of ocean near overseas colonies they had appropriated based on the Treaty of Tordesillas. His argument did not directly address the *Santa Catarina* affair (which had already been settled), but it sought to entrench and expand existing powers over overseas possessions on land and sea.
7. For a fascinating discussion on this topic, see Anne-Laure Amilhat-Szary (2020).
8. See the works of Paolo Cuttitta (2018), Polly Pallister-Wilkins (2015, 2018), and William Walters (2011).
9. For example, Leslie Gross-Wyrtzen and Zineb Rachdi El Yacoubi (2024) argue that the externalization of Europe's policy priorities in the areas of migration and border control have turned the Morocco-EU borderland into a "contact zone" where regional understandings of race, place, and membership are reworked. Much like Tendayi Achiume (2022), these authors see the border as a racial project but one where old and new forms of understanding race and belonging are constantly negotiated.
10. Geographer Xavier Ferrer-Gallardo has written extensively about the evolution of the Spanish-Moroccan border co-operation on land. See, for example, Ferrer-Gallardo (2008).

References

Achiume, Tendayi. 2022. "Racial Borders." *110 Georgetown Law Journal* 445 (2022). ssrn.com/abstract=3962563.
Agrela Romero, Belén and Sandra Gil Araújo. 2005. "Constructing Otherness: The Management of Migration and Diversity in the Spanish Context." *Migration: European Journal of International Migration and Ethnic Relations* 43–44: 9–33.
Al Jazeera. 2023a. "At Least 209 Pakistanis Among Victims of Greece Boat Wreck." June 22, 2023. aljazeera.com/amp/news/2023/6/22/at-least-209-pakistanis-among-victims-of-greece-boat-wreck.
———. 2023b. "UN Mission Accuses EU of Aiding Crimes Against Humanity in Libya." March 27, 2023. aljazeera.com/news/2023/3/27/un-mission-accuses-eu-of-aiding-crimes-against-humanity-in-libya-2.
Amilhat-Szary, Anne-Laure. 2020. *Géopolitique des frontières: Découper la terre, imposer une vision du monde*. Le Cavalier Bleu.
Anderson, Scott, Ivan Angelovski, and Mark Kelley. 2024. "The Deadly Dive to the Titanic." *CBC News*, March 28, 2024. cbc.ca/newsinteractives/features/deadly-dive-to-the-titanic.
APDHA (Asociación Pro Derechos Humanos de Andalucía). 2007. *Derechos humanos en la frontera sur 2006*. apdha.org/webanterior/media/fronterasur2006.pdf.
Araque Conde, Pilar. 2018. "Un superviviente de la tragedia de El Tarajal: 'La Guardia Civil disparaba a bocajarro.'" *Público*, February 5, 2018. publico.es/sociedad/aniversario-tarajal-superviviente-tragedia-tarajal-guardia-civil-disparaba-bocajarro.html.
Arbex, Juan Carlos. 2001. *El salvamento marítimo en España*. Madrid: Alcaná Libros.
Arencibia, Ángeles. 2020. "Las pateras y Canarias (1994–2020): 10 claves del fenómeno." *Tiempo de Canarias*, September 19, 2020. tiempodecanarias.com/reportaje/planeta/las-pateras-y-canarias-1996-2020-el-fenomeno-en-10-claves.
Ayuso, Silvia and José María Brunet. 2020. "European Court of Human Rights Backs Spain in Express Deportation Case." *El País*, February 14, 2020. english.elpais.com/spanish_news/2020-02-14/european-court-of-human-rights-backs-spain-in-express-deportation-case.html#.
Banos, Arnaud, Luna Vives, Camille Martel, Elizabeth Hessek, and Kira Williams. 2024. "Lorsque le contrôle des migrations prend le pas sur la sauvegarde de la vie en mer: l'émergence des frontières dans la zone de responsabilité SAR espagnole." *Criminologie*, 57(2): 27-55. https://doi.org/10.7202/1114783ar.
Blanco, Juan Carlos. 2014. "Los asaltos a las vallas de Ceuta y Melilla de 2005." *El País*, March 19, 2014. blogs.elpais.com/fondo-de-armario/2014/03/la-valla.html.
Boza Fii. 2023. "Rapport des départs du Sénégal / Juin – Octobre 2023." November 6, 2023. bozafii.org/index.php/2023/11/06/rapport-des-departs-du-senegal/.

Brito, Renata and Felipe Dana. 2023. "Adrift in the Atlantic, a Boat of Death and Lost Dreams." *Independent,* April 12, 2023. independent.co.uk/news/ap-tobago-mauritania-europe-atlantic-b2318178.html.

Bulman, May, Maud Julien, Tomas Statius, et al. 2024. "Desert Dumps." *Lighthouse Reports,* May 21, 2024. lighthousereports.com/investigation/desert-dumps/.

Camacho, Julia. 2013. "Cruzar el Estrecho en pateras de supermercado." *El Diario de Córdoba,* August 18, 2013. https://www.diariocordoba.com/sociedad/2013/08/18/cruzar-estrecho-pateras-supermercado-37347016.html.

Caminando Fronteras. 2023. *Monitoreo del derecho a la vida – Año 2023.* caminandofronteras.org/monitoreo/monitoreo-del-derecho-a-la-vida-ano-2023/.

Campling, Liam, and Alejandro Colás. 2021. *Capitalism and the Sea.* London and Brooklyn, NY: Verso.

Canarias7. 2023. "Mogán se planta y abre otro frente con Madrid: No pagará más entierros de inmigrantes." September 22, 2023. canarias7.es/politica/mogan-pagara-entierros-inmigrantes-abre-frencxte-madrid-20230922232556-nt.html

Capanema P. de Almeida, Silvia. 2011. "From Seaman João Cândido to the Black Admiral: Memorial Conflicts in the Construction of the Hero of a Centenary Revolt." *Revista Brasileira de História* 31(61): 61–83. doi https://doi.org/10.1590/S0102-01882011000100004.

Carvajal, Álvaro. 2019. "Vox propone en el Congreso levantar un muro en Ceuta y Melilla contra la invasión migratoria." *El Mundo,* September 12, 2019. elmundo.es/espana/2019/09/12/5d7a192ffc6c83426d8b4646.html.

Castellano, Nicolás. 2014. "Baijea abrió la ruta." *Cadena SER.* August 2014. cadenaser.com/especiales/seccion/espana/2014/inmigracion-canarias/#:~:text=Baijea%20abri%C3%B3%20la%20ruta,Salinas%20del%20Carmen%20(Fuerteventura).

———. 2023. "'Está dentro de la zona SAR nuestra': la SER accede a las grabaciones de Salvamento Marítimo del último naufragio en la ruta canaria." *Cadena SER.* June 22, 2023. https://cadenaser.com/nacional/2023/06/22/esta-dentro-de-la-zona-sar-nuestra-la-ser-accede-a-las-grabaciones-de-salvamento-maritimo-del-ultimo-naufragio-en-la-ruta-canaria-cadena-ser/.

CBC News. 2023. *Titan Sub Built by 'MacGyver-ing' Off-the-Shelf Parts: Journalist* [video file]. June 26, 2023. cbc.ca/player/play/video/1.6888642.

CEAR (Comisión Española de Ayuda al Refugiado). 2024. "Caso Tarajal: 14 muertes y diez años de impunidad." February 1, 2024. cear.es/caso-tarajal/.

Ceuta Actualidad. 2019. "Los musulmanes residentes en Ceuta constituyen en torno al 43% de la población, según UCIDE." February 21, 2019. ceutaactualidad.com/articulo/sociedad/musulmanes-residentes-ceuta-constituyen-torno-43-poblacion-datos-union-comunidades-islamicas-espana/20190221112243079267.html.

CGT (Confederación General del Trabajo). 2019. "SASEMAR consiente que Babcock reduzca el sueldo a sus plantillas a pesar de tener importantes ingresos — CGT — Confederal." *CGT.Org* May 10, 2019. CGT.org.es/SASEMAR-consiente-que-babcock-reduzca-el-sueldo-a-sus-plantillas-a-pesar-de-tener-importantes-ingresos/.

———. 2022. *Estatutos y reglamento de Congresos de la Confederación General del Trabajo.* Zaragoza: XIX Congreso Confederal del CGT. CGT.org.es/wp-content/uploads/2008/04/Estatutos-CGTactualizados-XIX-congreso.pdf.

Chester, Simon. 2009. "Grotius, Selden and 400 Years of Controversy." *Slaw,* November 1, 2009. slaw.ca/2009/11/01/grotius-selden-and-400-years-of-controversy/.

CNT (Confederación Nacional del Trabajo). n.d. "Diferencias entre CNT y CGT." *CNT València.* valencia.CNT.es/que-es-la-CNT/diferencias-entre-CNT-y-CGT/.

Couper, Alastair D. 1978. "Marine Resources and Environment." *Progress in Human Geography* 2, 2: 296–308. doi.org/10.1177/030913257800200205.

Crawley, Heaven and Dimitris Skleparis. 2018. "Refugees, Migrants, Neither, Both: Categorical Fetishism and the Politics of Bounding in Europe's 'Migration Crisis.'" *Journal of Ethnic and Migration Studies* 44(1), 48–64. doi.org/10.1080/1369183X.2017.1348224.

Crutchley, Commander William Caius. 1912. *My Life at Sea*. London: Chapman and Hall.

Cué, Carlos E. 2024. "Sánchez y Von der Leyen prometen más de 500 millones para desarrollar Mauritania y frenar los cayucos a Canarias." *El País*, February 8, 2024. https://elpais.com/espana/2024-02-08/sanchez-y-von-der-leyen-prometen-mas-de-500-millones-para-desarrollar-mauritania-y-frenar-los-cayucos-a-canarias.html

Cuttitta, Paolo. 2018. "Delocalization, Humanitarianism, and Human Rights: The Mediterranean Border Between Exclusion and Inclusion." *Antipode* 50, 3. doi:10.1111/anti.12337.

Delgado Sanz, Enrique. 2023. "El cuadrante que muestra la Cara B de la crisis de los Cayucos: Los rescatadores y las jornadas de 20 horas." *El Confidencial*, October 29, 2023. elconfidencial.com/espana/islas-canarias/2023-10-29/canarias-cayucos-salvamento-rescatadores-horas_3763085/.

Département de la Pêche Maritime. 2010. *Recherche et sauvetage des vies humaines en mer: Rapport national 2010*. Royaume du Maroc.

Dines, Nick, Nicola Montagna, and Elena Vacchelli. 2018. "Beyond Crisis Talk: Interrogating Migration and Crises in Europe." *Sociology*, 52(3), 439–447. doi.org/10.1177/0038038518767372.

Diome, Fatou. 2003. *Le ventre de l'Atlantique*. Le livre de poche.

Dirección General de Comunicación Exterior. 2006. *Plan África 2006-2008*. Ministerio De Asuntos Exteriores Y De Cooperación. June 2006. Madrid: Gobierno de España. crea-africa.org/wp-content/uploads/2008/09/LIBROPLANAFRICA.pdf.

Dirección General de la Guardia Civil. 2022. *Contratación de un servicio de mantenimiento integral para los despliegues fijos del Sistema Integrado de Vigilancia Exterior (SIVE)*. T/0073/P/21/2. Madrid: Gobierno de España.

EFE. 2020. "El defensor del pueblo denuncia que las 'importantes carencias' detectadas en la 'nave de la vergüenza' afectaron a la salud de los migrantes." *El Diario*, December 3, 2020. eldiario.es/canariasahora/migraciones/defensor-pueblo-denuncia-importantes-carencias-nave-verguenza-afectaron-salud-migrantes_1_6480593.html.

———. 2023. "Caminando fronteras pide a la fiscalía una investigación penal sobre la neumática hundida tras diez horas de espera." *EFE*, July 6, 2023. efe.com/canarias/2023-07-06/caminando-fronteras-pide-a-la-fiscalia-una-investigacion-penal-sobre-la-neumatica-hundida-tras-diez-horas-de-espera/.

El País. 2021. "Marruecos llama a consultas a su embajadora en España." May 18, 2021. elpais.com/espana/2021-05-18/espana-convoca-a-la-embajadora-de-marruecos.html.

———. 2023. "Lea el acuerdo de Coalición Canaria y el PSOE para la investidura de Sánchez." November 10, 2023. elpais.com/espana/2023-11-10/lea-el-acuerdo-de-coalicion-canaria-y-el-psoe-para-la-investidura-de-sanchez.html.

Endrina, Nieves, Juan C. Raseroa, and Dimitrios Konovessis. 2018. "Risk Analysis for RoPax vessels: A Case Study for the Strait of Gibraltar." *Ocean Engineering* 151 (2018).

Eroski Consumer. 2001. "La prestación social sustitutoria desaparecerá el 31 de Diciembre." *Consumer*, March 31, 2001. consumer.es/economia-domestica/la-prestacion-social-sustitutoria-desaparecera-el-31-de-diciembre.html.

Europa Press. 2015. "Lanzarote recuerda el naufragio de la patera de Los Cocoteros cuando se cumplen seis años." *El Dia*, February 15, 2012. eldia.es/canarias/2015-02-15/3-Lanzarote-recuerda-naufragio-patera-Cocoteros-cuando-cumplen-seis-anos.htm.

Europa Press Nacional. 2023. "CC ve a Sánchez proclive a nombrar un mando único del Gobierno ante el repunte de inmigración en las islas." *Europe Press*, October 11, 2023. europapress.es/nacional/noticia-cc-ve-sanchez-proclive-nombrar-mando-unico-gobierno-repunte-inmigracion-islas-20231011135611.html.

European Commission. 2000. *Partnership Agreement ACP-EC*. June 23, 2000. Benin: Cotonou.

———. 2020. "European Contact Group on Search and Rescue (E03752)." December 21, 2020. ec.europa.eu/transparency/expert-groups-register/screen/expert-groups/consult?lang=en&groupId=3752&fromMeetings=true&meetingId=27635.

———. 2024. "Search and Rescue." *Migration and Home Affairs*. May 7, 2024. home-affairs.ec.europa.eu/policies/migration-and-asylum/migration-management/search-and-rescue_en.

European Union. 2023. *EU Migration Support in Morocco*. eu/document/download/6690bcbf-3bec-40e1-b80e-f57a724cdf09_en?filename=EU_support_migration_morocco_Kostas.pdf.

Eurostat. 2023. *Autorisations délivrées pour travail saisonnier par secteur économique, sexe et nationalité* [Data set]. doi.org/10.2908/MIGR_RESSW2.

Ferrer-Gallardo, Xavier. 2008. "The Spanish–Moroccan Border Complex: Processes of Geopolitical, Functional and Symbolic Rebordering." *Political Geography*, 27 (3): 301–21. doi.org/10.1016/j.polgeo.2007.12.004

FIIAP (Fundación Internacional y para Iberoamericana de Administración y Políticas Públicas). 2024. "Rehabilitación de dos centros de atención temporal de extranjeros en situación irregular en Nuadibú y Nuakchott." March 19, 2024. fiiapp.org/noticias/rehabilitacion-de-dos-centros-de-atencion-temporal-de-extranjeros-en-situacion-irregular-en-nuadibu-y-nuakchott/

France 24. 2023. "Dozens of Migrants Dead, Fears for Hundreds Missing in Greece Shipwreck." June 14, 2023. france24.com/en/live-news/20230614-dozens-of-migrants-dead-100-rescued-as-boat-sinks-off-greece-1.

Frontex. 2009. *The Impact of the Global Economic Crisis on Illegal Migration to the EU*. Poland: Warsaw. europarl.europa.eu/meetdocs/2009_2014/documents/libe/dv/frontex_/frontex_en.pdf.

Fundación Raíces. 2021. "La justicia mantiene la suspensión de las repatriaciones de menores en Ceuta y desestima las alegaciones de la Abogacía del Estado." August 26, 2021. fundacionraices.org/?p=3250.

Furuseth, Andrew. 1914. *Safety of Life at Sea: Analysis and Explanatory Notes of the London Convention of the Safety of Life at Sea in Relation to the American Merchant Marine*. Collection Development Department. Widener Library. HCL. nrs.lib.harvard.edu/urn-3:fhcl:119592.

Gabella Maroto, Francisco. 2004. "Control de fronteras." Seminar delivered at the Instituto Universitario de Investigación sobre Seguridad Interior. iuisi.es/15_boletines/15_2005/doc028-2005.pdf.

Galán Caballero, Javier, Daniele Grasso, and Nacho Catalán. 2019. "España rescata a un tercio de los migrantes en aguas de responsabilidad marroquí." *El País*, March 28, 2019. elpais.com/politica/2019/03/26/actualidad/1553613053_040695.html.

Garcés Mascareñas, Blanca. 2022. "La necropolitica de la frontera." *CIDOB Opinión*, 704. cidob.org/publicaciones/la-necropolitica-de-la-frontera.

García Mira, Ricardo (ed.). 2013. *Lecturas sobre el desastre del prestige: Contribuciones desde las ciencias sociales*. A Coruña: Instituto de Estudios e Investigación Psicosocial Xoán Vicente Viqueira.

Gilmore, Ruth Wilson. 2007. *Golden Gulag: Prisons, Surplus, Crisis, and Opposition in Globalizing California*. Berkeley, CA: University of California Press.

———. 2022. *Abolition Geography: Essays towards Liberation*. Brooklyn, NY: Verso.

Gómez, Manuel V. 2019. "La mitad de los empleados públicos menores de 40 años son temporales." *El País*, August 17, 2019. elpais.com/economia/2019/08/14/actualidad/1565795704_566453.html.

Gordon, Edward. 2008. "Grotius and the Freedom of the Seas in the Seventeenth Century." *Willamette Journal of International Law and Dispute Resolution* 16 (2): 252-269. jstor.org/stable/26211640.

Greek Ombudsman Independent Authority. 2025. "Press Release: The Ombudsman's Report on the Pylos Shipwreck." theioi.org/downloads/4chl4/030225-PR-PYLOS-REPORT.pdf.

Gross-Wyrtzen, Leslie and Zineb Rachdi El Yacoubi. 2024. "Externalizing Otherness: The Racialization of Belonging in the Morocco-EU Border." *Geoforum* 155. doi.org/10.1016/j.geoforum.2022.103673.

de Haas, Hein. 2023. "Everything Politicians Tell You about Immigration is Wrong. This Is How It Actually Works." *The Guardian*, December 23, 2023. theguardian.com/commentisfree/2023/dec/29/politicians-immigration-wrong-cheap-labour.

Havern, Christopher B. 2012. "The Short Life and Tragic End of RMS Titanic." *Journal of Safety & Security at Sea. The Coast Guard Proceedings of the Marine Safety & Security Council* (Summer 2012). https://www.dco.uscg.mil/Portals/9/DCO%20Documents/Proceedings%20Magazine/Archive/2012/Vol69_No2_Sum2012.pdf?ver=2017-05-31-120748-633

Hegarty, Stephanie. 2018. "Migrant Slavery in Libya: Nigerians Tell of Being Used as Slaves." *BBC*, January 2, 2018. bbc.com/news/world-africa-42492687.

Heller, Charles, and Lorenzo Pezzani. "Forensic Oceanography: Tracing Violence Within and Against the Mediterranean Frontier's Aesthetic Regime". In *Moving Images: Mediating Migration as Crisis*, edited by K. Lynes, T. Morgenstern, and I. Alan Paul. Bielefeld: Transcript, 2020.

Hernández, José Antonio and Jesús Duva. 1995. "El fugitivo Luis Roldán, capturado en Laos." *El País*, February 27, 1995. elpais.com/diario/1995/02/28/espana/793926019_850215.html.

Hernando de Larramendi, Miguel and Ana I. Planet. 2007. "Las relaciones Hispano-Mauritanas (1960-2006)." *Anales de Historia Contemporánea* 23 (2007).

Herrera, Carlos. 2021. "El guardia civil que rescató al bebé en Ceuta, en COPE: 'Estaba helado, frío, no gesticulaba.'" *COPE*, May 19, 2021. cope.es/programas/herrera-en-cope/noticias/guardia-civil-que-rescato-bebe-ceuta-estaba-helado-frio-gesticulabafue-poco-traumatico-20210519_1297196.

Hyndman, Jennifer. 2008. "Conflict, Citizenship, and Human Security: Geographies of Protection." In *War, Citizenship, Territory*, edited by D. Cohen and E. Gilbert. New York: Routledge. pp. 241-57.

Instrucción Sobre el Modo y los Medios de Socorrer a los que se Ahogaren o Hallaren en Peligro en el Río de Sevilla. 1773. Sevilla: Imprenta del Doctor Don Geronymo de Castilla. Biblioteca de la Universidad de Sevilla. archive.org/details/ARes7850303.

International Conference of Safety of Life at Sea. 1914. *Text of the Convention for the Safety of Life at Sea*. London: United Kingdom. http://archive.org/details/textofconvention-00inte/page/n7/mode/2up?view=theater

IMO (International Maritime Organization). 1948. *Convention on the International Maritime Organization.* Geneva: Switzerland.
———. 1974. *International Convention for the Safety of Life at Sea (SOLAS).*
———. n.d. "SOLAS." imo.org/en/KnowledgeCentre/ConferencesMeetings/Pages/SOLAS.aspx.
———. 1979. International Convention on Maritime Search and Rescue (SAR).
Irídia and Novact. 2023. *Vulneración de derechos humanos en la Frontera Sur del Estado español 2021 – 2022.* iridia.cat/wp-content/uploads/2023/05/CAST-informe-FS.pdf.
IOM (International Organization for Migration). n.d. *Missing Migrants Project.* missingmigrants.iom.int/.
Kassam, Ashifa. 2023. "An Obscure Island Grave: Fate of Deadly EU Migration Route's Youngest Victim." *The Guardian,* December 8, 2023. theguardian.com/world/2023/dec/08/an-obscure-island-grave-fate-of-deadly-eu-migration-routes-youngest-victim.
Kropotkin, Peter. 1910 [1995] "'Anarchism', from the Encyclopaedia Britannica." In *Kropotkin: "The Conquest of Bread" and Other Writings,* edited by Marshall S. Shatz, 233–47. Cambridge Texts in the History of Political Thought. Cambridge: Cambridge University Press, 1995.
La Moncloa. 2018. "Creación de un mando único operativo para coordinar las actuaciones frente a la inmigración irregular en la zona del Estrecho de Gibraltar." August 3, 2018. lamoncloa.gob.es/consejodeministros/Paginas/enlaces/030818cm_mandoestrecho.aspx.
———. 2024. "El Gobierno constituye la comisión interministerial de inmigración." January 30, 2024. lamoncloa.gob.es/serviciosdeprensa/notasprensa/politica-territorial-memoria-democratica/Paginas/2024/300124-comision-interministerial-inmigracion.aspx.
Lantz, Jeffrey G. 2012. "Director's Perspective." *Journal of Safety & Security at Sea. The Coast Guard Proceedings of the Marine Safety & Security Council,* 2012. https://www.dco.uscg.mil/Portals/9/DCO%20Documents/Proceedings%20Magazine/Archive/2012/Vol69_No2_Sum2012.pdf?ver=2017-05-31-120748-633.
Lawrence, Felicity, Ashifa Kassam, Lorenzo Tondo, et al. 2023. "More than 1,000 Unmarked Graves Found along EU Migration Routes." *The Guardian,* December 8, 2023. theguardian.com/world/ng-interactive/2023/dec/08/revealed-more-than-1000-unmarked-graves-discovered-along-eu-migration-routes.
Linebaugh, Peter and Marcus Rediker. 2012. *The Many-Headed Hydra: The Hidden History of the Revolutionary Atlantic.* New York: Verso.
Lo Coco, Maite Daniela, Andrés G. Berrio, Clara Calderó Delgado, and Siham Jessica Korriche. 2022. *Vulneraciones de derechos en la respuesta institucional a las llegadas de personas migrantes en Canarias.* Barcelona: Iridia.
Lo Presti, Laura. 2019. "Terraqueous Necropolitics: Unfolding the Low-operational, Forensic, and Evocative Mapping of Mediterranean Sea Crossings in the Age of Lethal Borders." *ACME: An International Journal for Critical Geographies* 18, 6. doi.org/10.14288/acme.v18i6.1829.
López-Fonseca, Óscar and Juana Viúdez. 2024. "A Judge Investigates Possible Deficiencies in the Operation in Which Two Civil Guards Died in Barbate." *El País,* May 21, 2024. elpais.com/espana/2024-05-21/un-juez-investiga-posibles-deficiencias-en-el-operativo-en-el-que-murieron-dos-guardias-civiles-en-barbate.html.
Marín Silvestre, Dolors. 2005. *Ministros anarquistas: La CNT en el gobierno de la II República.* Barcelona: La Central.
Maritimes Crime. 2023. "Fishing in the Senegalese Waters, a Maritime Wealth Threatened." *Maritimes Crimes,* April 5, 2023. maritimescrimes.com/2023/04/05/senegalese-waters-a-maritime-wealth-threatened/.

Martín, María. 2020. "El defensor del pueblo: 'Confinar inmigrantes en Canarias no es la solución.'" *El País*, December 3, 2020. elpais.com/espana/2020-12-03/el-defensor-del-pueblo-confinar-inmigrantes-en-canarias-no-es-la-solucion.html.

———. 2021a. "Qué está pasando en Ceuta: Claves de la crisis migratoria entre España y Marruecos." *El País*, May 18, 2021. elpais.com/espana/2021-05-19/que-esta-pasando-en-ceuta-claves-de-la-crisis-entre-espana-y-marruecos.html.

———. 2021b. "Menores en primera línea del caos." *El País*, May 22, 2021. elpais.com/espana/2021-05-23/menores-en-primera-linea-del-caos.html.

———. 2024a. "El Gobierno demora la orden de la Audiencia Nacional de traer a España al sudanés que pidió asilo en Rabat." *El País*, April 10, 2024. elpais.com/espana/2024-04-11/el-gobierno-demora-la-orden-de-la-audiencia-nacional-de-trasladar-a-espana-al-sudanes-que-pidio-asilo-en-rabat.html.

———. 2024b. "El refugiado sudanés que ganó el pulso al Gobierno ya está en España." *El País*, May 23, 2024. elpais.com/espana/2024-05-24/el-refugiado-sudanes-que-gano-el-pulso-al-gobierno-ya-esta-en-espana.html.

———. 2025. "La muerte en la ruta migratoria hacia Canarias: Hallan dos nuevos cayucos perdidos en el Caribe." *El País,* January 31, 2025. elpais.com/espana/2025-02-01/la-muerte-en-la-ruta-migratoria-hacia-canarias-hallan-dos-cayucos-perdidos-en-el-caribe.html

Martín, María and Jesús A. Cañas. 2023. "Los narcos que trafican con migrantes imponen su ley en alta mar." *El País,* December 12, 2023. elpais.com/espana/2023-12-13/los-narcos-que-trafican-con-migrantes-imponen-su-ley-en-alta-mar.html?event_log=go.

Martín, María and Lola Hierro. 2024. "Los desembarcos en Canarias sitúan a España como el segundo país de la UE con más entradas irregulares." *El País*, January 1, 2024. elpais.com/espana/2024-01-02/los-desembarcos-en-canarias-situan-a-espana-como-el-segundo-pais-de-la-ue-con-mas-entradas-irregulares.html?event_log=go

Martín, María, Lola Hierro, and Diego Stacey. 2024. "Desterrados en el desierto." *El País*, May 21, 2024. elpais.com/internacional/2024-05-21/detenciones-masivas-y-traslados-forzosos-asi-se-destierra-con-dinero-europeo-a-migrantes-en-el-norte-de-africa.html.

Martín, María and Maud Jullien. 2023. "Survivors of the Shipwreck in the Mediterranean Accuse Greek Authorities: 'The Coast Guard Towed Us at High Speed, and We Capsized.'" *El País*, June 30, 2023. english.elpais.com/international/2023-06-30/survivors-of-the-shipwreck-in-the-mediterranean-accuse-greek-authorities-the-coast-guard-towed-us-at-high-speed-and-we-capsized.html.

Martínez Escamilla, Margarita. 2019. "La criminalización de la solidaridad." *Revista Crítica Penal y Poder* 18: 8-18. https://revistes.ub.edu/index.php/CriticaPenalPoder/article/view/30407.

———. 2020. "Devoluciones en caliente." *Rescoldos: Revista de diálogo social* 41:16. This is a radio interview published as part of an online magazine, available here: https://www.asociacioncandela.org/2020/02/29/devoluciones-en-caliente/.

Mau, Steffan, Fabian Gülzau, Lena Laube, and Natascha Zaun. 2015. "The Global Mobility Divide: How Visa Policies Have Evolved over Time." *Journal of Ethnic and Migration Studies* 41(8), 1192–1213. doi.org/10.1080/1369183X.2015.1005007.

Mbembe, Achille. 2019. *Necro-Politics*. Durham: Duke University Press.

Mediasanctuary. 2009. *Amiri Baraka "Why's/Wise"* [video file]. December 9, 2009. youtube.com/watch?v=mKfQNO66GPk&ab_channel=mediasanctuary.

Migreurop. 2020. "Hundreds of NGOs and Individuals Call for Revocation of Libya's SAR Zone." *Migreurop*, July 3, 2020. migreurop.org/article2997.html.

Ministerio de Transportes y Mobilidad Sostenible. 2024. *Plan anual de actuación 2024*. Sociedad de Salvamento y Seguridad Marítima. Gobierno de España. salvamentomaritimo.es/statics/multimedia/documents/2024/02/06/Plan_Anual_2024.pdf.

Ministerio del Interior. 2007. *Balance de la lucha contra la inmigración ilegal*. Gobierno de España. interior.gob.es/opencms/pdf/prensa/balances-e-informes/2007/Balance-de-la-lucha-contra-la-inmigracion-ilegal.pdf.

Ministerio de Justicia. 1988. *Real decreto 20/1988, de 15 de enero, por el que se aprueba el reglamento de la prestación social de los objetores de conciencia*. Gobierno de España. boe.es/buscar/doc.php?id=BOE-A-1988-1267.

Mountz, Alison. 2020. *The Death of Asylum: Hidden Geographies of the Enforcement Archipelago*. Minneapolis: University of Minnesota Press.

Motte, Bertille. 2024. "Migrant Death and Disappearability at Sea: Mediterranean Necropolitics as a European Strategy of Migration Deterrence." *Journal of Public and International Affairs*. April 22, 2024. https://jpia.princeton.edu/node/336.

Mouzo, Emiliano. 2015. "El naufragio que movió conciencias." *La Voz de Galicia*, October 4, 2015. lavozdegalicia.es/noticia/coruna/coruna/2015/10/04/naufragio-movio-conciencias/0003_201510H4C4993.htm.

Muñoz, Lucia and Sonia Moreno. 2019. "El gobierno ofrece barcos y formación a Marruecos para frenar las llegadas de migrantes a España." *El Diario*, April 4, 2019. eldiario.es/desalambre/salvamento-maritimo-embarcaciones-marruecos-naufragos_1_1619775.html.

Murillo, Pedro and María Martín. 2020. "Muere un bebé que nació en una patera con destino a Canarias." *El País*, January 8, 2020. elpais.com/politica/2020/01/08/actualidad/1578495302_198919.html.

Naranjo, Elena. 2021. "Así se desmanteló el 'muelle de la vergüenza.'" *14 Horas*, November 21, 2021. RTVE.

Newns, Lucinda. 2023. "Necropolitical Ecologies: Creative Articulations of Nature's Death-Work in the Borderzone." *Interventions* (2023) 26(1), 36–51. https://doi.org/10.1080/1369801X.2023.2190919.

Obokata, Tomoya. 2024. *Report of the Special Rapporteur on Contemporary Forms of Slavery, Including Its Causes and Consequences*. United Nations. documents.un.org/doc/undoc/gen/g24/120/97/pdf/g2412097.pdf.

Ocampo Aneiros, José Antonio. n.d. "Miguel Lobo y Malagamba." *Real Academia de la Historia*. dbe.rah.es/biografias/12232/miguel-lobo-y-malagamba.

O'Carroll, Lisa. 2024. "EU Leaders Unveil €210m Mauritania Deal in Bid to Curb People-smuggling." *The Guardian*, February 8, 2024. theguardian.com/world/2024/feb/08/spain-and-eu-to-sign-migration-deal-with-mauritania-as-people-smuggling-rises.

OLA (Office of Legal Affairs). 2024. "Codification and Progressive Development of International Law." *United Nations*. legal.un.org/cod/.

Pallister-Wilkins, Polly. 2015. "The Humanitarian Politics of European Border Policing: Frontex and Border Police in Evros." *International Political Sociology* 9, 1: 53–69. doi:10.1111/ips.12076.

———. 2018. "Hotspots and the Geographies of Humanitarianism." *Environment and Planning D: Society and Space* 38, 6: 991–1008. https://doi.org/10.1177/0263775818754884.

Palmer, Sarah. 2005. "Leaders and Followers: The Development of International Maritime Policy in the Nineteenth Century." *International Journal of Maritime History* 17, 2: 299-309. https://doi.org/10.1177/084387140501700217.

Parlamento de Andalucía. 2019. *Boletín oficial del parlamento de Andalucía 56*. April 8, 2019. parlamentodeandalucia.es/webdinamica/portal-web-parlamento/pdf.do?tipodoc=bopa&id=137774.

Peregil, Francisco and Miguel González. 2021. "El líder del Frente Polisario, hospitalizado en España." *El País*, April 23, 2021. elpais.com/espana/2021-04-23/el-lider-del-frente-polisario-hospitalizado-en-espana.html.

Philbrick, Nathaniel. 2000. *The Heart of the Sea: The Tragedy of the Whaleship Essex*. Viking Press.

Philippe, Charlier, Deo Saudamini and Annane Djillali. 2019. "Intra-rectal Tobacco Insufflation as a Resuscitation Method for Drowning Victims: A Gold-standard in the 18th Century." *Resuscitation* 142.

Piper, Imogen, Joyce Sohyun Lee, and Claire Parker. 2023. "Tracing a Tragedy: How Hundreds of Migrants Drowned on Greece's Watch." *The Washington Post*, July 5, 2023. washingtonpost.com/world/interactive/2023/greece-migrant-boat-coast-guard/.

Porter, Tim and Marianne Guenot. 2023. "The Missing Titanic Sub Fell Outside Safety Rules by Operating in International Waters Beyond the Law, Experts Say." *Business Insider*, June 21, 2023. businessinsider.com/titanic-sub-avoided-safety-rules-by-diving-in-international-waters-experts-2023-6.

Ramajo, Javier. 2018. "La imagen que abrió los ojos a la tragedia del Estrecho cumple 30 años: 'Era la primera vez y ponía los pelos de punta.'" *El Diario*, October 31, 2018. eldiario.es/andalucia/andalucia-primera-patera-pateras-migrantes-inmigracion-playa-los-lances_1_1877299.html.

Rittel, Horst W. J. and Melvin M. Webber. 1973. "Dilemmas in a General Theory of Planning." *Policy Sci* 4, 155–169. https://doi.org/10.1007/BF01405730.

Rodrigo, Sergio. 2021. *Paralelo 35°50* (Film). Entre Fronteras.

Rodríguez, Jorge A. 2022. "Muere Luis Roldán, el director de la Guardia Civil que se enriqueció con los fondos reservados." *El País*, March 24, 2022. elpais.com/espana/2022-03-24/muere-luis-roldan-el-director-de-la-guardia-civil-que-saqueo-los-fondos-reservados.html?event_log=regonetap.

Rodríguez, José María. 2024. "¿Un cayuco en Brasil? 1.500 migrantes han desaparecido en 2024 intentando llegar de Mauritania a Canarias." *EFE*, April 16, 2024. efe.com/canarias/2024-04-16/un-cayuco-en-brasil-1-500-migrantes-han-desaparecido-en-2023-intentando-llegar-de-mauritania-a-canarias/.

Rosati, Sara and María Martín. 2020. "El viaje del bebé que nació y murió en una patera." *El País*, February 1, 2020. elpais.com/politica/2020/02/01/actualidad/1580561759_101028.html.

Safety of Life at Sea: Hearings before the Committee on Foreign Relations. 1914. US Senate, 63rd Congress, 2nd Session.

Salama, José. 2020. "The Strait of Gibraltar, One of the Most Transited Sea Routes in the World." *José Salama & Co. Ltd*. April 1, 2020. salama.es/en/noticia/ver/id/79/title/the-strait-of-gibraltar-one-of-the-most-transited-sea-routes-in-the-world.html.

Salmi, Katya. 2014. "Abused and Expelled: Ill-treatment of Sub-Saharan African Migrants in Morocco." *Human Rights Watch*. hrw.org/report/2014/02/10/abused-and-expelled/ill-treatment-sub-saharan-african-migrants-morocco.

Sánchez, Nacho. 2019. "Interior centraliza en Málaga la gestión migratoria en el Sur." *El País*, March 9, 2019. elpais.com/politica/2019/03/08/actualidad/1552071835_698861.html.

Sapoch, Jack, Beatriz Ramalho da Silva, Bashar Deeb, et al. 2022. "Reconstructing the Melilla Massacre." *Lighthouse Reports*. lighthousereports.com/investigation//reconstructing-the-melilla-massacre/.

SASEMAR (Sociedad de Salvamento y Seguridad Marítima). 2006. *Plan nacional de servicios especiales de salvamento de la vida humana en la Mar y de la Lucha contra la contaminación del medio marino (2006 – 2009)*. Madrid: Gobierno de España.
_____. 2016. *Una Historia De Valor*. Madrid: Gobierno de España.
_____. n.d.a. "6 bases estratégicas de salvamento y lucha contra la contaminación marina." salvamentomaritimo.es/conocenos/nuestros-medios/6-bases-estrategicas-de-salvamento-y-lucha-contra-la-contaminacion-marina.
_____. n.d.b. "87 Unidades marítimas y aéreas." salvamentomaritimo.es/conocenos/nuestros-medios/87-unidades-maritimas-y-aereas.
Schmoll, Camille. 2015. "Introduction. Migrations en Méditerranée." In *Migrations en Méditerranée*, edited by H. Thiollet, C. Schmoll, C. Wihtol De Wenden. Paris: CNRS Éditions.
Sekimizu, Koji. 2012. "International Maritime Organization 100 Years after the *Titanic*." *The Coast Guard Journal of Safety & Security at Sea Proceedings* 69, 2. dco.uscg.mil/Featured-Content/Proceedings-Magazine/Proceedings-Archives-Delete/Proceedings-Archives/.
Serrano, Antonio. 2024. "Claves de la ILP que pretende regularizar migrantes: ¿Quién podría beneficiarse? ¿A cuántas personas afectaría?." *RTVE*, April 10, 2024. rtve.es/noticias/20240410/claves-ilp-pretende-regularizar-migrantes-quien-podria-beneficiarse/16053992.shtml.
South Pacific Logistics. 2024. "¿Qué es el Estrecho de Gibraltar y por qué destaca en el transporte marítimo?" January 12, 2024. web.splogistics.com/blog/post/1058/que-es-el-estrecho-de-gibraltar-y-por-que-destaca-en-el-transporte-maritimo.
Statewatch. 2019. *Aid, Border Security and EU-Morocco Cooperation on Migration Control*. November 2019. statewatch.org/media/documents/analyses/no-347-eu-morocco-aid-border-security.pdf.
Stevis-Gridneff, Matina and Karam Shoumali. 2023. "Everyone Knew the Migrant Ship Was Doomed. No One Helped." *The New York Times*, July 1, 2023. nytimes.com/2023/07/01/world/europe/greece-migrant-ship.html.
Steinberg, Philip E. 2001. *The Social Construction of the Sea*. New York: Cambridge University Press.
Thierry, Jean-Marie. 2020. "Société humaine des naufragés de Boulogne-sur-mer: Première station de sauvetage en France." *Voile et Moteur*, September 27, 2020. voileetmoteur.com/peche-en-mer/actualites-peche/societe-humaine-des-naufrages-de-boulogne-sur-mer-la-premiere-station-de-sauvetage-en-france/97937.
Trump, Donald. 2020. "Proclamation on Recognizing the Sovereignty of the Kingdom of Morocco over the Western Sahara." The White House, December 10, 2020. trumpwhitehouse.archives.gov/presidential-actions/proclamation-recognizing-sovereignty-kingdom-morocco-western-sahara/
Vargas, Jairo. 2018. "SOS de Salvamento Marítimo Al Gobierno: 'Estamos desbordados, necesitamos más personal y más medios.'" *Público*, July 21, 2018. publico.es/sociedad/rescate-pateras-sos-salvamento-maritimo-gobierno-desbordados-necesitamos-personal-medios.html.
_____. 2019. "Salvamento marítimo deja de informar en redes sobre pateras tras la irrupción de Vox." *Público*, January 4, 2019. publico.es/sociedad/salvamento-maritimo-salvamento-maritimo-deja-informar-redes-rescates-migrantes-llegada-vox-parlamento-andaluz.html.
Vargas, Natalia G. 2020a. "Un menor pasa nueve días perdido en el 'muelle de la vergüenza' de gran canaria tras ver a 16 personas morir en el mar rumbo a las

islas." *El Diario*, November 2, 2020. eldiario.es/canariasahora/migraciones/nino-pasa-nueve-dias-perdido-arguineguin-ver-16-personas-morir-mar-rumbo-canarias_1_6380636.html.

____. 2020b. "La 'Nave de la Vergüenza' Vuelve a Albergar a 79 Migrantes Sin Duchas ni Ventilación en el Puerto de Las Palmas." *El Diario,* October 21, 2020. eldiario.es/canariasahora/365-dias-de-migraciones/nave-vergueenza-vuelve-albergar-79-migrantes-duchas-ventilacion-puerto-palmas_132_6309202.html.

_____. 2023. "La 'Nave de la Vergüenza' de Lanzarote, el Símbolo de las Vulneraciones de Derechos a Migrantes en 2021." *El Diario,* November 7, 2023. eldiario.es/canariasahora/migraciones/nave-verguenza-lanzarote-simbolo-vulneraciones-derechos-migrantes-2021_1_10665912.html.

Vega, Guillermo and María Martín. 2020. "La descoordinación durante el rescate de un cayuco en Canarias: 'Estoy jugando con vidas ¡dime qué hago, ya!'" *El País*, September 22, 2020. elpais.com/espana/2020-09-22/la-descoordinacion-durante-el-rescate-de-un-cayuco-en-canarias-estoy-jugando-con-vidas-dime-que-hago-ya.html.

Villa Caro, Raúl. 2020. "Accidentes marítimos, recordando al reconvertido Urquiola." *Blog Naval de Exponav*. December 10, 2020. exponav.org/blog/historia-naval/accidentes-maritimos-recordando-al-reconvertido-urquiola/.

____. 2022. "Evolución del plan nacional de salvamento marítimo." *Blog Naval de Exponav*. December 12, 2022. exponav.org/blog/puertos-y-buques/plan-nacional-de-salvamento-maritimo/.

Vives, Luna. 2011. "White Europe: An Alternative Reading of the Southern EU Border." *Geopolítica(s). Revista de Estudios Sobre Espacio y Poder* 2 (1): 51–70. https://revistas.ucm.es/index.php/GEOP/article/view/36735.

Walters, William. 2011. "Foucault and Frontiers: Notes on the Birth of the Humanitarian Border." In *Governmentality: Current Issues and Future Challenges*, edited by U. Bröckling, S. Krassman, and T. Lemke. London: Routledge.

Weintraub, Hyman. 1959. *Andrew Furuseth: Emancipator of the Seamen*. Oakland, CA: University of California Press.

Index

Ábalos, José Luis, 106
abolitionism, border, 160–1, 182
Achiume, Tendayi, 15–16, 184n9
A Coruña, 51, 59–60, 64
Adriana, response to sinking of, 17, 21–3, 47–8
agricultural workers, women/youth as, 123–4, 127
Aegean Sea, oil spill from, 51, 59–62, 66, 80
Africa,
    blending borders/history with, 12, 83, 86–7, 91–4, 180–2
    border securitization, 89–90, 107–10, 134–6
    colonial power relations/tensions with, 9, 14–15, 174
    EU Emergency Trust Fund for, 107, 125
    sea migrants from, 1, 18–19, 41, 96, 118–20, 139
    Spain proximity to, xvii, 5–7, 107, 142
    see also cayucos
Africa Plan (Spain), 123
air crews,
    contracting out of, 68, 72, 77–8
    working conditions of, 76, 78, 138, 172
    see also helicopters; planes
Alarm Phone, viii, 22, 72, 100, 109, 133
Algeria,
    lack of cooperation with, 91, 99, 108, 125
    migration routes, 88–90, 96–8, 108
    zone of responsibility, 90, 108
Alioune (Senegalese man), 128–9
anarchism, 155
    in/after Franco dictatorship, 152–4, 156
    worker lack of identification with, 150, 159
anarcho-syndicalist union organizing, 18, 149–50, 152–3

paradoxes of, 156–8, 173
philosophies of, 154–5, 161, 165
Andalusia, 102, 184n2
    boats sinking near, 55, 164
    sea migration to, 56, 94, 97, 115
anti-immigration policies, 8, 112, 180
    search and rescue work and, 7, 90
Arbex, Juan Carlos, xi, 17, 57–61, 64
Arguineguín, port of, 115–17, 168
asylum seekers, 4, 21, 87–9, 114, 182; *see also* European Pact on Migration and Asylum
Atlantic Ocean/region, 171, 181
    deaths occurring in, 2, 15, 41, 48–9, 178
    international conventions on, 27, 31, 46
    repressing mobility in, 6, 8, 114, 125
    as sea migration route/zone, 8–10, 118–21, 128–30
    as zone of responsibility, 92, 96, 108, 121–3, 132–3, 138–45
    see also cayucos; *Titanic*
Aznar, José María, 65, 68

Balearic Islands, 89, 97
Bangoura, Alhassane, x, 1–2, 7, 178–9
Baraka, Amiri ("Why's/Wise"), 41
Barrionuevo Peña, José, 57–8, 60
Basir (Sudanese refugee), 88
Black people, 180
    on boat crews, 30, 48
    experiences on the move, 124, 136, 161
    racism facing, 15, 90, 96, 110, 119
    repression of mobility, 6, 15, 83, 110–11, 130
    see also racism
border control,
    EU versus Spanish, 11, 17–19, 53, 114, 143
    externalization/policies, 39–40, 89, 123–5, 132, 138, 184n9

merging rescue and, v, 11, 39, 52, 102–3, 175
technologies, 3, 6, 14, 107, 176
border crossings, undocumented, v, xvii, 98, 110, 132–4
racist narratives of, 90, 111
repressive approaches to, 3–4, 8, 88, 175–6, 182–3
war against, 3–4, 7
border(s), 132
abolition of, 46, 160–1, 182
anti-immigration focus at, 8, 32, 91, 112–14, 123–7, 182–3
concept of, 5, 12, 15
dehumanization at, 13, 84, 145, 180
externalization of, 5–6, 106–9, 112–14, 123–5
humanitarian, 81, 106, 175
infrastructure, 15–16, 95, 129, 149, 175, 182
racism at, 14–16, 110–11, 184n9
repressive, 6–7, 48, 107, 180–2
securitization of, 89–90, 107–10, 134–6
Borrell Fontelles, Josep, x, 17, 58–61, 65, 80
Britain, 62
colonial expansion, 36, 94
historical rescue innovations, 17, 43–5, 53
rescue efforts by, 21, 27

Cameroon(ians), 1, 15, 83, 110
Caminando Fronteras (Walking Borders), viii, 96, 141
data on migrants, 2, 96, 109, 120, 145
founding/mandate of, x, 1, 15, 132–3, 180
migrant calls to, 1–2, 100, 138–9
Campagne, Julie, xi, 2, 19, 178–80
Campling, Liam, 28, 36
Canada, 21, 57
temporary migration programs, 113–14
Canary Islands, 12, 142
cayucos to, 66–7, 71, 128–36
data on migrants to, xviii, 8, 67, 97
death/tragedy while en route to, x, 1–3, 144–5, 176
government migration control in, 8, 40, 71–3, 81
rescue efforts in, 75, 77–9, 134–8, 166–8, 175–6
sea migration to, xvii, 10, 115–26
see also Gran Canaria
Capa, Manuel, xi, xvi
as union/media spokesperson, 96–9, 164–6, 173, 180
views on rescue work, 105, 168–9, 171–2
capitalism, 150
exploitation of sea resources, 25, 28, 36
Castellano, Nicolás, 138, 148
CATEs (Centro de Atención Temporal de Extranjeros), viii, 116–18
cayucos,
abandoned/capsized, 115–16, 120, 128
death on, 120, 128, 135–7, 166, 168, 177
first crisis of, 66, 68, 121–5, 130
second crisis of, 71–2, 133–7
use by migrants, 119–20, 129–30
CCOE (Centro de Coordinación de Operaciones de Emergencia), viii, 106, 144
structure/functioning of, 68–9, 103–4
CCOO (Confederación Sindical de Comisiones Obreras), viii, 154–5
Ceuta (Spanish exclave in North Africa), border crossing at, 83–4, 87, 110–11, 130
geography/protection of, 85–7, 91, 130
SASEMAR zone of intervention around, 94, 108
Tarajal massacre and commemoration, 83–5, 87, 113
CGT (Confederación General del Trabajo), viii
anarchist commitments/goals of, 18, 150, 156–7
Mar y Puertos, *see* CGT Mar y Puertos
SASEMAR, *see* CGT SASEMAR
as smaller but vocal union, 154–5
structure of, 158–9
CGT Mar y Puertos,
collective struggles of, 169–70, 173
Noticias Marítimas newsletter, 160–3, 166
worker representation, viii, x, 147, 154, 158, 164–5
CGT SASEMAR, 160
collective organizing/growth of, 149–54, 169, 171–2, 181
Work Council, 154–5, 159, 173

worker representation, viii, x–xi, 102, 158–9, 163–6
see also SASEMAR
children, 92, 161
  migration deaths of, 2, 22, 76, 140–1, 176
  protection services for, 68, 138, 141, 181
  rhetoric of protection for, 4, 12, 110
CNT (Confederación Nacional del Trabajo), viii, 153, 155–7
Colás, Alejandro, 28, 36
Cold War, 36
colonialism, 181
  border/territorial policies rooted in, 15, 86–7, 141–2
  current legacies of, 9–10, 25, 122, 174
  human mobility impacts, 9, 87
  London Convention perpetuation of, 27–30
  ocean travel in, 33–5
colonies, former, 184n6
  international convention responses, 27, 36–8
  migration to Spain from, xvii, 16
Cons (Cameroonian migrant), 110
Conservative governments, 65–6, 68, 103
contiguous zones, 12, 37, 39, 46
conventions, international, 4, 23
  institutional implementation of, 26, 32, 37
  on rescue operations, 47–9
  SAR, see SAR Convention
  SOLAS, see SOLAS Convention
  UNCLOS, see UNCLOS Convention
corporal punishment, 29–30
Costa da Morte (Coast of Death), 51, 60, 63
Couper, Alastair D., 37–8
COVID-19 pandemic, 159
  steps to mitigate spread of, 116–17, 134, 142
  tourism amid, 116, 134
criminalization,
  of people on the move, 3–6, 79, 81, 144–5, 175
  of migrant rescue, 172, 182–3
  opposition to migrant, 18
  see also detention; smuggling
criminal networks,
  attempts to repress, 81, 98, 123, 128–9

institutional facilitation of, 113, 128–9, 132–3
migration industry, 3, 7, 98–9, 113, 136
see also narcolanchas; smuggling
Crutchley, William Caius (*My Life at Sea*), 16, 30

Daria (person giving birth), 1–2, 19
deaths at sea, 184n5
  cayuco, 120, 128, 135–7, 166, 168, 177
  children's, 2, 22, 76, 140–1, 176
  delayed responses to, 139–41
  historical/famous, 23–4, 41, 51
  honouring memories of, 2–3, 133, 176, 179–80
  migrants risking, 8, 96, 106, 116, 122, 127–8
  normalization/silencing of, 3–4, 11, 84, 140–1
  organized abandonment and 14–16, 21, 175–6
  racism and, 13, 174–5
  repressive migration/border policies and, 2–3, 7–8, 109, 120, 145
  rescue work to counter, 18, 76, 113–14, 171–2, 177–80
  see also drowning
Defensor del Pueblo, 114, 117, 141
deportation,
  cases of, 83, 111
  dehumanization and, 12–13, 49, 110
  failure as strategy, 6–7, 123–4, 180
  mass/summary, 84, 87–8, 114, 118, 129
  migration control through, 4–5, 49, 90–1, 112–13, 144, 183
  politician promises of, 6, 114
  rescue service involvement in, 102, 144
detention,
  cases of, 30, 58, 90
  facilities, 117–18, 125, 128, 181
  failure as strategy, 6–7, 124
  of people on the move, 5–6, 124, 144
  repressive migration system and, 13, 48–9, 180
Diome, Fatou, 41
Diouf, Saliou, 121
Djibril (Senegalese fisherman), 127–8
drowning, 141
  allowing migrant, 11, 84, 178

cases of, 2, 22, 83, 176
death rates from, 2, 99, 101, 109, 145
migrants risking, 41, 147, 172, 179
rescue work to mitigate, 42–3, 111, 149, 179–80, 182
Dutch East India Company, 34–5

Egypt, 21, 40, 88, 144
elite underwater unit, *see* GEAS
Emergency Operation Coordination Centre, *see* CCOE
emergency position-indicating radio beacons (EPIRBs), 11, 48
emergency services, 162
   alerts to, 1–2, 21, 100, 119, 138
   communication among, 24, 68, 72
   demand for expanded maritime, 57, 77
   Lanzarote (EMERLAN), viii, 176
environmental disasters, 51–2, 56, 60, 152
   organizational/governmental concern for, 17, 63–7, 80
   SASEMAR creation/focus amid, 17, 56, 62, 80, 174
environmental protection, mandates for, 24, 32, 67
Estrada, Oriol, xi, 152–3
   early search and rescue work, 69, 79, 94, 99, 168
European Border Surveillance System (EUROSUR), 95, 132
European Communities, *see* European Union
European Court of Human Rights (ECHR), viii, 87–9, 114
European Pact on Migration and Asylum, 70, 144, 180–2
European Union (EU),
   border regime, xvii–xviii, 6–7, 14–16, 61, 69–70, 87–90, 121
   externalization of border responsibilities, 5–6, 106–9, 112–14, 123–5
   funding of militarized repression, 6, 90–1, 95, 134, 179–83
   international convention involvement, 26–7, 32–3, 42, 45–7
   migration policy, 12–14, 23, 39–40, 129, 143–5
   non-European dehumanization, 12, 49, 86, 110–11, 141–3, 174
   Spain's entry to, xvii, 26, 45, 52, 80–1, 93

Spain's rescue services versus, 11, 17–18, 55, 58–60, 102, 171–3
undocumented entry into, 3, 8, 86–7, 94, 126
Exclusive Economic Zones (EEZs), 32–3, 39, 109, 142
externalization, migration,
   concept/purpose of, 5–6, 123–5, 184n9
   failure as strategy, 6–7, 129, 138–40, 177
   migration control through, 5, 89–90, 112–13, 143–4, 180

far right movements/political parties, 66, 72
   anti-immigrant sentiments, 91, 101–2, 105, 180
Felisberto, João Cândido, 30
Fernández, Patuca (Patricia), xi, 84
France, 34, 62
   rescue organizing in/from, 21, 43–4, 53, 171
Franco dictatorship,
   anarchism versus, 153–4, 156
   life after, 55, 57, 93
   sea rescue efforts amid, 45, 52–3, 86
French National Maritime Rescue Society, *see* SNSM
Frontex (European Border and Coast Guard),
   alerts to 21–2
   involvement in Spanish CCOE, 69, 80–1, 95, 102–3, 106
Furió Genovés, Ismael, 172–3
   as Secretary General, x, 99, 103, 157, 164–6, 180–1
   views on rescue work, v, xvi, xviii, 147, 169
Furuseth, Andrew, 16, 28–31

Gali, Brahim, 111
Galicia, 51
   boats sinking near, 50, 55, 59, 62–3
Gambia, The, 1, 119–20, 126
GEAS (Grupo Especial de Actividades Subacuáticas), 84, 111, 176
geopolitics, 19, 118
   European control in, 5, 15
   migrants as pawns in, 15, 109–10, 114, 141–3
   ocean, 33–6, 38

Gilmore, Ruth Wilson, 13–14, 16, 182
Global Approach to Migration and Mobility, 8
Global Maritime Distress Safety System (GMDSS), 62
global mobility divide, 7
Gordon, Edward, 34
governments,
  Canary Island migration control, 8, 40, 71–3, 81
  Conservative, 65–6, 68, 103
  environmental concerns, 17, 63–7, 80
  policies of, *see* migration policies
  Socialist, 54, 58, 66, 68, 103
Gran Canaria, 2, 115, 168
  cayuco/migrant arrival on, 134–5, 138, 147
  rescue coordination from, 71–2, 117, 130–1, 159, 167
Greece, 129
  Coast Guard rescue responses, 21–2, 48, 177
  in EU border regime, xvii–xviii, 5, 47
  migration to, 5, 162, 172
Grotius, Hugo, 16, 34–6
Guardamares, 131, 140
  fleet/capabilities of, 66, 74, 77, 130, 133
  workers/conditions on, x, xi, 77, 79, 97, 165–8
Guardia Civil Maritime Service (SEMAR), ix
  cases of rescue involvement, 50, 56, 111–12, 131–2, 176
  control of rescue operations, 17–18, 58–9, 81, 102–3, 106, 144
  SASEMAR coordination with, 68–70, 79–80
  surveillance by, 86–7, 93, 95–100, 123, 148
  Tarajal massacre involvement, 83–4, 87

Haas, Hein de, 129
helicopters, 175
  cases of dispatching, 1, 21, 60, 104, 123, 136
  crew working conditions, 75–9, 138–40, 172, 181
  government acquisition of, 46, 55–6, 62, 65–6, 150
  lack of (maintained), 50, 130, 164, 172
  rescue system, 46, 72, 74–9, 100–1, 181
  see also air crews
Hercules, 14, 50, 86
Hernández, Dácil Trujillo, x, 179–80
Hervé (Tarajal massacre survivor), 83–4
Hucks, Timothy, 90
humanitarian border, 81, 106, 175
humanitarianism, 5, 81, 175
hydraulic system of migration, 7–8, 118, 130

Iberian Peninsula, xvii, 33–5, 89
immigrant(s), 3, 180–1
  legal/political constructions of, 13, 93, 184n2
  precarious/low-paid employment, 14, 170
immigration, xvii
  law, *see* immigration law
  strategies to prohibit, *see* anti-immigration policies
immigration law, 90
  harshness of Spanish, 15–16, 93, 112
  jurisdictional limits of, 33, 39, 173
  Spanish creation of, 13, 49, 51–2
Integrated System for the Surveillance of the External Border, *see* SIVE
International Ice Patrol, 24, 31
international law,
  development of, 25, 27, 31, 33–4
  jurisdiction, 37, 39–40, 108, 142
  maritime versus public, 27, 31
  rescue operations, 21, 108
International Law Commission, 37
International Maritime Organization (IMO), 46, 96
  conventions of, 32, 51
  creation/functions of, 24–6, 31
Italy, 57, 162
  in EU border regime, xvii–xviii, 47, 101
  migration to, 21, 94, 129, 172
  rescue policies, 172, 177

Juanola, Aran Sol, x, 63–4
jurisdiction(s) at sea, 62, 124
  history shaping, 16, 38
  Morocco's claims to, 40, 105, 141
  ships as mobile, 28–30, 32–3, 69

Index

UNCLOS Conventions on, 32–3, 38–9, 42, 47
  see also contiguous zones; Exclusive Economic Zones

Kropotkin, Peter, 155

La Isla, sinking of, 50–1
Lampedusa (Italian island), 162
  shipwreck, 133, 172
Lanzarote, 117, 131, 134, 167
  emergency service (EMERLAN), viii, 176
  migrants buried in, x, 2, 178–9
  search/rescue cases near, x, 1–2, 170, 176–7
  see also Lanzarote's Network of Solidarity with Migrant People
Lanzarote's Network of Solidarity with Migrant People, xi, 2, 19, 170, 178
La Restinga, port of (in El Hierro), 115, 131, 135, 168
Latin America, 37
  Spanish migration to/from, xvii, 13–16
Libya, 46, 88, 162
  as EU border guard, 5–6, 14–15, 113, 144
Lobo y Malagamba, Miguel, 44–5
London, Jack (*Sea Wolf*), 41
London Convention, 26–31

Maleno, Helena, x, 1, 180
Mali, 120, 123
Malta, xviii, 47, 49, 177, 179
Mare Clausum (Selden), 35–6
Mare Liberum (Grotius), 35–6
Marichal Niebla, Haridian, x, 179–80
Marine Captaincies, 55, 57–8, 103
Maritime Rescue Coordination Centres (MRCCs), 60, 72–3, 100
Marthe, Laetitia, xi, 2, 19, 170, 178–80
Mauritania, 10, 171
  as EU border guard, 5–6, 113, 125, 140, 144
  migrants departing from, 71, 115, 119–20, 127–9, 134, 176
  Spain border monitoring with, 122–5, 177–8
Mayecor (Serer man), 126–8

Mbembe, Achille, 15–16
Médecins Sans Frontières (MSF), 171
media, 106
  narratives on migration, 8, 71, 88, 93, 110–12, 134, 180
  oil spill coverage, 65
  SASEMAR presence in, 73, 81, 101, 148–50, 163–6, 173
  see also social media
Melilla,
  border crossing at, 87–8, 110–11, 130
  geography/protection of, 85, 87, 91
  SASEMAR zone of intervention around, 108
Melville, Herman (*Moby Dick*), 41
migrants,
  child, *see* children
  data on, 2, 96, 109, 120, 145
  dehumanization of, xvii, 9, 12–13, 49, 180–1
  detention of, *see* detention
  as geopolitical pawns, 15, 109–10, 114, 141–3
  as politicized category, xvii, 13
  surveillance of, *see* surveillance, increased
  see also people on the move
migration,
  as dynamic, 8–9
  as hydraulic system, 7–8, 118, 130
  industry, 3, 7, 98–9, 113, 136, 176
  media narratives on, 8, 71, 88, 93, 110–12, 134, 180
  militarization of, *see* militarization, migration
  repression, *see* repression, migration
  sea, *see* sea migration
migration policies,
  EU border regime, 8–9, 14, 33, 39, 173
  simplified narratives of, 3–4, 8–9
  Spanish, 13, 15–16, 49, 51–2, 93, 112
migration route(s),
  Alboran Sea, 89, 95–7, 101, 103–4, 108, 163
  Algerian, 89–90, 96–9, 108
  Atlantic, 6–9, 118–21, 130, 132–5, 171–2
  blocking of, 15, 87, 133–4, 145, 182
  Central Mediterranean, 102, 118, 144, 162, 171–2, 177, 181

countries as border guards, 5, 114, 145
Eastern Mediterranean, 8, 118, 162, 171–2
as hydraulic system, 7–8, 118, 130
increasing danger in, 6–8, 96–100, 108–9, 120, 128–30, 178
rescue services on, 14, 68, 75, 130, 102–8, 141–4, 171–2
sea, 8–10, 81, 93–5, 122–3
Strait of Gibraltar, 89–90, 92–6
use of term, 8–11
Western Mediterranean, 6–8, 68–71, 89, 92–9, 118–22, 171–2
militarization, migration, 129, 163
deaths/harm from, 6–7, 89–90, 147–9, 159
detention facilities, 117–18
European strategy of, 4–6, 80–2, 124, 180
failure as strategy, 3, 6–7, 136, 183
resistance to, 89, 159, 183
stealth, 71–2, 92, 140
military,
dictatorship impacts, 50, 55, 57–8, 93, 152
elimination of mandatory service in, 53–4, 79
national demonstrations of, 33–6, 86–7, 147–9
SASEMAR distinction from, xvi, 17–18, 71, 104–6, 160, 172–5
search and rescue involvement, 58–61, 69–72, 103–7, 113, 144, 177
see also Single Operative Command
mobility, human, 92
criminalization of, 4–6, 48–9
divide, 7–8, 174
policy approaches, 8–9, 146
punitive narratives of, 10–11, 48, 130
state limiting of, 7, 9–12, 142
supposed crises of, 3–4, 9
wealth and, 7–8, 48–9
Modou (Lebou fisherman), 125–8
Morocco, 171
deportation to, 83, 87–90, 111, 140
developing rescue capacity of, 100–1, 105–9, 139–41
as EU border guard, 5–6, 83, 89–91, 112–14, 177–8, 184n9

geopolitical interests in, 40, 141–3
human rights violations in, 15, 88, 110–11, 114, 134
migrant journeys from, 1, 19, 87–90, 110–12, 176
National Rescue Plan, 100, 106
Royal Navy, 100, 104–6, 109, 113, 140, 144
Spain's colonial territory in, 12, 83–7, 90–1, 141–2
Spain's relations/borders with, 83–7, 105–9, 122–4, 130
varied migration routes from, 56, 71, 93–8, 110–11, 118–21
zones of responsibility, 46, 56, 89–90, 101–5, 108–9, 139–43
Mountz, Alison, 4, 141
multilateral co-operation, 25–27, 37, 106, 143–4
multipurpose boats, 66, 74, 150, 167
MUO (Mando Único Operativo), see Single Operative Command

narcolanchas, 92, 95, 97–9
National Rescue Coordination Centres (NRCCs), 72, 100, 144
National Rescue Plan(s) (Spain),
initial iteration, 53, 56–7, 60
lack of focus on sea migration, 56, 62, 66–70
later versions of, 61–2, 65–70
National Workers' Confederation, see CNT
Navy (Spain),
control of ports by, 55, 57
search and rescue work by, 51–3, 55–6, 70, 80
Ndour, Augustín, 180
necropolitics, 15–16, 175
NGO(s) (non-governmental organizations),
criticisms of government, 88–90, 114, 117
removal from Spanish zone of responsibility, 170–3, 177
rescue work of, 70, 102, 145, 161–2, 180–2
SASEMAR not an, xvi, 17, 49
see also Caminando Fronteras
Noticias Marítimas (CGT union newsletter), 160–3, 166
nuclear testing, ocean, 36–7

oil,
  chapapote on beaches from, 63–4
  sea-based extraction of, 38, 40
  spills, 57–60, 62–6, 74
  tankers, 51, 59–62, 66–7, 92, 96, 184n5
organized abandonment, 14–16, 47, 175
ownership, sea,
  claims of, 36, 141
  international conventions and, 23, 32–4, 39, 47

pateras, 119, 136
  migrant use of, 93–5, 111, 121, 134
people on the move,
  concept of, xvii
  deaths of, *see* deaths at sea; drowning
  detention of, *see* detention
  entitlement to protections, 4, 9, 88, 114, 129, 182
  narratives about, 11–13, 18, 110–11, 114
  precarious status of, 7, 14, 66, 77, 176, 182
  smuggling of, *see* smuggling
  see also migrants
Pia Boxes, 43
planes, 64, 124
  cases of dispatching, 1, 138, 174–5
  contracting out of, 68, 72, 77–8
  government acquisition of, 46, 61–2, 66
  lack of (maintained), 50, 66, 130, 172
  rescue system, 3, 74–9, 100, 130, 180
  see also air crews
Polisario Front (independence movement), 111, 142
Port and Merchant Marine Law (1992), 58, 60, 68
precarity,
  boats', 96, 108
  employment, 77, 182
  status, 7, 14, 66, 176
Prestige, oil spill from, 51, 62–3, 65–7, 103
Proactiva Open Arms, 162
Proem-Aid, 162

Queipo de Llano y Acuña Álvarez de las Asturias, Francisco, 52–3
race as border infrastructure, 15–16, 139, 184n9
racialization, 180
  othering based on, 12–13, 18, 110–11, 114
  rescuing based on, 49, 174–5, 179
  seafaring workers' exploitation and, 28, 32, 48–9, 169
racism,
  anti-Black, 15, 90, 96, 110–11, 119
  concepts of, 13–14, 16
Rackete, Carola, 162–3
Red Cross,
  of the Sea, *see* Red Cross of the Sea
  Spanish, *see* Spanish Red Cross
Red Cross of the Sea (Spain),
  establishment of, 52–3
  shrinking rescue work of, 56–7, 66, 74, 79
  volunteering for, 53–5, 133, 165, 181
refugees,
  narratives on, 4, 13, 88, 161
  state obligations toward, 9, 88, 114, 129, 182
regional coordination centres, 60–2, 73–5, 130–1, 135, 138–9, 147
REMOLMAR/REMASA (Remolques Marítimos Sociedad Anónima/Maritime Towing Inc.), 74, 153
  history as private company, 56, 72, 151
  state acquisition of, ix, 66–8
repression, migration, 134
  in EU border regime, 6–7, 48, 107, 180–2
  failure as strategy, 6–8, 136, 145–6
  government legitimizing of, 3–5, 48, 81
rescuers, 162
  code of, xviii, 18, 104–5
  experiences of, 96–9, 120
  former, 17, 67, 94
  militarization of work, 131, 141, 147–9
  SASEMAR, 72, 75–81, 102, 118, 132, 181
  training/capacity of, 43–4, 69, 135–8, 172
  working conditions/organizing of, 151–4, 164–72
resource extraction, sea-based,
  international conventions and, 27–8, 32, 36
  jurisdiction over, 33, 35–9, 141–2
  new technology for, 25, 37–8, 40
resuscitation methods, 2, 43–4

Rodríguez, José María, 134–5
Roldán Ibáñez, Juan Luis, 17, 57–9
Royal National Lifeboat Institution
   (Britain), 44, 53
Rush, Stockton, 20–1

Sailors' Union of the Pacific, 28–9
Salvamares,
   dimensions/capacity of, 56, 74, 97, 107,
      150, 167
   dispatching, 2, 104, 115, 147, 170
   SASEMAR fleet of, 66, 107, 115, 130,
      133–5
   workers on, xi, 77, 79, 104, 138, 164,
      167–8
Salvamento Marítimo, *see* SASEMAR
Salvamento Marítimo Humanitario (NGO),
   171
Sánchez, Pedro, 68, 71, 105
Santa Catarina, 34–5, 184n6
Santana, Txema, 134
SAR (Search and Rescue) Convention
   (1979/1985):
   enforcement of, 24, 26, 49, 70, 109, 143
   goals of, 21–3, 41–2, 45–7, 80–1
   principles/customs behind, 18, 42,
      45–6, 72, 173–5
   Spain implementation of, 49, 55–8, 100–4
SASEMAR (Sociedad Española de Salvamento Marítimo),
   air fleet, 66, 68, 72, 74–9, 139
   in cayuco crises, 130–3, 137
   contracting out services, 68, 72, 77–8
   coordination with various entities, 69,
      72–4, 76–80, 84, 103, 144
   creation of, 16–17, 55–6, 60–2, 67–8
   as European outlier, xviii, 80, 175, 177,
      181–3
   mandate/budget of, 16–17, 51–3, 65–70,
      77, 92, 149
   meeting with workers in, xvi, 78–9,
      94–5, 137
   migrant rescue work, 2, 11, 49, 67–70,
      74–81, 96–102, 115
   militarization of, 70–1, 104–5, 175
   Moroccan military rescue training by,
      104–6, 108
   regional coordination centres, 60–2,
      73–5, 130–1, 135, 138–9, 147

sea fleet, 2, 66, 72–4, 76
search and rescue principles of, xviii,
   81, 175, 177
types of vessels assisted, 11, 74–5, 119
workers for, 53–4, 57, 67–8, 72–9, 162
union for, *see* CGT SASEMAR
satellite phones, 119–21
seafarers, 120
   labour organizing, viii, 28–31, 154,
      158–60
   obligations of rescue, xviii, 41–3, 45–7
   working conditions of, 29–31, 169–70
Seamen's Act, 29–30
sea migration, 119, 137–8
   criminalization of, 3, 39, 45–8
   early patterns of, xvii, 56, 62, 93, 134,
      152
   framing as crisis/threat, 3–4, 9, 81–2,
      130, 145
   industry of, 3, 97–100, 116, 144
   international conventions on, 23, 47,
      175; *see also* UNCLOS Conventions
   political discourse on, xviii, 3–4, 11,
      99–103, 105, 159–61
   profiting from, 3–7, 14, 42, 98–9, 136,
      146, 176
   rates of, 3, 66–8, 71, 80, 121–6
Search and Rescue Regions (SRRs), 2–3,
   45–6, 139
search and rescue work,
   anti-immigration policies and, 7, 90
   criminalization of, 172, 182–3
   innovations, 17, 43–5, 53
   international conventions on, 4, 26; *see
      also* SAR Convention
   merging border control and, v, 11, 39,
      52, 102–3, 175
   migration control versus, 4–5, 48–9
   migration route, 14, 68, 75, 130, 102–8,
      141–4, 171–2
   military involvement in, 58–61, 69–72,
      103–7, 113, 144, 177
   NGO, 70, 102, 145, 161–2, 180–2
   obligations of, xviii, 41–3, 45–7
   for people on the move, 2, 11, 49,
      67–70, 74–81, 96–102, 115
   principles of, xviii, 81, 175, 177
   Spanish versus EU, 11, 17–18, 55,
      58–60, 102, 171–3

two-tier system of, xviii, 49, 68–9, 104, 114, 172, 175–7
see also rescuers; universal rescue
Second Republic (Spain), 152, 156
security,
  migration as threat to, 3–5, 81, 175
  national (security) versus human safety, 10–12, 49, 81–2, 97, 132, 183
  organizations/conventions for, 24, 32, 58
  training forces for state, 6, 39, 86, 95, 106, 124, 171
  violence in name of, 14, 98
Selden, John, 16, 35–6
SEMAR (Servicio Marítimo de la Guardia Civil), *see* Guardia Civil Maritime Service
Sena, Ildefonso, 93–4, 100
Senegal,
  colonial encroachment in, 9–10
  as European border guard, 5–6, 113, 140, 144, 177–8
  people on the move from, 1, 19, 71, 119–22, 181
  political/economic tensions in, 8, 123–30, 170
  Spain collaboration with, 122–5, 128–9
  young men leaving from, 8–10, 41, 122, 125–9, 134
shipping industry, 62, 67, 164
  accidents impacting, 52, 55
  changes for regulation of, 24–5, 32, 63
Single Operative Command (Mando Único Operativo, MUO), ix, 103–4, 106, 144
  creation of, 68–9, 71, 149
SIVE (Sistema Integrado de Vigilancia Exterior), 79, 95–6, 98, 132
smuggling, human, 177
  boats/equipment used in, 95–6, 118–19
  criminal networks operating, 3, 7–8, 14, 120, 123, 133
  experiences with, 127–9
  profitability/business of, 7, 97–9, 136, 145, 175–6
  restrictive border policies increasing, 6–8, 14, 123, 126–9, 133
  violence against migrants in, 22, 118
SNSM (Société nationale de sauvetage en mer), ix, 44, 53

Socialist governments, 54, 58, 66, 68, 103
Socialist Party, x, 71, 152
social media, 164
  CGT union presence on, 141, 150, 163
  updates on rescue operations via, 101, 139
Sociedad Española de Salvamento de Náufragos (SESN), 45, 51–3
Sociétés humaines et des Naufragés (France), 44
SOLAS (Safety of Life at Sea) Convention (1974/1980),
  adoption of, 26–7, 31–2
  Spain signing of, 49, 51, 56
  stipulations/framework of, 23, 32, 41–2, 47, 62
Soufi, Nawal, 21
Spain,
  building maritime rescue system, 26, 51–60, 65–6, 74–5, 80, 150–1
  history of human mobility, xvii, 56, 62, 93, 134, 152
  Instrucción rescue plan, 42–3
  Levante region, 97, 99
  mili service/volunteering, 53–4, 144
  National Rescue Plan, *see* National Rescue Plan(s)
  Navy, *see* Navy
  two-tier rescue system, xviii, 68–9, 104, 114, 172, 175–7
Spanish Civil War, 45, 51, 156
Spanish Red Cross, 52
  migrant processing facilities, 111, 115–17, 133, 181
  as part of rescue network, 68–9, 80, 104, 144, 150
Spanish Society for the Rescue of Shipwreck Victims, *see* Sociedad Española de Salvamento de Náufragos
Steinberg, Philip, 33, 35
Strait of Gibraltar,
  geography of, xvii, 85, 94
  migration routes of, 89–90, 92–6, 98
  mythology of, 14, 86
  surveillance/rescue operations in, 11, 69, 95–6, 99, 103, 108
surveillance, increased,
  developing systems of, 53, 64, 79, 106–8, 112, 131

206 THE GATES OF THE SEA

migrant attempts to avoid, 95–6, 120, 129, 133–6
technologies, 91, 95, 129, 144
see also European Border Surveillance System; SIVE

Tarajal massacre and commemoration, 83–5, 87, 89, 112–13
Tarrida, Enric, x, 17, 54–5, 161, 181
  initial search and rescue work, 67–8, 72, 102, 151–4, 168, 173
technology, 119
  border control, 3, 6, 14, 176
  marine vessel, 25, 31–2
  SASEMAR air/sea fleet, 73, 75, 172
  surveillance, 91, 95, 129, 144
  resource extraction, 38–40
Temporary Holding Centres for Foreigners, see CATEs
Tenerife, 131, 135–6, 148, 167–8
Thiaroye-sur-mer, 125–7
Titan, response to implosion of, 17, 20–4, 47–8
Titanic,
  (lessons from) sinking of, 16–17, 23–4, 26–7
  Titan implosion by, 20–1
tourism,
  benefits of functioning rescue system, 11, 55, 92, 133
  COVID-19 pandemic and, 116, 134
  migrant presence versus, 13, 93, 115–17, 126, 181
  National Rescue Plan and, 56–7
  two-tier rescue system for, xviii, 68–9, 104, 114, 172, 175–7
trafficking, 176
  drug, 92, 95, 97–9, 136
  human, 133, 145
  migrants facing violence by, 8, 32
TRAGSA (Empresa de Transformación Agraria), ix, 63
Trump, Donald, 91, 142–3
Tunisia, 5–6, 46, 144
Türkiye,
  as EU border guard, 5, 15, 40, 107, 113, 144
  migrants from, 162, 177

UGT (Unión General de Trabajadores), ix, 152–5
UNCLOS Conventions (UN Convention on the Law of the Sea, 1982/1994),
  clarifying jurisdiction, 23, 32–3, 38–9, 42, 47
  maritime rescue provisions, 26
  reinforcing global/colonial inequalities via, 27–8, 34, 36–8
  Spain's signing of, 49
union(s),
  Comisiones Obreras, see CCOO
  Mar y Puertos, see CGT Mar y Puertos
  National Workers' Confederation, see CNT
  opposition to London Convention, 28
  SASEMAR, see CGT SASEMAR
  Unión General de Trabajadores, see UGT
  Unión Sindical Obrera, see USO
United Kingdom, see Britain
United Nations, 22, 37, 114, 141
  Convention on the Law of the Sea, see UNCLOS Conventions
  creation of, 25
United States, 24
  border control in, 3, 91, 183
  geopolitical interests, 36–7, 142
  on international conventions, 27–32
  migrant detention in, 6, 90, 183
  rescue involvement, 20–1, 24, 57
universal rescue (principle of),
  commitments to, 45, 171, 177
  erosion of, 103–4, 175, 178
USO (Unión Sindical Obrera), ix, 154–5
UVSE (Unidad de Voluntarios de Socorro y Emergencias), ix, 56

Valido, Cristina, 71
Villa Caro, Raúl, 55
violence against people on the move,
  border policies increasing, 7–8, 82, 176, 180
  domestic, 110, 129
  fleeing, 129, 182
  migration route, 6–7, 99
  in name of security, 14, 98
  normalization of, 3, 12–13
  outsourcing of, 14–15, 184n3

racialized, 14, 49
sexual, 7, 145
in smuggling, 22, 118
structural, 14, 16, 19
trafficking, 8, 32

Walcott, Derek Alton, 174
Western Mediterranean region, 132 171–2
    criminalization of mobility in, 6, 81, 84, 89, 114
    deaths in, 84, 96, 109, 113, 120, 178
    migration routes, 8, 71, 89, 92–9, 105, 118–22
    rescue operations in, 68–9, 75, 102, 141–4, 175, 178
    zone of responsibility, 46, 70–3, 104, 108, 125, 149
Western Sahara, 111
    migration routes, 40, 71, 118–21, 134, 138, 176
    Moroccan/disputed territory of, 40, 91, 122, 139, 141–3
Workers' Union Coalition, *see* USO
World War I, 25, 31
World War II, 25, 32, 37–8, 168

xenophobia, 6, 29, 49

zone(s) of responsibility, 132–3
    Algerian, 90, 108
    concept of, 2–3, 32–3
    deaths/harm in, 2, 21, 89–90, 143
    Moroccan, 100–1, 104–5, 108, 139–42
    rescue operations in, 43–4, 67–8, 71–3, 79, 143–5, 161
    SAR Convention on, 45–7, 109
    shared, 101, 104–5, 108, 143
    Spain's, 71–3, 81, 92, 149, 163, 170–2
    see also Search and Rescue Regions